USA

NATIONAL
PARKS

USA
NATIONAL
PARKS

LANDS OF WONDER

CONTENTS

The sense of freedom afforded by these spectacular landscapes is unparalleled, whether exploring the country's oldest national park or its youngest wild wonderland. We've organized the 62 national parks in order of establishment, each a vital part in the country's narrative.

Right A hike in Zion National Park leads you through a labyrinth of towering pinnacles in shades of fiery red

Left At Redwood National Park, some of the world's largest original redwood forests offer tranquility and incite moments of awe

Bottom Left Yellowstone National Park is home to the Grand Prismatic Spring and meandering bison

Left The Pipiwai Trail passes through a bamboo forest in Haleakalā National Park

Below Glacier Bay National Park offers truly spectacular views from its icy waters

Bottom Right Double Arch is a striking landmark in Arches National Park

INTRODUCTION

You'll find every imaginable landscape awaiting exploration in the national parks of the United States. Icy monoliths looming in Alaska's Denali, rugged and romantic coastline sweeping through Maine's Acadia, craggy volcanic peaks piercing the sky in California's Pinnacles, lush tropics abuzz with wildlife in Florida's Everglades—and this is just scratching the surface.

In *USA National Parks: Lands of Wonder*, we celebrate the past, present, and future of the great American wilderness. We begin with The Story *(p12)*, exploring the history of the national parks, starting with the land's American Indian heritage, the migration of the Pioneers, the trailblazers previously written out of history, and the birth of the National Park Service (NPS) in the early 20th century. This federal agency was established in response to a renewed respect for nature, and a desire to protect it for future generations. This mission is more crucial than ever. Our planet is experiencing difficult times—the effects of climate change, a war on plastic, and much more besides. In The Story, we delve into how the NPS and its rangers are responding

to our changing environment and the unprecedented popularity of the parks, while simultaneously welcoming visitors of all backgrounds and safeguarding the parks for the future. And who wouldn't want to explore and savor these vast open spaces? They are beautiful, and we know they are essential to our health and wellness. In The Parks *(p32)*, we showcase the 62 stars of the show, each extraordinary and unique in its own right. Within this chapter you'll find all sorts of inspiration for your next outdoor adventure—from backcountry hikes and cycling routes, to stargazing, caving, and wildlife watching. Plus, we've gathered gorgeous photography and thought-provoking tidbits to spark your curiosity and give a flavor of the breathtaking diversity that awaits you.

These national parks belong to everyone—nature doesn't care about your age, race, mobility, or education. So, leaf through this book and don your hiking boots, grab your binoculars, forget about your cell phone, and immerse yourself in these true lands of wonder.

Alaska

- KOBUK VALLEY
- GATES OF THE ARCTIC
- DENALI
- WRANGELL–ST. ELIAS
- LAKE CLARK
- KENAI FJORDS
- KATMAI
- GLACIER BAY

Arctic Ocean

CANADA

ALASKA

Pacific Ocean

Hawaii

HAWAII

- HALEAKALĀ
- HAWAI'I VOLCANOES

Pacific Ocean

Pacific Ocean

Pacific Ocean

USA

HAWAII

INDONESIA

- NATIONAL PARK OF AMERICAN SAMOA

FIJI

AUSTRALIA

NEW ZEALAND

The Caribbean

USA

Atlantic Ocean

MEXICO

CUBA

- VIRGIN ISLANDS

Pacific Ocean

- OLYMPIC
- NORTH CASCADES
- GLACIER
- MOUNT RAINIER
- YELLOWSTONE
- GRAND TETON
- CRATER LAKE
- REDWOOD
- LASSEN VOLCANIC
- GREAT BASIN
- ARCHES
- CANYONLANDS
- CAPITOL REEF
- YOSEMITE
- ZION
- BRYCE CANYON
- KINGS CANYON
- PINNACLES
- SEQUOIA
- DEATH VALLEY
- GRAND CANYON
- CHANNEL ISLANDS
- JOSHUA TREE
- PETRIFIED FOREST
- SAGUARO

WASHINGTON

OREGON

MONTANA

IDAHO

NEVADA

UTAH

CALIFORNIA

ARIZONA

Pacific Ocean

PLOTTING THE PARKS

The immensity and range of America's wide-open spaces are truly staggering—and they're all waiting for you to explore. Use this map to plot your next adventure across the country's national parks, from the showstoppers to the lesser-known gems, and everything in between.

Left The Grand
Canyon is spectacular
from both the ground
and the sky

The Story

AN ENDURING LEGACY

Many of the national parks in the United States preserve land and historic sites once occupied by American Indian tribes, whose legacy is most tangible in the parks of the American West.

Preserving the works of man

The stewardship we celebrate in the present has deep roots in the traditions and people of the past. The earliest inhabitants of the New World existed by hunting animals and cultivating crops, their lives in rhythm with the changing seasons. Though most of these American Indian tribes were displaced or removed by force in the Plains Wars, from the 1850s through the early 1920s, a number of parks and monuments retain the heritage of cultures spanning thousands of years.

Above The more fortunate Lakota Sioux survived the Battle of Wounded Knee

Left The Cliff Palace, in Mesa Verde National Park, is the largest cliff dwelling in North America

A visit to the dwellings of the Ancestral Puebloans at Mesa Verde National Park (p60) brings you closer to the people who flourished here centuries before the voyage of Christopher Columbus and the colonization of North America. Established in 1906 under the Antiquities Act by President Theodore Roosevelt, Mesa Verde was the first national park set aside specifically to "preserve the works of man," as a desire to protect both the natural environment and the cultural legacy of indigenous peoples grew in the national conscience.

In the years that followed, many more American Indian sites were designated monuments and parks under the Antiquities Act. In addition to their natural beauty, areas that include the Grand Canyon, the Petrified Forest, and Zion were also protected for the preservation of artifacts from the Paiute, Shoshone, and Zuni.

The human cost

Tragically, a number of these historic sites saw native people forced from their land and many massacred. Yosemite, Yellowstone, and Grand Teton were a few of the parks created at the expense of American Indian tribes who were forced to relocate to reservations. But there were those who refused to relent or disarm. In 1890, near what is now Badlands National Park, almost 400 Lakota Sioux were killed or injured in an act of military aggression by the US Army. At the site today called Wounded Knee, a national monument stands to remind us of past injustices and to recognize the people whose land we are obligated to preserve.

INSPIRING IDEAS

American Indian Culture

There are many ways to experience American Indian culture in the parks.

Ceremonial Dances
Feel the pulse as tribal communities exhibit traditional music, singing, and dancing at the Grand Canyon (p90), Denali (p86), and Mesa Verde (p60).

Petroglyphs and Rock Art
Look for intricate ancient drawings on stone walls at Canyonlands (p156) and Arches (p170).

Crafts
Learn a skill at a cultural site, as local artists share their creativity in intricate basket making, beadwork, and pottery.

Explore Dwellings
Crawl through tunnels and scramble up ladders while exploring the incredible cliff dwellings in Mesa Verde National Park.

BUILDING
A HOME

North America's pioneers were not rich—they were looking for a better life and land to call their own. But the American Dream came at a cost.

Crossing the Western frontier

In 1803, President Thomas Jefferson made the Louisiana Purchase from France, a portentous move that doubled the size of the United States. In the late 1830s, those living on the East Coast migrated west, crossing the Mississippi in large numbers to live in this "new" land, which had for centuries been occupied by American Indians. The plains and mountains acquired in the Louisiana Purchase and considered too harsh to settle in were set aside as "Indian Territory"—Oklahoma today—with American Indian tribes made to relocate here.

Settlers by the thousand headed toward the fertile West Coast valleys on the Oregon Trail (from 1836), California Trail (from 1843), and Mormon Trail (from 1847), traveling in huge covered wagon trains across the Great Plains. Families made the crossing—which could take six months or longer—with just a handful of possessions, risking extremes of weather, numerous diseases, and occasional conflicts with American Indians.

In 1849, the California Gold Rush provided an extra, albeit short-lived, inducement, but the main draw was the promise of land. The Donation Land Claim Act of 1850 allocated pioneers free lots in the Oregon Territory and, in 1862, the first Homestead Act opened up millions of acres to settlement by any US citizen (including, in theory, African Americans). All you had to do was reside on the land for five years, and show evidence of having made improvements. In 1869, The First Transcontinental Railroad was completed, making the journey west faster, cheaper, and safer.

All of this was a disaster for American Indians, the first people of the land. Most tribes were at least partly nomadic, making it easy for settlers to claim "uninhabited" land. Eventually, even Indian Territory was given away in the Oklahoma Land Runs of 1889, and a year later the frontier was officially declared "closed." Abandoned cabins and wagons in the likes of Grand Teton (p110), Capitol Reef (p168), and Death Valley (p220) national parks act as reminders of this.

Pioneers in popular imagination

The romanticizing of pioneer life had begun back in the 1860s, with cheap "dime novels" that featured thrilling stories of cowboy

Above Homesteaders were hopeful to file claims for land, often standing in line for hours

INSPIRING IDEAS
Pioneer History

Though national parks are best known for their scenery, many also preserve remnants of pioneer history, especially in the West.

Capitol Reef National Park
Wander the streets of Fruita, established in 1880 by Mormon pioneers and now a ghost town (p168).

Joshua Tree National Park
Join a ranger-led tour at the Keys Ranch, where homesteaders once lived (p228).

Rocky Mountain National Park
Visit the Holzwarth Historic Site, a homestead built in 1917 (p77).

Grand Teton National Park
See early pioneer homes at Menors Ferry Historic District and Mormon Row (p110).

Yosemite National Park
Explore the homestead cabins at the Pioneer Yosemite History Museum (p40).

derring-do. Buffalo Bill Cody opened his first "Wild West" show in 1883, and when Hollywood movies ramped up in the 1920s, a new genre of "Westerns" emerged. The image of confidently self-reliant pioneer communities was cemented by popular books such as Willa Cather's *O Pioneers!* (1913), and Laura Ingalls Wilder's *Little House on the Prairie* series (from 1932). American Indians were portrayed negatively or not at all, the annexation of their homeland conveniently ignored.

Yet there's little doubt that the modern United States would not exist without those early settlers. And, as the frontier disappeared and the 20th century waited just around the corner, a new age was dawning, with the country experiencing a renewed appreciation for the beauty of the American wilderness.

Below *Emigrants Crossing the Plains,* (1866) a lithograph by Currier & Ives, shows droves of settlers traveling in wagons, with American Indians looking on

THE BIRTH OF AN IDEA

Romanticism—with its focus on nature and the great outdoors—and the efforts of visionary individuals laid the foundations for the creation of the National Park Service.

Celebrating the natural world

Attitudes toward nature had been shifting since the start of the Romantic era in the late 18th century, when artists began to draw inspiration from the natural world. From the 1830s, writers such as Walt Whitman, Ralph Waldo Emerson, and Henry David Thoreau urged their fellow citizens to see land as more than just a commodity, while artists of the Hudson River School—Thomas Cole, Thomas Moran, and Albert Bierstadt—began to create romantic images of the American landscape on vast canvasses.

Influenced by this growing movement, surveyor Ferdinand V. Hayden—aided by Moran's paintings—helped persuade Congress to declare Yellowstone *(p34)* the nation's first national park in 1872. The land was set apart "for the benefit and enjoyment of the people," though the American Indians who had been custodians of the land for centuries were notably not allowed to visit.

Father of the national parks

Born in Scotland in 1838, John Muir immigrated to the US with his family when

Below The Grand Canyon of the Yellowstone (1872) by Thomas Moran captures the artist's adoration for the great outdoors

he was 11. He spent much of his 20s wandering North America's wilderness, increasingly drawn to botany and the great outdoors. In 1864, President Abraham Lincoln assigned Yosemite to the state of California—the first time the federal government had set aside land specifically for preservation and public use. Having fallen in love with Yosemite's landscape, Muir spent the rest of his life campaigning to protect it, and he became a passionate advocate for America's national parks. He lived in Yosemite for several years and wrote essays that contributed to the establishment of Yosemite National Park in 1890 *(p40)*. He also cofounded the

Sierra Club in 1892, an environmental organization that is still in existence today.

In 1903, Muir took President Theodore Roosevelt on a camping trip to Yosemite in an effort to convince him to expand the national park system. It worked, and by 1916 the Department of the Interior was managing 35 national parks and monuments—a mammoth task. It wasn't just men leading the charge for conservation in the 20th century. Muir's lifelong mentor was Jeanne Carr, one of his university professors and a lover of nature, while activist Rosalie Edge founded Hawk Mountain Sanctuary, the world's first preserve for birds of prey, in 1934. There were many more besides.

To more effectively handle the conservation of the parks, President Woodrow Wilson created the National Park Service (NPS) as a separate agency later in 1916. The NPS continued to expand over the next century, and it continues to grow even today, with its 62nd national park—White Sands *(p246)*—added to the family in 2019.

Above Scottish-born John Muir adored the natural world, especially Yosemite, and campaigned for its conservation

> " Only by going alone in silence, without baggage, can one truly get into the heart of the wilderness. All other travel is mere dust and hotels and baggage and chatter. "

JOHN MUIR, 1888

UNSUNG HEROES

Individuals from different walks of life worked to preserve our natural heritage through the 19th and 20th centuries. Few received the credit they deserved, but the contributions of these unsung heroes are part of this great legacy.

African American contributions

Before emancipation, in 1863, African American guides led tours through the many features of what is now Mammoth Cave National Park, in central Kentucky. Best known among them was Stephen Bishop, who is credited with discovering and exploring many sections of the longest

cave system in the world *(p137)*. Bishop created the first maps and named many of the cave's most prominent landmarks. He was buried in the national park.

In 1903, more than 400 African American men of the US Cavalry were dispatched from their military base at the Presidio in San Francisco to patrol the newly established national parks of Yosemite *(p40)* and Sequoia *(p46)*. Led by Captain Charles Young, this regiment—considered part of the Buffalo Soldiers—performed many of the same duties that park rangers do today. For three summers, until 1906, they built roads, trails, and campgrounds that visitors still use and enjoy.

Trailblazers of the 20th century

George Melendez Wright was a young naturalist of Hispanic descent who, in 1933, he was appointed the first chief of the National Park Service Wildlife Division. Using his own funds, he conducted a four-year study of park sites ranging from Yosemite to the Everglades. With an eye toward restoring parks to their natural state, Wright pushed for the creation and enforcement of policies that restricted the

Above Left Selena LaMarr was famous for educating visitors and Lassen Volcanic National Park staff about the skilled craftsmanship of American Indians

Above Right Buffalo Soldiers of the 9th Cavalry were stationed at Yosemite National Park, under the leadership of Captain Charles Young

Above Captain Charles Young was the first African American national park superintendent

feeding of bears and the killing of predators to encourage ecological balance.

Later in the 20th century, Selena LaMarr shared her Atsugewi tribal customs as an interpretive ranger at Lassen Volcanic National Park (p81). For 20 years, starting in 1952, she gave demonstrations of traditional basket weaving and food preparation to show visitors the culture of a civilization that might otherwise be lost in the past. Dressed in the clothing and beadwork of her ancestors, LaMarr embodied the living memory of an ancient people.

Lancelot Jones was a popular fishing guide and private landowner on Biscayne Bay (p190). Having inherited the property from his formerly enslaved father, Israel Lafayette Jones, the charismatic entrepreneur courted the favor of the millionaires who vacationed there. But when developers attempted to buy up the land to create an exclusive resort community, Lancelot Jones insisted that the environment stay exactly as it was. His resistance contributed to the creation of a national monument in 1968 before Biscayne was designated a national park in 1980.

> " If Martin Luther King were alive today, he would be first and foremost to say we as a people need to go to Yellowstone, we need to go to the Grand Canyon. Because if this is America's best idea and we played a role in this creation, how dare we not choose that for ourselves. "
>
> SHELTON JOHNSON, YOSEMITE NATIONAL PARK INTERPRETIVE RANGER, 2013

INSPIRING IDEAS

Celebrate the Heroes

The NPS has several monuments and celebrations to its unsung heroes.

Buffalo Soldier Speaks

In summer, watch beloved interpretive ranger Shelton Johnson tell the story of the Buffalo Soldiers at the Yosemite Theater (p40).

Old Guides Cemetery

Pay your respects at Stephen Bishop's grave in the cemetery at Mammoth Cave National Park (p136).

Women's History Month

Throughout March, women conservationists and pioneers—both past and present— are celebrated across all the national parks.

Snap the Parks

Try recreating the iconic works of these photographers:

Edward Weston
Echo the sculptural lines snaking across the dunes at White Sands *(p246)*.

Stephen Wilkes
If you're patient, try Wilkes' 2015 day-to-night time-lapse of the Grand Canyon *(p90)*.

Ansel Adams
Adams captured the same frame from Yosemite's Inspiration Point in summer and winter. Can you?

Above Mary Colter designed this house in the Grand Canyon

INSPIRING A GENERATION

The creation of the National Park Service sparked a tourism boom that has yet to subside. Landscape photography drew the public's interest and, as more parks were added, a road trip to a national park became the default summer vacation.

Clever campaigning

Before a National Parks Service could exist, Americans had to believe in it as an idea. With this in mind, parks advocate Stephen Mather teamed up with photographer Robert Sterling Yard in 1915. The two embarked on a publicity campaign designed to persuade the American public that these wild places were theirs to discover and care for. Yard collected stunning photographs of the first established national parks, taken by some of the country's best photographers. With these he created promotional pamphlets and sent them to every member of Congress, plus 275,000 Americans. The NPS was born the following year.

Visionary photography

Perhaps the most influential early park photographers were the Kolb brothers *(p91)*. In 1904, Emery and Ellsworth Kolb established a photo studio at the Grand Canyon—though in reality this was a makeshift tent on the rim above the Bright Angel Trail. By 1906 the tent studio had become a small wooden house, and the brothers were running a healthy business taking and selling photos of park visitors. As adventurous as they were marketing-savvy, the Kolbs would take snapshots of tourists at the canyon's rim, then race down the steep trail to process the images in the river water below, before rushing them back up to the studio ready to sell before the visitors left the park.

The Kolb brothers explored the canyon far and wide, capturing landscapes the likes of which most Americans had never seen. They even made an early motion picture while running the Colorado River, which they presented on lecture tours around the US; that adventure was described in a special issue of *National Geographic*, cementing the Kolbs' reputation and helping spread the word about the incredible natural beauty of the Grand Canyon. Today visitors can take a look inside the ramshackle Kolb Studio, which stands safely in its original location, preserved by the Historic Sites Act, in spite of some officials having campaigned to tear down the studio.

Ansel Adams *(p43)* meanwhile took some of his most famous photographs at Yosemite in the 1920s and 1930s. He first visited the park at the age of 14 and—much like John Muir and Yosemite—it left an indelible impression. He returned with his camera as soon as he was able. In the wilderness Adams found beauty and spirituality, which he aimed to share through

his photography. Adams was more successful than he could ever have predicted. His masterly photographs introduced a generation to the splendor of the western landscape, and mass tourism followed.

Harmonious architecture

Photographers aren't the only ones who shaped the way we see our national parks. Architect Mary Colter (p92) is largely

> " A great photograph is one that fully expresses what one feels, in the deepest sense, about what is being photographed. "
>
> ANSEL ADAMS, 1982

responsible for the distinctive look of the structures in most parks today: how they blend in with the environment, use local and therefore sustainable materials, and look charmingly hand-built. The best examples of Colter's work include several buildings from 1905 through 1932, and cling to the South Rim of the Grand Canyon. These demonstrate how Colter took inspiration from the surrounding landscapes, as well as from American Indian design; her Desert View Watchtower echoes the silhouette of an Anasazi tower, for example, while the Hopi House resembles a traditional dwelling, with its tiny windows and red sandstone walls. The particular style she developed spread to other parks and became known as "National Park Service rustic"—or "parkitecture."

Above Left Emery and Elsworth Kolb did anything to capture that perfect photograph, even being suspended in a crevasse over the Grand Canyon as here, in 1908

Above Right The Kolb brothers loved Grand Canyon's landscape, here showing a man and his donkey on Tanner Ledge, c. 1913

SEND A
RANGER

Park rangers are the face of the national parks—they welcome visitors, keep order, and protect the wilderness. Those familiar uniforms are both reassuring and nostalgic, representing a long tradition of park stewardship.

The early park protectors

The first national park ranger was Harry Yount, the gamekeeper at Yellowstone National Park, who held the position for a year. He was hired in 1880 to manage wildlife in the park and keep hunters and poachers out, as well as to guide prestigious visitors around the land. On leaving, Yount suggested that the territory was too big for just one person to oversee, and that several officers should be stationed in various corners of the park. And so the role of a ranger was born. Previous stewards of the land predate the National Park System, with the likes of the Buffalo Soldiers patrolling parks (p20). Early park stewards were charged with protecting the wilderness from timber thieves, forest fires, and poachers, but they also built roads and trails. With the establishment of the National Park Service in 1916, the role began to take real shape, and today it applies to any NPS employee who wears the iconic uniform and hat. The latter was first worn in Yellowstone in 1929 and it immediately became part of NPS lore.

Rangers and their trainees

Today, the duties of a ranger vary as widely as the parks they work in, and 20,000 rangers work across all NPS sites (plus 2 million volunteers). The shared goal of all rangers

Below Junior Rangers learn new skills and are rewarded with badges

" If a trail is to be blazed, it is 'send a ranger.' If an animal is floundering in the snow, a ranger is sent to pull him out; if a bear is in the hotel, if a fire threatens a forest, if someone is to be saved, it is 'send a ranger. "

STEPHEN T. MATHER, FIRST NPS DIRECTOR, 1929

across NPS parks and monuments is to protect the country's beautiful lands for future generations—which naturally includes the preservation of flora and fauna—while also ensuring visitors are kept safe. But rangers also specialize in either interpretation and visitor services—including providing the best experience for visitors of all backgrounds, and less able-bodied visitors—or law enforcement and protection, which includes wildfire management, emergency services, and search and rescue. All disciplines require extensive training and education, meaning rangers are experts in their fields. Badges on the rangers' uniforms indicate the areas of their skill and responsibility.

Keeping young people engaged with the parks is a crucial part of the ranger role, and the NPS runs a Junior Ranger Program whose motto is "Explore. Learn. Protect," which well summarizes the role of ranger. The program is activity based, and nearly every national park offers children—generally aged 5 to 13—the opportunity to become a Junior Ranger. Curious kids can complete a number of activities in a national park and discuss their findings with a park ranger. The range of activities is wide, encompassing everything from searching for wildlife on a nature walk and hunting for a hidden treasure on a fossils dig, to exploring the cosmos hanging in the night sky. Junior rangers track their activities in an official booklet, and at the end of the program they get a Junior Ranger patch.

INSPIRING IDEAS
Meet the Rangers

There are lots of ways to get involved with the park rangers.

Yellowstone National Park
In summer, rangers lead walks to look for wildlife and hidden geysers. Evening programs are also available (p34).

Grand Canyon National Park
Geology, fossils, and American Indian culture are some of the topics explored on ranger-led hikes at the Grand Canyon (p90).

Glacier National Park
Rangers lead two-hour snowshoe hikes in winter from the Apgar Visitor Center (p66).

Shenandoah National Park
This is one of several parks that offer weekly raptor programs, where visitors can get up-close with birds (p122).

Everglades National Park
Rangers conduct tours on foot, bicycle, canoe, or tram. Don't miss the meteor-shower bike rides (p142).

Top Canyonlands ranger Diane Tom enjoys working with the Junior Rangers

Bottom Park rangers are experts, and can answer all kinds of questions

Alternative Parks

Try these lesser-known but just as lovely parks.

North Cascades
With glacier-fed alpine lakes, excellent backpacking, and wildlife, this *(p162)* is a great alternative to Glacier.

Shenandoah
The sweeping, wooded mountains and misty waterfalls here *(p122)* are similar to Great Smoky Mountains.

Saguaro
If you're considering Joshua Tree, visit here *(p224)* instead. You'll find cactus forests, a diverse ecosystem, and poetic, starlit nights.

Sequoia or Kings Canyon
Want to walk among the giants? Give Yosemite a miss, and head to one of these *(p46* or *p132)* instead.

Lassen Volcanic
Witness geothermal activity to rival Yellowstone here *(p78)*.

Capitol Reef
Often overlooked, this park *(p168)* has the same ruddy cliffs, canyons, and sandstone spires as Zion.

PRESERVING OUR PARKS

The National Parks Service was created in the early 20th century to protect the country's beautiful natural lands. And though many landscapes have changed dramatically since then, this mission statement remains the same.

Rising temperatures

As with all of our planet, the biggest conservation challenge facing the National Park Service today is climate change. Warmer temperatures are recorded at national parks each year. This has a notable visual impact on parks such as Glacier *(p66)*, where glaciers are melting at an unprecedented rate. Scientists predict that—sadly—these icons of the park could disappear altogether by 2030. Additionally, warm and dry weather created by global warming impacts wildlife populations and increases the likelihood of wildfires in national parks. This was seen in the Rim Fire of 2014, which destroyed tens of thousands of acres in Yosemite *(p40)*. The NPS established a central task force devoted to monitoring the environmental impact of climate change in 2010, and is continuing in its efforts to combat the effects. Its conservation efforts include lighting prescribed fires and tree thinning to reduce the chance of wildfires in parks such as Yosemite.

Project of the century

A key challenge is understanding how wildlife and delicate ecosystems can be protected. Rewilding initiatives have been implemented

Above Yellowstone is celebrated for its gray wolves, reintroduced in 1995

within many national parks to save dwindling species. In the 1990s, for example, Yellowstone began rewilding gray wolves, a species that was near the brink of extinction. The park's last wild wolf pack had been killed in 1926 by NPS employees, thanks to a policy to eliminate predators. Without the wolves, coyotes ran rampant and the elk population exploded, which in turn meant overgrazing, leading to a decline in bird and beaver populations, plus river erosion. Scientists realized that top predators were needed to balance the ecosystem in Yellowstone, and so 14 gray wolves were introduced to the park in 1995. Within 10 years, the willow and aspen groves rebounded, the river banks and bird and beaver populations stabilized, and rare species such as foxes, badgers, and eagles returned. Yellowstone was rehabilitated through rewilding and the initiative has become one of the most celebrated success stories of the NPS. This is just one example, and various other research studies and initiatives are taking place. In Glacier, scientists are tracking dwindling harlequin ducks, while plans are afoot to move bison from the Grand Canyon, as the creatures overgraze meadows, contaminate water sources, and trample across ancient sites.

Play your part

Over-tourism naturally impacts the wildlife and environment of the national parks. Summer sees particularly high numbers, and visitors flock to the giants—such as Yellowstone and Yosemite. The NPS has established various programs to counterbalance the effects of this, such as permit systems to scale Half Dome in Yosemite. You can play a part in preserving the parks. For a start, there are 62 parks to choose from, including lesser-known gems with equally breathtaking landscapes. Visit the NPS website for more, or turn to p253 for tips.

Right Paths run throughout Yosemite, and the parks generally, to ensure wildlife is undisturbed and protected

ACCESSIBLE FOR ALL

There's a spirit of inclusion in all NPS programs, facilities, and lodges, and the service works tirelessly to make these amazing spaces accessible to all. Here are a few ideas to inspire you—turn to p253 for more information.

For the hearing impaired

The parks really are for everyone, and deaf visitors will discover various initiatives to enhance their visit. Most park visitor centers have captioned videos and assistive listening devices to fully orient deaf visitors and help

bring the parks to life. In Yosemite *(p40)*, interpreters and assistive listening devices are available for ranger-led hikes. One favorite hike begins behind the sumptuous Ahwahnee Hotel and winds through the surrounding thick forest. Assisted listening devices are also available for the magical evening campfire programs at Sequoia *(p46)* and Kings Canyon *(p132)* national parks.

For the visually impaired

Many national parks have Braille and large-print transcriptions of their maps and guides. Individual parks also have specific programs and facilities. Blind visitors to the Grand Canyon *(p90)*, for example, can experience this natural wonder through the sense of touch on the Trail of Time. The trail runs along the canyon rim and presents a geologic timeline of the park, with touchable rock samples adding a sensory experience. Likewise, the Chapin Mesa Archaeological Museum in Mesa Verde National Park *(p60)* has artifacts like bone tools available for tactile investigation. Blind visitors to Mammoth Cave *(p136)* can visualize the park's mystical caverns thanks to a tactile sculpture in the visitor center. And in Shenandoah *(p122)*, the official park app includes vivid audio descriptions of the overlooks along gorgeous Skyline Drive.

Traveling by foot or wheelchair

As for exploring the parks on foot or by wheelchair, there's a world of possibilities. In Death Valley National Park *(p220)*, slow

Below Wheelchair users will find all kinds of scenery awaiting them, such as at Glacier National Park

Above Visitors can watch and listen to the eruption of Old Faithful in Yellowstone

walkers can explore the ruins at Harmony Borax Works, which produced borax in the 1880s. A slightly graded, hard-packed dirt trail leads around the abandoned equipment, bringing you closer to the park's history. Over in Mount Rainier National Park (p50), slow walkers can enjoy the charmingly named Trail of the Shadows, which winds through the forest, past beaver lodges. The hard-packed trail is generally level, and features interpretive plaques about Mount Rainier's eruption.

If you're wanting to take more of a back seat, Crater Lake Trolley Tours in Crater Lake (p54) gives slow walkers a chance to rest their feet and enjoy a scenic ride around the lake while learning about its history. Over in Arches National Park (p174),

meanwhile, slow walkers can take a stroll on the South Window Trail. The hard-packed dirt trail is fairly level, though there are a few steps leading up to an overlook, which offers an impressive red-rock view.

In Yellowstone (p34), wheelchair users can get a front row seat for Old Faithful's electrifying eruption on the barrier-free boardwalk near the geyser. Alternatively they can watch it through the floor-to-ceiling windows in the wheelchair-accessible visitor center. The Sterling Munro Boardwalk at Mount Rainier is also wheelchair-accessible. The half-mile (1 km) trail winds through the forest to a viewpoint offering a panoramic view of the Picket Range.

For something a little different, Great Sand Dunes (p236) and Indiana Dunes (p244) both offer loaner beach wheelchairs, so wheelchair users can still explore the dunes. Lovers of wildlife can board a red bus tour in Glacier National Park, equipped with onboard cameras to bring you closer to resident mammals, from bison to bighorn sheep.

> **"It's just a matter of the Park Service reaching out to all sectors of the community to make sure every citizen has the opportunity to learn a little bit more."**
>
> ROBERT STANTON, PAST NPS DIRECTOR, 1997

INSPIRING IDEAS

Accessible Adventures

There's no shortage of wheelchair-accessible adventures.

Relish the Water
Enjoy the healing waters at Sol Duc Hot Springs in Olympic National Park (p126).

Sleep Outside
Pitch your tent at a backcountry campsite at Rocky Mountain (p72), or camp in an accessible tent cabin at Yosemite's Tuolumne Meadows Lodge (p40).

Enjoy the View
Admire the Grand Canyon (p90) on an accessible airplane tour, or view the Bryce Canyon amphitheater from Bryce Point (p104).

Go Underground
Tour the underground chambers at Carlsbad Caverns (p112) or Mammoth Cave (p136).

Ride the Rails
Hop aboard Cuyahoga Falls Scenic Railway for a slow ramble (p232).

LOOKING TO THE FUTURE

The NPS has expanded and the parks have evolved, but they remain an essential means of escape from our busy lives, and a vital resource to preserve for future generations.

Approaching the next 250 years

The year 2026 will see the 250th anniversary of the Declaration of Independence. This document embodied the American vision of a new, free land—though many did lose their homes and lives in the process. Little did the Signers of the Declaration know that, more than 200 years later, the American people would become stewards of the country's mountains, forests, deserts, and wetlands—essentially making every American citizen a park ranger. And that these lands of wonder would be officially protected by the National Park Service. There is certainly much to mourn and learn, but there is also much to celebrate and remember as we approach the next 250 years and look to protect the wilderness for future generations.

The NPS continues to work hard to foster diversity and inclusion, and acknowledges that there is more work to be done here over the coming years. The national parks are—after all—for everyone. Initiatives such as Women's History Month cast a spotlight on those who have been written out of history, while partnerships with American Indian organizations connect

Below Left Navajo dance performances remind us of the Grand Canyon's long history

Below Center Children of the future will hopefully enjoy parks like Redwood

Below Right Joshua Tree is just one park in which you can switch off

visitors with the parklands' rich heritage. Likewise, climate change is having a physical impact on the natural world, and the NPS continues to research ways to safeguard the parks and their wildlife for years to come.

The power of nature

In the National Park Service's earliest days, the American people flocked to the parks to enjoy a break from their daily lives and revel in being in nature. Times have little changed—this sense of escapism is needed more than ever, as our lives are more hectic than ever. Studies show that spending time in nature increases our health and overall sense of well-being. Exploring the national parks by foot, climbing their cliffsides, and cycling their mountain trails are a wonderful way to experience the natural scenery. And the parks are also perfect for pursuing wellness of a different kind: yoga, stargazing, and forest bathing allow us to find stillness and calm in the wilderness.

The United States has changed dramatically since 1872, when Yellowstone was established as the very first national park. But the NPS mission has remained steadfast and history is still being written, as "new" parks are being welcomed into the fold, such as White Sands in 2019. You're part of the story moving forward. So flip through the following pages and contemplate your future relationship with these lands of wonder.

> **" These beautiful things from the past carry us into the future. "**
>
> GROWING THUNDER FAMILY (JOYCE, JUANITA, AND JESSA RAE), 2019

Left Mount Rainier
National Park is awash
with color in spring

The
Parks

FOCUS ON
Forces of Nature

Yellowstone sits above two vast bodies of magma (molten rock), lying miles under the surface. The superhot temperatures heat the groundwater, which bubbles up as pressure builds. Geysers form when narrow underground chambers constrict the water, which reaches temperatures of 244°F (118°C). Once the pressure is too great, it sends the pent-up steam and boiling water bursting out of the earth in a dramatic plume.

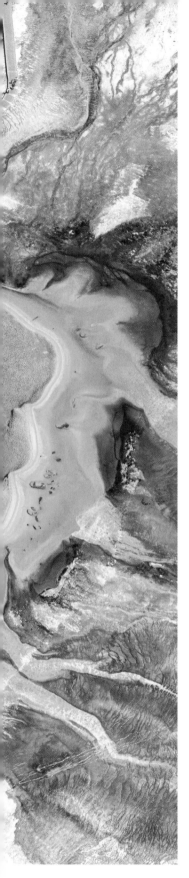

Left Its almost psychedelic colors make Grand Prismatic Spring a photographer's dream

Wyoming • Montana • Idaho

YELLOWSTONE

ESTABLISHED 1872

With gushing geysers, geothermal wonders, a wealth of large wildlife, and superlative Rocky Mountain landscapes, America's first national park remains one of the most spectacular places in the world.

Set atop a dormant supervolcano, Yellowstone contains more than half the world's geysers and hydrothermal features. Early 19th-century explorers described it as a place of fire and brimstone, and their reports of boiling mud and petrified trees were dismissed as tall tales or a touch of lunacy. Later, when the unique features and environmental importance of this incredible landscape were realized, Yellowstone became the first national park. In 1978, it was made a UNESCO World Heritage Site.

A wild wonderland

Today, you might describe Yellowstone as nature's ultimate spa. You can walk amid bubbling mudpots, hissing fumaroles, and sizzling hot springs in a remarkable, otherworldly landscape that glows in the sunlight with seemingly unnatural, fluorescent hues. In some places, the sulfurous smell of rotten eggs will wrinkle your nose. At the park's many geysers, the underground cauldron erupts in awesome towers of steam that billow into the clouds.

And there's more. The park comprises several regions, and its geologic wonders include deep, rugged canyons, torrential waterfalls, vast alpine lakes, towering peaks, splendid travertine terraces, and the mighty Yellowstone River. Its forests and grasslands are home to a staggering array of wildlife, including wolves, bears, and the largest public bison herd in the country.

Star showstopper

Yellowstone's amazing geothermal features are what make this national park unique. And none is more famous than the iconic geyser Old Faithful. Most geysers are unpredictable, but this one, named by explorers in 1870, is one of a handful tracked by park rangers. It erupts about 20 times a day, approximately every 90 minutes, although the intervals can vary up to half an hour. Predicted eruptions are posted at park buildings, or just look out for the gathering crowd.

You'll have to be quick for a ringside seat at Old Faithful, but the magnificent plume of thundering steam shoots up 185 ft (56 m), an awesome sight stretching far beyond the viewing deck. Each jaw-dropping eruption, which lasts under five minutes, sprays 3,700–8,400 gal (14,000–32,000 l) of boiling water into the sky.

Old Faithful is the star of Yellowstone's Upper Geyser Basin, but it's not the biggest in the park. The largest in the world is Steamboat Geyser, with major eruptions that can soar 300–400 ft (90–120 m) high. In fact, there are more than 500 active geysers here, clustered in fascinating geyser basins.

Nature's wizardry

Venturing onto the trails at Norris Geyser Basin, Yellowstone's hottest and oldest thermal area, is like walking into a wizard's cauldron. The rank odors of sulfurous gases belch from bubbling mudpots. Minerals and bacteria turn the crust near the roiling hot pools a rainbow of colors. It's a primeval scene you'll see nowhere else.

Midway Geyser Basin is home to the world's third-largest hot spring, the Grand Prismatic Spring, a gigantic sizzling pool of electric blue flanked by fiery bands of

Above Steam rises from the Norris Geyser Basin, even as a snow dusting covers the boardwalk

Above Bison serenely munch on grasses as the geyser Old Faithful waterworks perform behind

Wildlife Haven

Bison have lived here since prehistoric times. In the 1900s, the park was key in bringing them back from near extinction. Today, it provides habitat for other threatened species too:

▽ **Grizzly bears** The park is one of the last refuges for these awesome bears. Look for them in the Hayden and Lamar valleys, the north slopes of Mount Washburn, and from Fishing Bridge to the east entrance.

▷ **Bison** From fewer than 50 individuals in 1902, the free-ranging Yellowstone bison herd now numbers 4,900, the country's largest bison herd on public lands. The Lamar Valley is the best place to see them.

△ **Gray wolves** Yellowstone helped ensure the survival of this endangered species when they were reintroduced here in 1995. They now roam freely through the park, and are best seen at sunrise and sunset in the northern range.

△ **Canadian lynx** Yellowstone provides critical habitat for the elusive Canadian lynx, noted for its silver-brown fur and black-tufted ears. A group lives in the conifer forests and preys on snowshoe hare.

orange, yellow, and green. The springs get their dazzling hues from thermophiles, tiny organisms that thrive in the extreme heat. At Roaring Mountain, you'll hear the hissing of a mountainside covered in steaming fumaroles venting from the netherworld.

BEST FOR
Cool Places to Stay

Nothing beats the thrill of watching the eruption of the world's most famous geyser from the hotel sundeck of the Old Faithful Inn. Built in 1903–04, this rustic masterpiece is among the last log hotels in the country, and sports gabled dormers jutting from a seven-story roof, a 65-ft (20-m) rock fireplace in the lobby, pine-railed balconies, and cozy rooms.

World of wildlife

Yellowstone's spellbinding geyser basins also provide warmth for the park's wildlife. Bison in particular winter in thermal areas when deep snow covers their summer grazing grounds. Most of the rest of the park is covered in forest, which, along with the grasslands, provides a haven for a vast range of animals and birds.

Yellowstone has the finest habitat for megafauna (large animals) in the Lower 48. Wildlife jams are frequent along park roads, as cars stop to watch bears, moose, and bison. You are likely to see elk and deer and, if lucky, a coyote or wolf running through a clearing. Look for mountain goats and bighorn sheep on rocky ledges. Your best chance of seeing animals of all sizes is on a quiet hiking trail. Wherever you go in the park, wildlife watching is one of Yellowstone's biggest attractions.

3,472

The size of the park in square miles (8,991 sq km), which is larger than either Rhode Island or Delaware.

900

In miles (1,450 km), the total length of the hiking trails throughout the park.

4

The number of visitors, in millions, that the park welcomes a year.

Endless exploration

If you did nothing more than marvel at Old Faithful and spot some of the park's wildlife, you would leave Yellowstone happy. But there is so much more to explore.

Perhaps the best way to experience the park is along its vast hiking trails, which wind down into the canyons and up Rocky Mountain peaks standing up to 11,000 ft (3,350 m) high. From these lofty heights, survey the park's many splendors.

In the center of the park is Yellowstone Lake, one of the world's largest alpine lakes. As you gaze across its tranquil waters, consider that it was created by a volcanic explosion and the collapse of the Yellowstone caldera 174,000 years ago. Paddle, sail, or cruise onto it from marinas on the shore.

The mighty torrent carves out the Grand Canyon of the Yellowstone. Twenty miles (32 km) long and 1,000 ft (300 m) deep, this narrow cleft reveals layers of geologic color in the rock walls and bursts

Below The dense forested walls bring a vivid green to the lower part of the park's Grand Canyon

July and August are the best months for camping, when temperatures are warm enough to pitch a tent and sleep under the stars.

of steam from hydrothermal features. Take in the views from drives along the north and south rims. Ospreys nest on the canyon's pinnacles, and you may spy them soaring aloft or feeding their chicks. The canyon ends at the Tower waterfall, which plunges into a hanging valley between lava-rock columns.

In the north of the park, nature has fashioned remarkable travertine terraces at Mammoth Hot Springs. Once again, hydrothermal forces are at play, depositing layer upon layer of dissolved limestone in a staircase of chalky white and burnt orange that resembles a frozen waterfall.

Activities in abundance

You can enjoy outdoor pursuits year-round. Licensed outfitters offer guided horseback trips, and during spring and fall, cycling is permitted on designated park roads. In winter, explore a magical wonderland on snowshoes or skis along groomed trails.

Superb fly-fishing for brown and rainbow trout draws anglers from all over, and there are many idyllic rivers where you can cast your line. None is finer than the Yellowstone River, the longest free-flowing river below the Canadian border. From aptly named viewpoints such as Inspiration Point and Artist Point, you'll have breathtaking vistas of the river plummeting over the Upper Falls and the even larger Lower Falls, its roaring white water like a geyser in reverse.

Best Day Hikes

Mountain hike ▷ Bunsen Peak, 4.6 miles (7 km) round trip. A moderately steep switchback trail leads up through meadows and forest to the summit, where there are stunning panoramic views of the Yellowstone River valley.

Canyon hike ▷ Seven Mile Hole Trail, 10 miles (16 km) round trip. Enjoy splendid views of Silver Cord Cascade from the canyon rim before descending 1,000 ft (300 m) into the Grand Canyon of the Yellowstone.

Lake hike Yellowstone Lake Overlook Trail, 1.7 miles (2.7 km) round trip. After a steep ascent that passes thermal features, you'll reach a high mountain meadow with grand views over the West Thumb area of the lake.

Waterfall and geysers hike ▷ Fairy Falls Trail, 6.7 miles (11 km) round trip. Hike to one of the park's finest waterfalls, then carry on past steaming hot springs to Spray and Imperial geysers.

Left The spectacular Mammoth Hot Springs terraces have been described as an "inside-out cave"

Did You Know?

Yellowstone has more than 10,000 hydrothermal features.

California

YOSEMITE

ESTABLISHED 1890

The name Yosemite conjures images of looming
mountains and riotous meadows, pure lakes and
rushing waterfalls, and, of course, those giant sequoias.
This second-oldest park delivers on all its promises.

Yosemite National Park is about grandeur. Among its countless spectacular waterfalls is Yosemite Falls, at 2,425 ft (739 m) the highest in North America. Thirty-one peaks reach above 12,000 ft (3,658 m), and the age of many redwood trees is measured in thousands of years. The soaring cliffs of the Half Dome and El Capitan combine with this wilderness to lend Yosemite its incomparable beauty. High up on Tuolumne Meadows in the Sierra Nevada, you can see a dazzling display of wildflowers in July and August, when the plants shake off the winter snows.

Majestic flora

A rare mix of topography, climate, and soil creates the range of native plants found at Yosemite. Explore the different terrains and look out for mountain willow, sky-blue alpine asters, and verdant-green sedges. Standing tall among them all are the trees: at lower elevations, blue oak and gray pine, while elsewhere the incense of cedar fills the air. And, of course, the arboreal movie stars are the giant sequoias. In Mariposa Grove, trees have their own names, such as the Fallen Monarch and Grizzly Giant.

FLORA AND FAUNA
Yosemite Toads

Native to the Sierra Nevada mountains, this threatened species likes to sun itself on warm rocks. Don't be tempted to touch: they emit a toxin to deter predators.

Eyes are close-set, with horizontal pupils

Only females have spots and splotches

Above The world's largest tree, the giant sequoia goes by other names: Sierra redwood and just plain big tree

Left A UNESCO World Heritage Site, Yosemite is awash with color in the warm sunshine

Through the lens

It was American photographer Ansel Adams who showed the world that Yosemite's most remarkable features are its mighty mountains and imposing rock formations. He was drawn again and again to photograph places like El Capitan and the Half Dome, capturing them in different lights and seasons to show their changing moods.

It's hard to single out one feature, but perhaps the aptly named El Capitan shows the best of Yosemite. The perfect sighting of its sheer cliff face is from Tunnel View, on Highway 41—of course, you'll be sharing this with many other onlookers. Still, if this is your first experience of Yosemite, it's a jaw-dropper of a view, also introducing you to the Half Dome and the Bridalveil Fall.

For a more personal experience, tackle El Capitan Trail, which starts near Yosemite Village and is a tough 14-mile (23-km) round trip to the top of El Capitan. It is a challenge, though not as much as your other option: the 3,000-ft (914-m) climb of its sheer granite face. If the views from the bottom are awe-inspiring, just consider what the views from the top are like.

Half Dome was another Adams favorite, a granite formation 8,836 ft (2,693 m) high that does indeed look like a rock dome that has been sliced in half. Standing above the

Sunset is the best time for atmospheric shots, when the fog rolls in and blankets the peaks.

Below Visitors admire the mesmerizing views of Half Dome and the valley from Glacier Point

valley floor, the silhouette of this cliff has become the symbol of Yosemite. One of the easiest ways to see it is from Mirror Lake, a short hike from Yosemite Village; one of the toughest and most exhilarating is to climb to the top. The latter requires a full day to cover the 15-mile (24-km) round trip, starting from the valley floor. It begins as a pleasant, even idyllic, hike through woodland, with the serenade of warblers, the chatter of sparrows, and possibly even the rat-a-tat-tat of a woodpecker.

When you emerge from the woods, however, you face the last section, up the side of the dome itself, hauling yourself up

using twin cables bolted into the rock. It becomes increasingly obvious why Half Dome was once considered totally inaccessible. Today, aided by the cables, the fully fit hiker can pull their way to the top. One feature here is the so-called "Diving Board" from which Ansel Adams took the shot he rightly called "Monolith, the Face of Half Dome."

At 10,916 ft (3,327 m), Cathedral Peak is over 2,000 ft (610 m) higher than Half Dome and it's yet another of Yosemite's distinctive shapes. Here, you may have to settle for the view, unless you're an experienced climber, but you can still hike the Climber's Approach Trail to soak up the scenery from the bottom and capture some amazing photos of dare-devil rock-climbers who take to the bare, rocky surfaces like mountain goats.

Above El Capitan is a mercurial creature, changing its look to suit the weather and season

PARK PIONEERS
Ansel Adams

Ansel Adams was 14 years old when he first visited Yosemite with his family in 1916. By age 20, he had become successful for his black-and-white images of the park, pushing physical and technical boundaries to get the perfect shot of El Capitan and the Half Dome. He became one of America's best photographers and continued to share his love for Yosemite by conducting workshops there (p22).

Left The powerful waters of Yosemite Falls plunge down into the conifer woodlands of the Yosemite Valley

Mighty waters

If there's one feature that makes people go "Wow!" in Yosemite, it's the triple-decker Yosemite Falls. This is especially so in the spring, when the falls are at their height, thundering with the added water of the melting mountain snows. It's the highest waterfall in the park, its waters plunging 2,425 ft (739 m) before crashing into pools and against rocks to create three separate sections. Tumbling in two great leaps, Upper and Lower Yosemite Falls are at their most spectacular in May and June. By September, however, the falls often dry up due to the hot summer weather, and tend not to flow again for a few months.

Yosemite Falls may be the highest and most impressive falls, but the park is filled with water features easily accessible from Yosemite Village. These include the Bridalveil Fall, a short (but steep) hike from the parking lot to a mighty 617-ft (188-m) plunge, which runs all year.

With dozens of falls to choose from, it's not hard to find isolated spots. Relatively few people see the Wapama Falls, in the beautiful Hetch Hetchy Valley. A little over

Three-quarters of visitors arrive May through October, and some trails close in winter, so April offers the best balance of activities and peacefulness.

Above Located in the northwest of the park is the remote Hetch Hetchy Reservoir

an hour's drive up pine-lined roads from Yosemite Village brings you to the serene blue expanse of Hetch Hetchy Reservoir.

The Wapama Falls are visible in the distance from the parking lot at the O'Shaughnessy Dam, and the trail there runs beside the reservoir's sparkling waters. You'll splash your way through several streams, and if you come too early in the year those streams will make the track impassable. Listen for the crash in the woods that might just be a bear running, and watch where you tread—rattlesnakes live here, too. At journey's end, you'll be upclose with these dramatic falls, which can be so fierce in spring that they engulf the bridge at their base.

Reflected views

Falls are not the only water features in the park. Visit the hauntingly beautiful Mono Lake. Covering an area of 70 sq miles (181 sq km), the lake is at least 760,000 years old. There are pleasures to be had year-round: a clear winter's day is the perfect time to observe the gnarled tufa towers jutting from the water; in spring and fall, millions of birds make it their home; and in summer you can swim in its dense, ultra-salty waters.

Not surprisingly, the waters of the aptly named Mirror Lake make superb reflections of the cliffs behind in the water. This lake can be reached by a trail that weaves through woodland from Yosemite Village. It lacks the scale of Mono Lake, and in drier weather may even disappear completely, but when filled in late summer, it makes the perfect tranquil spot to enjoy the views of mountains and forests.

90

The percentage of visitors who don't venture beyond Yosemite Valley, which makes up just 1 percent of the park.

209

Height of the Grizzly Giant, the tallest tree, in ft (64 m). It's also the oldest.

13,114

In ft (3,997 m), the height of Mount Lyell, the highest point in Yosemite.

Right A lone hiker surveys the lunar landscape at the dried up Mono Lake

Right Climbing one
of the park's eastern
mountains, like Alta Peak,
affords superb views

California

SEQUOIA

ESTABLISHED 1890

The call of the wild is strong here. Preserving the
earth's largest living trees, towering granite peaks,
and alluring lakes, Sequoia National Park is a colossal
adventure land that takes the breath away.

There's something inherently magical about
a park named after 2,000-year-old sequoia
trees, a species that John Muir *(p19)* saluted
as "the very gods of the forest." And godly
this park is, harboring a 10,000-year-old
cave complex deep beneath the earth and
the highest peak in the Lower 48 states.

FAMILY FUN
Ranger for a Day

For just one day every year the park
invites children ages six and up to
earn a Junior Ranger badge. Become a
ranger and enjoy a host of activities
for all ages, including learning how
to be a mule-packer or working with
the park fire service.

On top of the world

The eastern half of Sequoia is where the
park's famed peak, Mount Whitney, sits at
a height of 14,505 ft (4,421 m). Although this
is one of the few mountains of its size that
you can hike without any mountaineering
skills, the trek to the top is no mean feat.
Once you get your permit, you'll want to do
some training at high altitudes, as thinner
air at the upper elevations will leave you
breathless. For those up to the challenge,
it's an experience like no other, covering a
distance of 22 miles (35 km) that can take
up to 16 hours, so set off before sunrise.

Mount Langley is almost as high at
14,032 ft (4,277 m), but attracts fewer
hikers to its intense 21-mile (34-km)
ascent, making it a more serene adventure.
If you prefer easier hikes, then do what
the pioneers did, and head west.

The Sequoias

Sequoias are among the longest-living organisms on earth, which is why they get so big: they just keep on growing, and they develop quickly compared to other trees. They have surprisingly shallow roots in order to collect all the water they need to keep them alive, most of which they gather from melting winter snows. Their thick bark also protects them from all but the fiercest fires.

Below The sequoia trees rise commandingly over the green meadows, humbling visitors with their sheer size

Namesake trees

Defining the landscape in the western half of the park are the renowned and striking enormous sequoias. Giant among them is the General Sherman Tree, the largest known tree on the planet when measured by volume, standing 275 ft (84 m) high and thought to be 2,300–2,700 years old.

This gargantuan tree is in the park's aptly named Giant Forest, which is home to five of the ten biggest trees on earth. Walking through whole groves of sequoias, some as tall as a 26-story building, is a humbling and awe-inspiring experience.

The land through the trees

While the giant sequoias are the undeniable draw here, the park is imbued with natural wonders and dramatically diverse landscapes in abundance. Deep beneath your feet lies a network of subterranean caves and tunnels. The most majestic and rightfully beloved of these is Crystal Cave, which welcomes hardy explorers from May to September. If you can bear the steep hike up through woodland and alongside ravines to the cave entrance, plus another 45 minutes of walking on the guided tour, this underground wonderland reveals its hidden pools, surreal rock formations, and a stream that has been polished like marble.

Water features make up an incredible landscape above ground, too. Here you will meander past rivers that are part of the National Wild and Scenic Rivers system. Though majestic, these rivers become dangerous during spring and early summer, when melting snow from nearby peaks reduces the temperature to a hazardous icy cold. More calming are the lakes and ponds—over 3,200—that are essential to the survival of the park's wildlife, including coyotes, cougars, wolverines, beavers, black bears, and amphibians like the endangered yellow-legged frog. Precipice Lake, almost in the very center of the park, is arguably the most astonishing, with a backdrop of strange rock formations that make for an otherworldly image.

To truly immerse yourself in the park's mesmerizing water spectacles nestled within the lush landscape, embark on the Little Five Lakes Trail, a loop trail of around 30 miles (48 km) that starts in the subalpine glacial valley of Mineral King. It's worth the strenuous trek not only for the lakes, but for the dramatic waterfalls, vivid wildflower meadows, dense forests, and winding rivers along the route. Another exhilarating and challenging hike is the Big Five Lakes Trail. Leading through a glacial valley and woodland, here you'll pass five gorgeous lakes as alpine peaks rise majestically around you. Even taking on the shortest and easiest hiking paths that are on offer in this park will have you in awe of Mother Nature's creations.

Above Precipice Lake is almost an ethereal vision, its calming turquoise waters reflecting the jagged granite cliffs

Three Hikes

Popular ▷ Big Trees Trail, 1.3-mile (2.1-km) loop trail. Discover the significance of giant sequoias and the area's ecology on this short and paved hike near Three Rivers. Have your camera at the ready for monumental low-angle shots of the famed golden trees.

Peaceful Big Baldy Ridge Trail, 6 miles (10 km) round trip. Let colorful wildflowers lead you to spectacular viewpoints from the summit of Big Baldy in the late spring.

Remote ▷ Little Baldy Trail, 1.7 miles (2.7 km) round trip. Surprisingly one of the lesser-known trails in the park, the steep climb to the top of Little Baldy offers 360-degree views over the park.

Did You Know?

Of the 25 park glaciers, Emmons is the largest.

14,411

Elevation in ft (4,392 m) of the summit.

964

The number of plant species in the park.

1895

The last year the volcano erupted.

Washington

MOUNT RAINIER

ESTABLISHED 1899

Named for the active volcano that dominates the area, Mount Rainier National Park holds a mythic status among city-dwellers from nearby Seattle, beckoning visitors with its breathtaking scenery, abundant wildlife, and historic inns.

Nestled against the south side of Mount Rainier is the perfectly named Paradise, an area filled with accessible trails that wind up the mountainside through technicolor fields of wildflowers. Here you gaze across the epic views of Unicorn Peak and its row of neighbors to the south. The twisting, turning road from the Nisqually Entrance reveals rushing waterfalls and evergreen-framed peaks at every turn—and offers an up-close look at Mount Rainier.

Hiker's paradise

Hiking options abound, from afternoon strolls to serious climbing, offering something for everyone—a crowd-pleasing choice is the Skyline Trail to Panorama Point, a 5.5-mile (9-km) round trip. On a clear day, not only is there an unimpeded view of Mount Rainier, but mounts Adams, St. Helens, and Hood stand out on the horizon, too. The road to Paradise is usually open in winter, so when trails are snow-covered, pack your skis or snowshoes. The 93-mile (150-km) Wonderland Trail is a classic backpacking loop that encircles the mountain; sections can be done as day hikes. For the really experienced climber, a trek to the summit with a mountaineering guide is fantastic. Wherever you go, bring your good camera—and a wide-angle lens.

Above The easy slopes of the Skyline Trail make it possible to focus entirely on the beautiful surrounds

Far Left One of the best parts of the Skyline Trail is called Panorama Point—which says it all

Left A lavish grand lobby is just one reason the Paradise Inn is a National Historic Landmark

PARK PIONEERS
Dee Molenaar

Dee Molenaar was a ranger devoted to Mount Rainier. He climbed it more than 50 times, wrote books about it, and spent his 100th birthday in his wheelchair at its base. He was one of the climbers saved in 1953 by "The Belay," Pete Schoening's hair-raising group of six roped climbers who fell while descending K2 in the Karakoram Range in Pakistan.

The past in the present

Each corner of the enormous Mount Rainier National Park offers up its own delights. Longmire—namesake of homesteader James Longmire—is the gateway to Paradise and a designated historic district. Longmire built the first guest cabins here in 1889, soon adding a hotel and clubhouse, which is the oldest remaining building here. A self-guided walking tour among the historic buildings leads you through the district's early days. Starting here, too, is the Trail of the Shadows, an accessible walk past hot springs and an early homestead. Longer treks include the 9-mile (15-km) Narada Falls Trail, with three waterfalls set deep in dense forest.

Cowlitz country

In the park's southeast corner, Ohanapecosh is named for an ancient Taidnapam (Upper Cowlitz tribe) site meaning "standing at the edge." Drier and warmer than Paradise, it's famous for gorgeous fall colors and

old-growth trees. Gentle trails meander among towering Douglas firs, Western hemlock, and red cedars, while following the glacial Ohanapecosh River. Longer hikes pass rushing waterfalls, while a jaunt along Hot Springs Trail leads to tiny hot-springs pools—too small to bathe in, but a sure sign of the forces that churn beneath.

In the northeast corner is the bustling Sunrise area. At 6,400 ft (1,950 m), this is the highest point in the park accessible by car. Visitors are met with 360-degree views of Mount Rainier and Emmons Glacier.

And then there's "the quiet corner"— Carbon River and Mowich Lake. In the park's early days, the area attracted dubious mining claims, some of which were land grabs by settlers or even poachers. None of the mines struck it rich, and preservationists won out when Congress ended mining in the park.

This corner's charms lie in its peacefulness—the mellow, mossy hikes through temperate forest and pretty lakeside campsites at Mowich Lake. It's an excellent place to cycle, particularly along the old Carbon River Road, which leads hikers and cyclists to an isolated backcountry campground.

Above The park has four suspension bridges, three of which are footbridges only

Through the Seasons

Spring The park awakes from its winter slumber in April—the perfect time for bracing hikes at lower elevations and seeing breathtaking waterfalls gushing at peak flow until June.

Summer ▷ July and August offer up an unparalleled chance to cherish the sight of colorful wildflowers blooming across every alpine field. Stroll through picturesque meadows to spot daisies, asters, lilies, and more varieties.

Fall ▷ September and October are the best months to explore popular trails. Slow down to admire towering trees that have stood for a thousand years on the Grove of the Patriarchs hike, a 1-mile (1.6-km) loop that takes you over the Ohanapecosh River.

Winter ▷ Although most roads are closed, the snow-cloaked park remains open from November through May. Ski or snowshoe from Narada Falls parking lot to see Mount Rainier's white-topped peak mirrored in the still waters of Reflection Lake. A sledding hill just above the upper parking lot at Paradise is the perfect playground for fun.

Left The Carbon River valley has been shaped by both glaciers and volcanic activity

Did You Know?

The Paradise area once held the world record for measured snowfall in a single year: 93½ ft (28.5 m) in 1971–2.

WASHINGTON

○ Portland

OREGON

Eugene ○

IDAHO

■ CRATER LAKE

Medford ○

CALIFORNIA | NEVADA

Oregon

CRATER LAKE

ESTABLISHED 1902

Famous for the startling color and clarity
of its lake, the caldera of what was once
Mount Mazama is the crown jewel of Oregon's
only national park, surrounded by
equally beautiful forestland.

Crater Lake's serene surface belies its dramatic origins. The lake came into existence when a monumental 12,000-ft (3,650-m) volcano called Mount Mazama erupted 7,700 years ago, devastating the pristine landscape and forming a caldera that gradually—over 250 years—filled with a supply of rainwater.

Above Visitors wait for the ferryboat to shuttle them across the lake

The eruption that formed Crater Lake was cataclysmic and fast—geologists say it took hours, or at most a few days—but it wasn't the first eruption. The indigenous Klamath peoples who inhabited the area had witnessed thousands of years of volcanic activity from Mount Mazama. When this last violent episode occurred, they saw it as an epic battle between the sky god, Skell, and the god of the world below, Llao, who inhabited the mountain. Details vary, but in most versions of the story the gods were battling over a woman, and the battle ended when Skell forced Llao back into the mountain, which then destroyed itself. Afterward, the Klamath considered the lake sacred; only shamans could look at it, and they kept it a secret from the white settlers. Its existence wasn't recorded officially until 1862, when Oregon prospector Chauncey Nye wrote a newspaper column about seeing the deep-blue lake.

Above A snow-covered Wizard Island sits in the middle of Crater Lake, the deepest lake in the United States

Did You Know?

The name Mazama comes from an American Indian word for mountain goat, derived from an Aztec word for "small deer."

1,943

The deepest point in ft (592 m) of Crater Lake.

6

The diameter in miles (10 km) of the lake.

44

The average annual snowfall in ft (14 m).

1949

The last year it was cold enough for the lake to freeze over.

Unexplained mysteries

Three mysterious shapes pierce Crater Lake's placid surface. The biggest is Wizard Island, a cinder cone that sticks 755 ft (230 m) above the water, created by one of several smaller eruptions on the caldera floor after Mount Mazama imploded. Visible from the southeast side of the rim is the Phantom Ship, a gnarled rock formation resembling a spooky pirate vessel, especially when glimpsed through fog. Weirdest of all is the Old Man of the Lake, a 30-ft (9-m) tree stump that bobs around the water, jutting 4 ft (1 m) into the air and traveling freely. It can go miles in a day, sometimes moving against the wind. In the 1980s, scientists leashed the Old Man to the shore while exploring the lake with submarines; immediately, a snowstorm blew in—in August. As soon as someone freed the log, the storm cleared, and the mystery of the Old Man continued.

If you have...

An hour ▷ Head for the Steel Information Center near the park entrance to pick up a map. Then start your journey by car, heading to Rim Drive, where you can drink in the views from Crater Lake Lodge.

A day Follow the full 33-mile (53-km) Rim Drive, stopping at various overlooks to gulp in fresh air and enjoy the scenery. Better yet, make the loop by bicycle.

A weekend ▷ Follow the Rim Drive by car or bicycle, camp overnight at charming Mazama Village or the rustic Lost Creek campground, then hike down to the water for a boat tour on day two.

Experiencing the majesty

One look at the breathtakingly clear blue water of Crater Lake and you'll want to get into it as quickly as possible. Because of the caldera's sheer walls, this isn't an easy task. The only feasible (and legal) way to access the lake's shore is by hiking down the Cleetwood Cove Trail on the northern rim, accessible mid-June through October. The trail is a mile (1.5 km) long, and rugged.

Once at the shore, you can swim in the pristine waters, fish for salmon and trout, or take a boat tour around the lake. To explore Wizard Island, the boat tour is the only way to go. After docking, another challenging trek over loose gravel and lava rocks awaits. The trail to the top rises 700 ft (213 m), but once you reach the peak, you'll be rewarded with panoramic views and the singular opportunity to stand atop a caldera within a caldera. Choose between two hiking trails on the cone, or venture a little farther away from the top to luxuriate in the quiet stillness of the island.

Sightseeing by bicycle

Cycling the complete circuit of Rim Drive is another popular way to take in the lake. The steep, high-elevation route is physically

Above Dedicated cyclists complete the scenic tour round the breathtaking Crater Lake in a day

demanding, and riders can take breaks along the way to appreciate the spectacular scenery at any of the 30 overlooks. Start and end your ride at the historic Crater Lake Lodge. If you ride clockwise, you'll soon reach the Watchman parking area, with its bird's-eye view of Wizard Island. Cloudcap is another good stop, where you'll find the trailhead to Mount Scott, the park's highest point at 8,929 ft (2,721 m). Pause, too, at Kerr Notch, with its picture-perfect framed view of the Phantom Ship.

Hardcore enthusiasts might consider the Century Ride, a 100-mile (160-km) route that begins at Fort Klamath Museum. Mountain bikers should head to Grayback Drive for 8 miles (13 km) of unpaved bliss.

Below Hillman Peak, a basalt pinnacle on the western rim of Crater Lake, is slightly higher than Watchman Peak

Beyond the Lake

The main attraction is undoubtedly the lake, but you'll be spoiled for choice with the number of breathtaking natural wonders and outdoor adventures to enjoy. Nighttime and off-season can be some of the best times to see another side of the park.

▷ **The Pinnacles**
These needlelike formations in Sand Creek Canyon, off well-marked Pinnacles Road, make a fascinating counterpoint to the lake.

◁ **Plaikni Falls**
This is an easy, mile-long (1.6 km), accessible trail that runs through old-growth forest and ends at a stunning waterfall.

▷ **Stargazing and night-sky photography**
There's very little light pollution in the park, making it perfect for counting constellations.

◁ **Skiing and snowshoeing**
In winter, the Rim Drive is closed to traffic, but open to snowshoers and skiers. The 90 miles (145 km) of trails allow camping year-round.

▷ **Watchman Peak**
This is a prime spot for viewing the magical sunsets over the crater. You can trek on your own to the top, join a ranger-led hike, or just drive to the lookout.

South Dakota

WIND CAVE

ESTABLISHED 1903

From deep inside the earth, a hissing wind blows, traveling the length of one of the world's longest cave systems before bursting onto the bright, grassy plains of the Black Hills.

It's unclear what force first drew the indigenous peoples of the area to the dark passageways and whistling winds of Wind Cave, but the cave was discovered long ago by the Lakota. Wind Cave is central to their emergence narrative, which explains how humans came to be. The complicated tale is

filled with trickery, love, and hardship and tells how people were taken up from the underworld and taught to hunt and survive in the land above.

Wonders that lie beneath

Wind Cave only became known to the wider world in 1881, when two brothers, Tom and Jesse Bingham, stumbled upon the cave's entrance after following the direction of a loud whooshing sound. Today, 140 miles (225 km) of labyrinthine corridors have been mapped, revealing unique geological wonders, such as needlelike growths known as frostwork, knobby "popcorn" calcite structures, and—webbed across the cave's ceilings—the world's largest and perhaps finest example of boxwork formations.

FOCUS ON
A Culture of Stories

The oral tradition of storytelling is strong in American Indian culture, and is how community history and legend have historically been shared. One such story of the Oglala Lakota tells of Wind Cave, a sacred place. In the Lakota language, *"Oniya Oshoka"* refers to an area where the planet "breathes inside," transferring wisdom through a passageway between worlds.

5

Percentage of the cave that has been mapped.

———

95

Large percentage of the world's boxwork formations found at Wind Cave.

———

300

Age of the cave in millions of years—it is among the oldest on Earth.

Left The sweeping landscape above Wind Cave provides perfect photograph material

If you have...

An hour Take a self-guided wildlife drive on Highway 385.

A day ▷ Explore Wind Cave on a ranger-guided tour. Excursions vary in length, and are moderate to strenuous.

What lies above

Above ground, the Black Hills are home to the abundant prairie wildlife that made the Dakota Territory an especially popular hunting ground in the late 1800s. Prairie falcons and other birds, pronghorn antelopes, coyotes, prairie dogs, and the iconic American bison are all here in huge numbers. Driving along US Highway 385 and South Dakota Highway 87, it is virtually impossible *not* to spot wildlife.

The plains are also famous for changing weather, with afternoon storms serving up color-rich skies that stretch above swaying grasslands. In spring, fields of wildflowers add an even more vibrant color pop to the above-ground world of Wind Cave—a world that in terms of "wow factor" holds its own with its subterranean counterpart.

Above The dry climate of the cave is perfect for the formation of the calcite-rich, honeycomblike boxwork

Wind Cave | Established 1903 **59**

Virginia Donaghe McClurg

In 1882, journalist Virginia Donaghe McClurg became one of the first white women to see the cliff dwellings at Mesa Verde. She founded the Colorado Cliff Dwellings Association and worked to protect these cultural treasures through her writing, lecturing, and fundraising. With activist Lucy Peabody, "the mother of Mesa Verde," she rallied support through the Federation of Women's Clubs and the press. Their work was vital in the creation of Mesa Verde National Park.

Right Balcony House, a largely intact Ancestral Puebloan dwelling, can be reached by ladder

Colorado

MESA VERDE

ESTABLISHED 1906

Magnificent and mysterious, Mesa Verde is an archeological wonder where you can explore ancient Puebloan dwellings etched into the park's looming cliffsides.

Step back into an ancient world in Mesa Verde. Centuries before European explorers reached this continent, the Ancestral Puebloans thrived among the steep cliffs and rocky mesa tops for 700 years. They built 600 remarkable cliff dwellings in the sandstone alcoves, hidden and protected by the overhanging bluffs, and dug round ceremonial centers, called kivas, deep into the rock. These are some of the best-preserved archeological sites anywhere, and as you walk among them, picturing the vibrant community that existed here, the ruins seem to spring to life once more.

Most impressive of all is the massive Cliff Palace, with more than 150 rooms. Stunning to look at, it's even more exciting to climb wooden ladders like the ancestors did and explore its warren of tiny rooms on a ranger-guided tour. Take a tour, too, of

Balcony House and Long House. Scenic roads and trails lead to other villages on the mesa—small sites that can be explored in an intimate setting. The Chapin Mesa Archeological Museum houses relics that illuminate this long-ago way of life. The building itself is something of an artifact—hewn from the same type of rock the Puebloans used to create their own homes.

Get a fabulous photo of the labyrinthine Spruce Tree House from overlooks near the Chapin Mesa Archeological Museum.

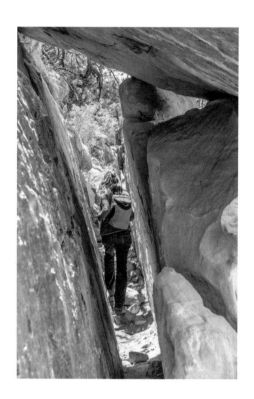

Above These narrow canyon-rock trails are early village sidewalks

A story in artifacts

It was Spanish explorers who gave Mesa Verde its present-day name, which means "green table." Centuries earlier, long before European explorers thought of the New World, early indigenous people settled these high, flat-topped cliffs.

Around AD 550, a group called the Basketmakers gave up nomadic life and built pithouses several feet below ground on the mesa top and in the recesses of the cliffs. Over the next two centuries, their villages flourished, as they learned to farm and make pottery. Their move from pithouse dwellings to multistoried stone houses marked the start of the Pueblo era. Although they left no written records, around three million objects—stone tools, weapons, pottery, and baskets—have been found at Mesa Verde. These artifacts give a fascinating glimpse into the lives of the Ancestral Puebloans.

Then, at the height of their prosperity the Puebloans began constructing the elaborate cliff dwellings you see today. In the 1200s, whether for defense, protection from the elements, or other reasons, they moved off the mesa top and into these hidden villages. The tall, straight walls, made of carefully fitted sandstone blocks, show their skill as master builders. The buildings range from small family units to complexes with mazes of chambers for living and storing food. Many rooms are plastered and painted with designs.

Sophisticated infrastructure

When you stand amid these remarkable ruins, imagine daily life among the Ancestral Puebloans. They continued to grow corn, beans, and squash on the mesa top, climbing up to their fields using hand- and toeholds chiseled into the rock. Trails led down into the canyon for hunting game and drawing water. Open courtyards echoed with the sounds of domesticated dogs, turkeys, and village activities. The people sun-dried foods to last through the harsh winters and made beautiful pottery and crafts. Intriguing, too, are the kivas, where religious ceremonies, healing rites, and even weaving "bees" were held.

History Timeline

Mesa Verde's history stretches back to prehistoric times. Early inhabitants endured centuries of hardship to develop the skills needed to survive the rigors of life in this unforgiving climate.

AD 750

▽ Ancestral Puebloans emerge from Basketmaker culture. They build the first dwellings above ground, and farming becomes their primary means of subsistence.

7500 BC

▷ Mesa Verde is seasonally inhabited by Paleo-Indians, a nomadic people who moved throughout the Southwest and hunted game with spears.

C. AD 550

△ Basketmaker culture settles at Mesa Verde, so named because of the many baskets discovered at archeological sites from this era. Their rock art is found across the area.

1190s–1270s

△ As the population expands, extensive, interconnected pueblo complexes are built, including some 600 cliff dwellings.

Did You Know?

Building cliff dwellings without ground-floor doors and windows provided protection against invaders.

And then... gone

Yet, by 1285, the cliff dwellings were inexplicably abandoned. For a long time, it was believed that the Ancestral Puebloans simply vanished. Theories that they were wiped out by disease or warfare prevailed. It's more likely that they were victims of early climate change. The 13th century brought regional drought and crop failure, and it's now thought they migrated south to join Pueblo communities in New Mexico and Arizona, where their descendants live today. What they left behind helps us reconstruct the story of their lives.

Above The intricate compound of Cliff Palace is formed by linked-up living spaces

1285

▽ Mesa Verde is abandoned. Prolonged droughts likely made farming unviable, and the people moved to join relatives in other Pueblo communities in the region.

1906

△ After intense lobbying by activists such as Lucy Peabody and Virginia McClurg, Mesa Verde is established as a national park by President Theodore Roosevelt.

1978

▽ Mesa Verde becomes a designated UNESCO World Heritage Cultural Site, one of the first World Heritage sites in the United States.

1996–2003

△ Wildfires destroy forests and damage archeological sites, including rock artworks, but the clearing of dense undergrowth reveals many undiscovered sites in the park.

2006

▽ Excavated American Indian remains and grave goods dug up during early archeological explorations are reburied in religious ceremonies held by related tribal elders.

Exploring the ruins

Mesa Verde encompasses two separate areas—Chapin Mesa and Wetherill Mesa—each with its special charms. Drive the winding, scenic roads from the park entrance to the end of Chapin Mesa, where you'll find Cliff Palace, Balcony House, and Spruce Tree House. Along the way, stop at the overlooks and peer down into the canyons to get great views of the cliff dwellings, mesa-top villages, and surrounding landscape. The road traversing Wetherill Mesa has fabulous vistas of deep canyons and sandstone cliffs.

The best way to experience the cliff dwellings is to take a ranger-guided tour of Cliff Palace or Balcony House, or Long House on Wetherill Mesa. These take you right inside the great complexes, where you will climb up ladders, walk down stone steps, and even crawl through a tunnel, just

Below Steps and terraces lead to the top of Step House on Wetherill Mesa

as the Ancestral Puebloans once did. Even more special are the Cliff Palace twilight tours and the sunrise tours of Balcony House, when the soft light and contrasting shadows make the ruins most atmospheric.

Sign up for backcountry tours that will get you acquainted with Mug House, Oak Tree House, and other lesser-known sites. Rangers also give evening campfire talks on the natural and cultural history of Mesa Verde at the Morefield Campground.

Many sites can be visited on self-guided tours. Some, such as Square Tower House, are reached along short, paved trails off Mesa Top Loop Road. These include Kodak House on Wetherill Mesa, so named because a Swedish researcher left his camera here in 1891.

To really connect with the breathtaking landscape of Mesa Verde, follow hiking trails to Step House and Far View House, where you will discover pithouses, kivas,

Did You Know?

An estimated 20,000 people lived in the Mesa Verde region in the 13th century. A century later, it was all but deserted.

petroglyphs, farming terraces, and lookout towers. These sites are much less visited, and you'll be able to linger and enjoy the peaceful surroundings.

Paths to follow

The only national park created to protect cultural and historic sites, rather than natural features, Mesa Verde's fragile archeological treasures are treated with care, and activities are structured accordingly. Still, outdoor adventures abound, and you can cycle on most roads, over steep hills and winding curves that may test your endurance, and there are lots of ranger-led bike and hike tours to join.

In winter, when the snow dusts the ridges above the cliff dwellings, Mesa Verde is magical. You can cross-country ski and snowshoe on groomed park trails, or simply walk through the frosty wonderland as the ancient cliff dwellers once did.

Above Views extend for miles and miles in every direction from the Soda Canyon overlook

Best Hikes

Petroglyph Point Trail ▷ 2.4-mile (4-km) loop trail. Although it's rugged and narrow and includes several steep drop-offs along the canyon wall, this hike is well worth the effort. The chance to see the rock art panel with handprints, spirals, hunting scenes, and other petroglyphs makes this scenic trail very popular.

Badger House Community Trail 2.3 miles (4.8 km) round trip. Beginning at the information kiosk on Wetherill Mesa, this moderately easy trail is both paved and gravel, and leads you through four sites on the mesa top that span 600 years of history.

Point Lookout Trail ▷ 2.2 miles (3.5 km) round trip. For fabulous views of Montezuma and Mancos valleys and the surrounding countryside, hike the switchbacks up the back of Point Lookout and across the mesa top on this short but steep route.

Soda Canyon Overlook ▷ 1.2 miles (2 km) round trip. This easy walk to the edge of the canyon through an open area gives you some fantastic views of the park. It offers a particularly splendid look at Balcony House and great views of other archeological sites. It's a quick route and the trail is flanked by sage brush and other local flora.

Spruce Canyon Trail ▷ 2.4 miles (4 km) round trip. Starting at the trailhead near the Chapin Mesa Archeological Museum, this moderately difficult hike takes you down to the bottom of the canyon and across a small stream in season.

Montana

GLACIER

ESTABLISHED 1910

The fearsomely beautiful Glacier National Park is best appreciated from the dizzying heights of Going-to-the-Sun Road, an engineering marvel that snakes precariously along the valley wall, with views that will leave you awestruck at the power of nature.

Nearly two million people a year journey to Glacier, in the far north of Montana, to witness the grandeur of the glaciers and the solitude and adventure of the park's extensive, often challenging hiking trails. The 26 active glaciers are a huge draw, but the "Crown of the Continent" also offers magnificent wildlife and turquoise lakes, formed when age-old glaciers scraped hollows in the land. Many of those icy lakes are so clear you can see right to the lake bed.

Protecting the glaciers

Rising temperatures have, sadly, led to a steep decline in the park's namesake features. When Glacier was established in 1910, it was home to more than 100 glaciers; today, three-quarters are gone. Protecting what remains is why it's so important to enjoy Glacier responsibly. It's also the best way to experience the park. For example, picture rolling into West Glacier on Amtrak, then hopping onto a free shuttle to Apgar Village, where you stop to admire the peak-encircled Lake McDonald. Next, a bus whisks you up Going-to-the-Sun Road to take in the incredible and serene scenery. The bus stops at all the key spots, including Logan Pass, with its 700-plus miles (1,127 km) of hiking trails—maximum sightseeing, with minimum carbon footprint.

George Bird Grinnell

George Bird Grinnell was a young editor at *Forest and Stream* when he first visited this region in 1885. Awestruck by the raw, unspoiled nature, Grinnell used the magazine's influence to campaign for the creation of Glacier as a national park. A founder of the Audubon Society and friend of President Theodore Roosevelt, he was dubbed "the father of American conservation." Grinnell wrote dozens of books on the American West, many about the Plains Indians. Today, Grinnell Glacier bears his name.

762

The total number of lakes in the park. The largest is Lake McDonald.

Above Rocky Mountain goats are at home in their high-altitude element, where they sometimes cross paths with visitors on trails and overlooks

FLORA AND FAUNA
Mountain Goats

Rocky Mountain goats are the official symbol of Glacier. Living on craggy cliffs, they are perfectly suited to their tough home terrain. Sticky, flexible hoof pads allow the goats to prance effortlessly up near-vertical slopes and across uneven boulders. A double-layer wool coat protects them from 100-mph (160-kph) winds and bitter cold—temperatures here can dip to –50°F (–45°C).

Top-flight hikes

Apgar Village, at the foot of Lake McDonald, is the most accessible entry point to the park, although the area known as Many Glacier also draws its share of visitors, with a historic lodge, string of lakes, and dozens of hiking trails, including the deservedly popular hike to Grinnell Lake and Grinnell Glacier. This hike, consistently rated one of the most spectacular in the US, is best done in the fall, when the park is more peaceful. It can be a relatively strenuous trek, but you will be rewarded with incredible scenery, a famous glacier, and

an iridescent turquoise lake. You're also likely to see some of the park's abundant wildlife along the way, including mountain goats, bighorn sheep, black bears, and grizzly bears.

For a novel way to start the hike, book passage on a shuttle boat to the trail. This gives you a 3.4-mile (5.5-km) head start—and you can enjoy the 360-degree views of the surrounding peaks while bobbing on the water. You can hop on the boat at the Many Glacier Hotel dock, before changing to a second boat that takes you across Lake Josephine, where you catch the main trail.

Grizzly country

It's not uncommon for boat passengers to spot grizzly bears munching away amid the berry bushes on the lakeshore, often startlingly close to groups of hikers. Grizzlies are a threatened species in the United States and endangered in Canada, but they have a strong presence at Glacier—an estimated 300 live in the park. They're imposing creatures, standing well over 6 ft (1.8 m) tall when upright. Unsurprisingly, rangers and park signs emphasize bear safety, for the bears' sake as much as for your own. In general, though, grizzly bears keep to themselves and eat berries, seeds, roots, and grasses, plus trout, carrion, and the occasional elk calf. In winter, when food is scarce, the

Above An adult grizzly lumbers through a meadow in bloom

bears move to higher ground to hibernate. They steer clear of humans when they can; the key to safe hiking in bear country is to avoid surprising a bear, generally by making plenty of noise. Rangers recommend hiking in groups of at least three or four. Some of the busiest trails in Glacier National Park cut through ideal bear habitat, so pay attention to safety tips and be aware that you're walking through their front yard.

Black bears are also common at Glacier, and are easily mistaken for grizzlies. Both range in color from blond to dark brown; black bears are typically smaller, and they don't have the large, intimidating shoulder hump that distinguishes a grizzly.

Best Off-Season Hikes

The majority of park visitors arrive in the summer. If you want to avoid the peak-season crowds, try these off-season hikes.

▽ **Winter** Do the 10-mile (16-km) Apgar Lookout hike on skis or snowshoes November through April, when the road to the trailhead is still snowed in. Rangers lead weekend walks.

▷ **Spring** To see bright wildflowers bursting forth and spot reemerging wildlife, take the 7-mile (11-km) Fish Creek Trail along Lake McDonald West Shore. It stays level the whole way.

△ **Fall** September provides a good opportunity to tackle the more popular hikes, in relative quiet, but before the cold sets in. If you've been dreaming of the Grinnell Glacier Trail, now's the time.

△ **Winter** Clip on your snowshoes or skis and venture onto the 4-mile (6.5-km), mostly flat trail that starts at McDonald Lodge and ends at McDonald Falls, one of 200 falls in the park.

Early in the day during the fall is prime time to see the shimmering turquoise lakes. Crowds thin by mid-August, and bears aren't yet out and about.

Jagged mountain peaks

Glacier National Park covers a massive area of nearly a million acres (405,000 ha) and has widely spaced hubs of activity. Lake McDonald, with Apgar Village at its base, is the main entry point on the park's west side, and you can reach it nearly year-round. Many hikes begin here, including one that follows the lake's western shore. The views from the dock across Lake McDonald alone, with a backdrop of rugged mountain peaks, make the trip worthwhile. Viewing is at its finest in the early morning or late afternoon light.

Another key area is Logan Pass—the park's highest point reachable by car or bus, with correspondingly fantastic views and, especially between late June and mid-August, rainbow-colored carpets of wildflowers that are set off by the mountain background. Here you'll find the starting point for hikes of all levels. The area is laced with paved trails that help make it accessible for visitors of varying physical abilities. If you're traveling the full length of the Going-to-the-Sun Road, this is an excellent place to stop for a while and drink it all in.

Indigenous cultures

St. Mary Valley, the park's eastern entrance, is notable for the beautiful

Above A solitary hiker takes in the scenery from a trail at Logan Pass

St. Mary Lake, which spans nearly 10 miles (16 km) and is streaked with turquoise from glacial runoff. The St. Mary Valley borders the Blackfeet Indian Reservation, home to about 8,600 tribal members, and the area has a rich history of Blackfeet, Salish, Pend d'Oreille, and Kootenai cultures. Tribal members, including musicians, speakers, drummers, and dancers, share their knowledge of local history and culture in the park's annual "Native America Speaks" programs, held throughout the summer. There are also interpretive bus tours of the park that shed light onto the rich history and culture of the Blackfeet.

Historically, the Blackfeet lived in the prairies on the east side of what is now Glacier National Park. On the more forested

Glacier Itinerary

Many of the park's glaciers are tucked away in remote locations that require considerable hiking chops if you want to explore them. Fortunately, there are easier, more accessible excursions that can be completed in a couple of days.

Easy ▷ Sperry Glacier. Shuttle to Logan Pass, the high point along Going-to-the-Sun Road, then follow the marked 1.3-mile (2-km) hike, which is mostly on boardwalk, from the pass.

Easy Jackson Glacier. This is the easiest glacier to see in the park, and it's visible from the Going-to-the-Sun Road's Jackson Glacier Overlook, which is the next stop down from Logan Pass.

Easy ▷ Salamander Glacier. You can spy this glacier from the car on the drive into the Many Glacier area. It sits just above Grinnell Glacier.

Moderate to difficult
Grinnell Glacier. This glacier will greet you at the end of a challenging, but rewarding, hike from the trailhead at Many Glacier. The hike is 5 miles (8 km) each way.

west side of the park were the Salish, Kootenai, and Pend d'Oreille tribes. The Blackfeet were traditionally buffalo hunters, but they also knew about and extensivly used hundreds of species of plant for food and medicine.

Trade with white fur trappers started as early as the 1700s, although Blackfeet culture continued to dominate the region until the 1870s. When the railroad was completed in 1891, however, white settlers flooded into the area, and the Blackfeet were forced to cede mountainous parts of their lands. Tourism wasn't far behind, and by 1892 you could arrive via the Great Northern Railway, rent a cabin at Lake McDonald, and enjoy a guided tour by boat or packhorse.

2,865

The total number in miles (4,610 km) of all the Glacier streams.

410

Size in acres (166 ha) of Harrison Glacier.

6,646

Elevation in ft (2,026 m) of Logan Pass, the highest spot on Going-to-the-Sun Road.

FOCUS ON
The Continental Divide

The Rocky Mountains straddle the Continental
Divide, a geologic watershed that runs from
the Bering Strait in Alaska down to the tip
of South America. It creates a fascinating
phenomenon: rivers and streams on the eastern
slopes run toward the Atlantic Ocean; on
the western slopes, they run to the Pacific.
This creates a vortex at the equator.

Left Surrounded by mountain scenery, Estes Park has long been seen as the gateway to the park

WYOMING
NEBRASKA
ROCKY MOUNTAIN ○ Fort Collins
UTAH ○ Denver
○ Grand Junction ○ Colorado Springs
COLORADO
NEW MEXICO

Colorado

ROCKY MOUNTAIN

ESTABLISHED 1915

The best of the Rockies is on display as you cross the Continental Divide on the highest continuously paved road in North America: lakes and forests, glaciers and tundra, and a wealth of wildlife lie before you.

Stretching from the Canadian border into northern New Mexico, the Rocky Mountains form one of the country's most dramatic landscapes. At the national park, you're surrounded by the best of their scenic wonders. More than 60 peaks soar over 12,000 ft (3,658 m)—nowhere else will you find such a magnificent concentration of towering summits in such a compact area. The region's glacier-carved past is showcased throughout: rugged faces of granite cliffs, deep emerald-green valleys, sparkling alpine lakes, and rocky moraines.

To see all this and more, drive the high-winding Trail Ridge Road, which follows a path used by American Indians for centuries. Thrilling milestones along the

way include crossing the Continental Divide and catching a glimpse of the Colorado River. This mighty river begins in the park as a shallow stream, steadily gathering force as it thunders south to carve out the Grand Canyon.

Nature at the top

Rocky Mountain is the highest national park in the country, with one-third of its land above the tree line. At the Alpine Visitor Center, pick up a trail that leads you across stark, sweeping tundra. This fragile terrain, dotted with weather-hardy mosses and tiny alpine flowers, is the only such ecosystem below the Arctic Circle. Walking through it, you feel like you're on top of the world.

Accessible Adventures

The park has trails for nearly every ability. The 1-mile (1.6-km) Coyote Valley follows the Colorado River and features moose-spotting. The half-mile (1-km) Sprague Lake Trail has a backdrop of mountain peaks, a fishing pier, and a picnic area. Lily Lake Trail loops 1 mile (1.6 km) around the lake, with a fishing pier and grand views of Longs Peak.

The park has several entrance points, but Trail Ridge Road (US Highway 34) is the only road that will take you across the entire park. Covering 48 miles (77 km) from the historic pioneer town of Estes Park in the east to Grand Lake in the west, it's an exhilarating drive that climbs sharply up the switchbacks and around hairpin curves. There are pull-offs all along the way, perfect places to drink in the spectacular views and capture timeless photographs of valleys ringed by snowcapped peaks.

Among the best stops is Many Parks Curve, situated on the edge of a hairpin turn. From the bowed wooden boardwalk, gaze onto a 180-degree view of key eastern sections of the park, such as Mummy Range, Beaver Meadows, and Moraine Park. At Forest Canyon Overlook, peer into a 2,000-ft (600-m) chasm that was carved by a glacier and is one of the wildest places in the park. On the greener, western side, Farview Curve looks out on magnificent vistas of the Colorado River and the aspen-filled Kawuneeche Valley, which glows in radiant color in fall.

Trail Ridge hiking

No matter where you stop, the bracing, pine-scented air and high-altitude sunshine make it hard to get back in the car. The park has numerous hiking trails, from easy half-day hikes to challenging backcountry treks that take you to hidden sapphire lakes and plunging waterfalls, or deep into rugged canyons and verdant valleys. If you just want to stretch your legs and explore the scenery, several trailheads lie along Trail Ridge Road. The popular Rock Cut Overlook is the starting point for the half-mile (1-km) Tundra Communities Trail, which

Below From the highest paved road in the US, Trail Ridge Road, the views are showstoppers

Sunrise and sunset are the best times to see wildlife, and the park will be peaceful.

has interpretive signs highlighting the plant life of this delicate alpine landscape.

South of Trail Ridge Road, Bear Lake Road winds through one of the most stunning regions of the park. Rocky ridges, called moraines, were deposited here by moving glaciers. Dozens of glacier-carved lakes dot the southern half of the land, their icy-blue waters sparkling in the sun. Many can only be reached along hiking trails, but Bear Lake is easily accessible. Glistening beneath the towering Hallett Peak, its lovely wooded shoreline is a natural viewing platform for several other park giants, including Longs Peak, at 14,259 ft (4,346 m) the highest in the park.

In Wild Basin, tucked in the southeast corner, are more lakes, winding creeks, and waterfalls. On the Wild Basin Trail, you'll pass several waterfalls and cascades in less than 2 miles (3 km) while hiking through pristine mountains and forests. The area is off the main roads, so crowds are sparse—perfect for a Rocky Mountain adventure.

Three Hikes

Popular ▷ Bear Lake Loop Trail, half mile (1 km) round trip. Walk along the shoreline of a pretty glacial lake on this easy hike. Relax on a bench and enjoy fabulous views of the surrounding summits.

Peaceful ▷ Bridal Veil Falls Trail, 6.4 miles (10 km) round trip. This moderately difficult trail passes a trickling stream, meanders through a serene wooded valley and aspen forest, and ends at a lovely waterfall.

Solitary ▷ Long Lake Trail, 12.4 miles (20 km) round trip. This strenuous hike offers sublime wilderness solitude as it follows the Roaring River and climbs to a big subalpine lake in the Mummy Range.

Above Spring clouds gather over a narrow section of the popular Trail Ridge Road

Left Trails in the park vary in level of difficulty, with plenty of boardwalks for easy hikes

Wildlife watching

As magnificent as the scenery is in Rocky Mountain National Park, the most thrilling thing about a visit here is the chance to see wildlife—big wildlife—in its natural home. You may not see elusive creatures like the black bear or cougar unless you venture into remote areas, but other large mammals are commonly spotted.

Elk are among the park's most famous residents. During the summer, large herds graze on the alpine tundra along Trail Ridge Road, particularly near the Rock Cut

Through the Seasons

Spring Spot moose, elk, and other animals with their newborn young feeding in the lower valleys in the spring. Bighorn sheep and mule deer migrate to green grasslands.

Summer ▷ The park's meadows and valleys are bursting with colorful wildflowers in the summer months. Look for mountain iris, red and yellow Indian paintbrush, and Colorado blue columbine, the state flower.

Fall Glorious fall colors paint the landscape, as the leaves of the aspen trees turn bright yellow. Listen for the strange, high-pitched mating calls of bull elks echoing through the park.

Winter ▷ Activities such as snowshoeing, sledding, and cross-country skiing reveal sparkling new views of the park's landscape. The seasonal lack of vegetation makes it easier to see coyotes, moose, and other big mammals.

Overlook. In this open country, the up-close sight of a bull elk, its enormous antlers raised against the bright blue sky like a majestic crown, is unforgettable.

In the fall, the elk move to the lower meadows for the breeding season. Then, the park resounds with their bizarre mating calls, known as "bugling," which sound like high-pitched shrieks. You're most likely to hear the calls in the early morning or evening. Moraine Park is one of the best places to observe the rutting ritual.

Although they are lone creatures, moose are often seen in the park, especially at lower elevations, where there are wetlands, willows, and lush vegetation around lakes and rivers. Good viewing spots are Lily Lake and Kawuneeche Valley.

It can be tricky to see Rocky Mountain bighorn sheep, the largest wild sheep on the continent, as they blend so perfectly into the rock ridges where they live. But in late spring and summer, they come down from the Mummy Range to graze at Sheep Lakes in Horseshoe Park. If you're lucky, you'll hit the "Bighorn Crossing Zone" at the same time they do.

Throughout the park, you'll see lots of birds, raptors, and small mammals, such as hamsterlike picas. Forest Canyon Overlook is full of pudgy yellow-bellied marmots, who whistle, trill, and chuck when alarmed.

Human history

Rocky Mountain National Park has had human residents, too, and some 150 historic structures are still standing. One of the easiest to visit is the Holzwarth Historic Site, where German immigrant John Holzwarth and his family homesteaded in the early 1900s and later built a popular dude ranch. During the summer months, you can take a tour of the rustic log cabins and buildings.

Farther north in the Kawuneeche Valley, follow the Colorado River Trail to the site of Lulu City. It sprang up after silver was discovered here in 1879, but mining costs were high, the ore quality was low, and within five years the town was abandoned. The remaining ruins are listed on the National Register of Historic Places.

Above This big bull elk is at the peak of his powers in fall rutting season; in winter, he'll shed his antlers

PARK PIONEERS
Imogene Green MacPherson

Imogene Green MacPherson began homesteading in the Moraine Park area in 1903. In a few years, she built a main lodge, dining room, stables, and cabins, later opening the Moraine Park Lodge in 1910. After she married, she continued to run the resort and other area businesses herself. In 1931, three years after her death, the National Park Service purchased the property. The historic log-and-stone lodge remains and now houses the Moraine Park Discovery Center.

California

LASSEN VOLCANIC

ESTABLISHED 1916

Witness Earth's geothermic power at Lassen Volcanic, where belching steam vents, bubbling mudpots, and scalding hot springs erupt in a primeval roar.

Arriving in Lassen, you feel like you're stepping into an alpine wonderland, complete with wildflower-speckled meadows and snow-dusted mountains. But the jagged peaks in the distance tell the tale of the park's eruptive past, when the serene mountains of today were once roiling volcanoes.

Lassen Volcanic National Park was formed over hundreds of thousands of years by volcanic heat and plate tectonics. Around 825,000 BC, a ring of plug dome volcanoes erupted violently, forming the Lassen Volcanic Center. Lassen is rare, in that it's one of the few places on Earth where all four types of volcanoes—shield, composite, cinder cone, and plug dome— exist side by side. The iconic Lassen Peak, the park's dominant feature, is one of the world's largest plug-dome volcanoes and is still an active force to be reckoned with.

Land of plenty

For centuries, Lassen was the hunting and fishing grounds of regional tribes such as the Atsugewi, Yana, Yahi, and Maidu. These nomadic peoples didn't live in Lassen year-round—the winter climate was too harsh. Instead, they migrated to the area in the summer months, when deer grazed in abundance, creeks teemed with trout, and the fertile volcanic soil served up a feast of berries, nuts, and seeds.

In the California Gold Rush of 1848–1855, white settlers came to the region and established many of the current routes through the park. Danish blacksmith Peter

10,456

In ft (3,187 m), the height of Lassen Peak.

30

The number of volcanoes in the park.

216

The number of bird species found here.

Lassen guided pioneers through the Cascade Mountains to the Sacramento Valley, and Lassen Peak bears his name. While gold was never discovered within the park boundary, prospectors grew rich from nearby claims, and towns followed.

Rocky top

In 1914, in a belch of steam, Lassen Peak sprang back to life after 27,000 years, forming a new crater on its rocky dome. The mountain continued to erupt periodically for years, with the largest blast in 1915, when it exploded in a devastating burst of lava and ash.

Above Lake Helen, with Lassen Peak in the background, sits at such a high altitude it may get snow in summer

Natural and Human History

Stories of this geologic marvel's fiery past show us how the Earth's forces carved the landscape, and how the original American Indian inhabitants and the European pioneers who came later shaped its future.

825,000 BC

A 9-mile (15-km) ring of plug-dome volcanoes erupts, spewing ash and lava and forming the Lassen Volcanic Center.

600,000– 350,000 BC

The stratovolcano Mount Tehama explodes, creating a caldera 2 miles (3 km) wide.

1500s– present

◁ For centuries, Lassen is the fertile hunting and fishing grounds for American Indian tribes such as the Yana.

1850s

The first settlers arrive with the California Gold Rush. Pioneers Peter Lassen and William Nobles build the area's first trails.

1907

Lassen Peak and Cinder Cone are established as National Monuments under President Theodore Roosevelt.

1914

◁ After a 27,000-year nap, Lassen Peak Volcano awakens with a bang. A series of eruptions take place until 1917.

1916

▷ This active volcano park is established as a national park on August 9, in the midst of its three-year volcanic run.

Thanks to the area's volcanic activity and
the stark beauty of its mountains, Lassen
Peak and the surrounding volcanos were
declared a national park in 1916. To entice
visitors to the new park, the Main Park
Road was constructed between 1925 and
1935. An architectural feat in its time, the
29-mile (47-km) highway snakes up to an
impressive 9,692 ft (2,954 m), making it the
highest road in the Cascade Mountains.

A haven for hikers

Much has changed since Lassen's explosive
beginnings. While the land still fumes and
belches, these days you can delight in the
awesome geothermic features of Lassen
safely. Visit Bumpass Hell Basin on a
moderate 3-mile (5-km) trail, with views of
Lassen Peak and a raised boardwalk that
unfurls over simmering mudpots and
boiling springs. Take care not to step off
the trail—the mud is as hot as ever.

Renowned for its hiking opportunities,
the park offers miles of trails that make
their way through evergreen forests to the
peaks of dormant volcanoes. You can stroll
through wildflower-carpeted meadows
toward dazzling waterfalls on easy-to-reach
family hikes, while thrill-seekers take the
climb to the top of Lassen Peak.

Below Pine trees
sprout up in the Fantastic
Lava Beds, seen near
Cinder Cone trailhead

**Visit in the early morning,
when steam from
geothermal activity rises
in the crisp air and dew
covers the meadows.**

Above Bumpass Hell gets its salty name from pioneer Kendall Bumpass, who fell into scalding mud and lost a leg

Seasonal pleasures

Lassen Volcanic National Park is a year-round destination, and the landscape changes dramatically with the seasons. Springtime brings dazzling displays of local flora, with a spectacular show of multihued wildflowers blanketing the meadows of the valleys. Lassen in the summer, meanwhile, is mountain living at its best, with superb hiking trails leading to volcanic peaks, glacial-blue alpine lakes jumping with fish, and campgrounds cloaked in expansive starry skies.

When the leaves change with the crisp fall air, the park is painted in bright splashes of orange, yellow, and red, and leaf peepers and aspiring photographers abound. On these cold, clear nights, mountain splendor is there for the taking in blessed serenity. Lassen Volcanic National Park receives some of the heaviest snowfall in California, and in the winter the park

Through the Seasons

Spring ▷ The spring months are an idyllic time to explore Lassen, with a display of vivid flowers and thunderous waterfalls that is unparalleled. Witness both on the fantastic Kings Creek Falls Trail, which wends past carpets of purple lupine and yellow mule's ears to the 30-ft (9-m) falls.

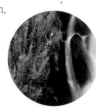

Summer ▷ Manzanita Lake, at the heart of Lassen, offers swimming, kayaking, and fishing in its unforgettable, glacial-blue water in the summer months. Warmer weather makes this season a great time for hiking, too, so try out the Bumpass Hell trail, which is usually not open before July.

Fall ▷ Have the park to yourself in this peaceful period, thanks to milder temperatures and autumnal colors painting the landscape. This is a fantastic time for camping, and the clear nights are perfect for campfire conversations.

Winter ▷ When snow blankets the Sierra Nevada, the park becomes a chilly, joyous playground. As well as snowshoeing opportunities, there's also skiing around the Sulphur Works hydrothermal area. And don't forget sledding and snow camping.

quiets down under its enchanting white cover. The snow also softens the rugged contours of Lassen's volcanic peaks and reflects back a burnished alpine glow. Here's a chance to follow ranger-led snowshoe hikes of the backcountry in the beautiful Manzanita Lake Area or set out on your own to discover the winter wonderland through your own eyes.

Pacific
Ocean

Honolulu○

○Kahului

HAWAII

HAWAI'I VOLCANOES

Hawaii

HAWAI'I VOLCANOES

ESTABLISHED 1916

Active volcanoes give an edge to the thrill at this park, where you can feel that the ground is alive beneath your feet as you gaze at the epic landscapes.

Viewing the majestic Mauna Loa from a distance is in itself humbling, but ascending to the 13,679-ft (4,169-m) summit of the Earth's largest volcano is an exhilarating experience in a category of its own.

Of the two paths to the top, one takes up to five days, and the shorter option is a nearly 20-mile (31-km) test of endurance—even the fittest person will need 14 hours to complete the trek. But the rewards are rich: views of Mauna Kea, Hawai'i's highest peak, and the exhilaration of conquering a volcano that's been active a million years.

On the lower mountain slopes is the Kapāpala Canoe Forest. This 1,257-acre (509-ha) preserve is part of the much larger wao akua forest (forest of the gods), which protects the acacia koa tree used in traditional canoe making. It's not hard to imagine these tall, slender trunks reaching up to touch their gods.

2018

The year the Kīlauea crater doubled in size, after the May eruption.

5

The length in miles (8 km) of the longest cat-proof fence in the US, built to protect the Hawaiian petrel.

1,653

The number of endangered species in Hawai'i—a third of all those in the US.

Ways to Explore

Enjoy by car ▷ A trip around Chain of Craters Road and Crater Rim Drive is like going through an enormous drive-through museum—one that's on another planet.

Tour the craters ▷ Get a close-up view of the Kīlauea and Kīlauea Iki craters, which last erupted in 1959. A steep, rocky descent through lush rain forest opens onto the moonscape of the hardened lava lake bed—magnificent.

Go on a hike Two must-do short hikes are Halemaʻumaʻu Trail, near a crater that still emits sulfur steams, and the aptly named Devastation Trail, through ash-covered remains of rain forest wiped out in the eruption of 1959.

Take an easy walk ▷ Wander the path of the Thurston Lava Tube, a now fern-lined tunnel that formed after an underground river of lava drained away.

Left During an eruption, a stream of lava gushes from a height of 60 ft (18 m), causing the heat and pressure of the superheated water to create a giant explosion

Ever-evolving landscape

With volcanic explosions happening as recently as May 2018—which closed major parts of the park for four months—you know that any visit to Hawai'i Volcanoes National Park is something special.

On one the park's iconic drives, such as the Chain of Craters Road, the dramatic landscape becomes a monumental drive-through museum, unfolding at every turn. As you set out, the winding roads skirt through pretty woodland forest, but then suddenly the trees end and you are surrounded by black lava rock lining the road, evidence of a violent eruption. Overlooks reveal what those trees conceal, allowing you to look out over these vast craters created long ago by the Earth's mighty upheavals. The oldest volcano in the Hawaiian-Emperor seamount chain, to which these volcanoes belong, dates back 81 million years, and within the park three volcanoes are active. Indeed, Kīlauea is so active that one stretch or another of the 19-mile (31-km) Chain of Craters Road is covered by lava almost every year.

A crater within a crater

The best view of the crater is from the Kīlauea Iki Overlook on the Crater Rim Drive, another 11 miles (18 km) of woods giving way to overlooks across vast expanses of lava, breathing out blasts of steam. If time allows, take the trail from the Kīlauea Iki Overlook to get even closer to the heart of the action.

So big is the Kīlauea crater, and so vigorous its activity through the centuries, that it contains another crater within it: Halema'uma'u. Its name means house of the 'āma'u fern, and this unusual local plant likes colonizing lava flows. You'll see lots of them on the Halema'uma'u Trail, which

Above Crater Rim Drive is a circular route offering spectacular views of the volcanic landscape

---

> FOCUS ON
>
> ## The First Hawaiians
>
> Hawaiian lore tells the stories of the islands' past, where the people came from, and how the culture was created from the shared input of far-flung ancestors. It's thought that the islands were settled starting in AD 300 by people from other Pacific islands, including the Marquesas Islands, Bora Bora, and Tahiti. Each brought their own customs and beliefs, which initially caused strife, but eventually blended to create the unique culture of modern Hawai'i.

History Timeline

Hawaii's volcanoes are even more awe-inspiring when you consider their earliest activity occurred 5.1 million years ago—two in the Emperor seamount chain are still very much alive.

1924
▽ After more than 50 explosions at Kīlauea in over two weeks, Halema'uma'u, the largest crater in the caldera, doubles in diameter and is considerably deeper.

1790
▷ A huge eruption of Kīlauea traps many local villagers who couldn't escape its fury. The footprints they make as they frantically tried to flee are still visible.

1916
△ A proposal to make this area, already popular with tourists, a national park is put forward in 1903. It is signed into law in 1916 by President Woodrow Wilson.

1959
△ Between November 14 and December 20, 16 separate explosions take place next to the Kīlauea caldera, creating a completely new crater named ī Kīlauea Iki.

starts at the Volcano House hotel. It's a 1.6-mile (2.6-km) round trip through rain forest filled with ferns, leafy trees, and huge lichen-covered rocks, some of which were spewed out in past eruptions.

The trail leads into the crater, a visual contrast to the lushness of the forest. It's a stark lunar landscape stretching before you, with a sulfurous smell of the gases that seep from cracks and fissures filling the air. How far you can walk on the trail depends on how restless the volcano is. Within the main caldera, you'll come face to face with Halema'uma'u crater, which Hawaiians consider home to Pele, goddess of fire and volcanoes and creator of the Hawaiian islands. In this vast and surreal landscape, the story makes perfect sense.

Above At the Kamokuna Viewing Area, a ranger offers insights on the park's history and volcanic phenomena

1980

▽ The national park is made an International Biosphere Reserve, creating a living laboratory to preserve its ecosystem and control alien species.

1987

▽ The park becomes a UNESCO World Heritage Site in the same year as the Acropolis in Athens, Greece, and the archeological site of Palenque in Mexico.

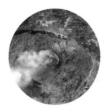

2018

▽ On May 11, the park closes because of excessive activity, after which Kīlauea volcano erupts and the lava flows for three months, destroying more than 700 homes.

1983

△ On April 30, Kīlauea begins erupting again, with explosions lasting 15 hours. Temperatures between 2,075°F and 2,102°F (1,135°C and 1,150°C) are recorded.

2008

△ On March 19, a small earthquake shakes Kīlauea's summit. No lava is emitted, but there is enough ash to close Crater Rim Drive and blanket nearby communities.

Alaska

DENALI

ESTABLISHED 1917

The power of nature takes on a whole new meaning in this immense national park. Here, under Alaska's dramatic sky, is one of the last frontiers, a land of tundra, cloud-piercing mountains, and wilderness like no other.

The icy arctic sun shines over the Alaskan tundra, igniting the landscape in bursts of purple, green, lavender, and orange. The air is frigid, and the energy electric. And when the high clouds part, and the towering massif of North America's tallest peak reveals itself, it's a no-holds-barred showstopper. This is Denali National Park and Preserve—the quintessence of great adventures in America's Great Land.

A trip to Denali absolutely belongs on the bucket list. The highlight, of course, is the namesake peak, rechristened from Mount McKinley in 2015 to its original Athabascan name, which fittingly means "the great one." This is a shy peak, so it may take a few days for her to poke her

head through the clouds. When she does, you will be treated to a spellbinding view that's completely out of this world.

Nature's playground

Here is wilderness at its wildest. As you explore the tundra, taiga forest, meadows, and streams, you will no doubt have myriad encounters with North America's most iconic species and apex predators. You are virtually guaranteed to spot moose and Dall sheep, or perhaps a wolf, grizzly, or caribou.

169

The number of bird species living in the park, including many birds of prey.

-99

The coldest temperature in °F (-73 °C) recorded in Denali.

Wildlife Sanctuary

Denali was created specifically to protect the rare wildlife of the Alaska Range, which includes 39 species of mammals, a range of birds—keep your eyes peeled for golden and bald eagles, gray jays, and ptarmigan—and the "Big Five"—moose, Dall sheep, caribou, wolves, and grizzly bears.

▷ **Grizzly bears** Nothing says Alaska quite like the majestic grizzly. Take the Park Road tour bus in the summer and you're likely to spot a mama and her cubs.

◁ **Dall sheep** Look to the hills for these playful climbers. Rams have especially jaunty headgear—if you listen carefully, you may even hear them butting heads in the rut.

▷ **Caribou** In the 1920s, 20,000 caribou made up the herd living east of Foraker River and north of the Alaska Range. Now, there are 1,700. You may still spot one, especially from the air.

◁ **Wolves** This is one of the best places on Earth to observe wolves in their wild habitats. There are hundreds of sightings here each year, especially in the eastern part of the park.

▷ **Moose** These ungainly ungulates are often found in marshes and around lakes. The alpha males can weigh up to 1,400 lb (635 kg) and stand 6 ft (1.8 m) tall at the shoulder.

The last frontier

Visiting Denali is a little more complicated than taking a trip to most national parks down in the Lower 48. There are fewer services here, limited established trails, and just a whole lot of big open wilderness waiting for you. Whether you spend two days on your adventure or take on a 10-day backpack trip, Denali has tons of activities that will keep your adrenaline redlined and take you to the back of beyond in one of the world's last great frontiers.

Above Mountaineering on Mount McKinley is world-class, offering up otherworldly glaciers and picturesque vistas

Left The vivid picture of Aurora Borealis as seen from Denali says it all

Star light, star bright

Most visitors come to Denali in summer, but some choose winter, specifically because they want to witness the unmatched spectacle of the Aurora Borealis (Northern Lights). The clear Alaskan skies are almost devoid of light pollution, and they put on an unrivaled light show.

Hiking utopia

There are few established trails in Denali National Park, so instead of following well-worn paths, most hikers head to the backcountry—across fields, streams, meadows, and brooks. For the novice, one option is to start with the direct, but steep, hike on the Mount Healy Overlook Trail. After the lung-pounding 2.7-mile (4.4-km) ascent, climbing 1,700 ft (520 m) past alder, spruce, and aspen forest, you're rewarded with some of the best views of Denali from terra firma.

Another day-hiking option takes you over 10 miles (16 km) through verdant

FOCUS ON
Planning Your Trip

Just the journey to Denali can take half a day, so plan in advance to make the most of your visit. If staying overnight, landing a camping spot at Wonder Lake Campground requires booking well ahead, but views of the Alaska Range and Denali reward the effort. No matter what you do, hop aboard the Denali Star train line, one of the best sightseeing train routes in the world.

spruce forest and across busy creeks, as you wend your way to the "Triple Lakes." The rolling hike affords awesome views of the river and lake systems, and it's the perfect launching point for bigger adventures farther afield.

The best hikes, though, are done on your own. No trails, no signs, no cellphone towers: nothing but nature. All you need is a compass and a map (and the know-how to use them), and you can head out from the Park Road in any direction and find your little slice of heaven. As you head for the horizon along open ridgelines, you'll see Alaska's great lands, but no sign of human civilization. Hop and skip across creeks, get your feet damp in wet tundra, and nestle up to nature in a way that's not possible amid crowds and lined-up hikes found on more organized nature tours.

To take trail-less hiking to new level, get a backcountry permit for a multiday trek deep into the park's interior. Thanks to the well-oiled permit system, access is staggered so that you're unlikely to encounter another soul on your journey. The park is about the size of Vermont, so the backcountry options are truly limitless.

Spectacle from the skies

Nothing beats a tour of Alaska from the air. Up here, you can see Denali and the Alaska Range in its pure, unadulterated immensity. Circle around glaciers (or even land on one for an afternoon of summer sledding), follow the migrating caribou, or just marvel at the unbridled grandeur that unfolds below. On the right day, you may just see a climber or two making their summit bid from Denali's top ridges.

Above Nothing can beat the aerial take on the Alaskan landscape

If you have...

Two days ▷ Plan a bus tour, camping, and a quick hike. When wildlife watching in Denali, you don't need to leave the park road to see the famous furry inhabitants. On the 92-mile (148-km) Park Road to the visitor center—eight hours by bus—you'll no doubt run into iconic wildlife and countless birds. On day two, hike the Triple Lakes Trail.

Five days ▷ Count on backpacking, flight-seeing, and a lodge stay. Start your visit with the shuttle bus to Wonder Lake Campground. Stay a night or two here before heading out on a two- to four-day backpack into the wilds beyond the park road. For your final day, treat yourself to a flight-seeing tour around Denali. Want to glam it? Reserve a spot at Camp Denali, a private reserve established in 1954 that's deep within the park's boundaries.

UTAH
NEVADA
GRAND
CANYON
○ Flagstaff
CALIFORNIA
ARIZONA
NEW
MEXICO
Phoenix ○
Tucson ○
MEXICO

Arizona

GRAND CANYON

ESTABLISHED 1919

Stand on the canyon rim and gaze at the vast, river-carved landscape of battered buttes and rugged pinnacles stretching away into the horizon, and you'll know you are looking at one of the most incredible vistas in the world.

Few places can leave you speechless, but this is one of them. Words like magnificent and stupendous pale in comparison to the scene that stretches as far as your eyes can see. No matter how many pictures you've seen, nothing prepares you for the unparalleled beauty of the Grand Canyon.

Millions of years in the making

The immensity of it is overwhelming. Sculpted buttes rise layer upon layer from the canyon floor, fading into distant, flat-topped mesas. From some viewpoints, it's just possible to make out the pencil-thin ribbon of blue that is the Colorado River, a mile below. Over millions of years, this mighty river carved out a giant chasm in the Colorado Plateau. Wind, rain, frost, and snow did the rest, eroding the rugged

bluffs into singular peaks with such whimsical names as Wotan's Throne, Cheops Pyramid, and Buddha Temple. When you admire the striated cliffs of sandstone, limestone, and shale, you are looking at two billion years of the Earth's geologic backstory.

Along the canyon's South Rim, humans, too, have made their mark, with distinctive, historic architecture that complements the park's natural beauty. Here, and across the chasm on the quieter North Rim, hiking trails and other pursuits let you immerse yourself in these glorious surroundings.

Above The canyon offers an embarrassment of riches at every turn— here, a stunning sunset over the Colorado River

Did You Know?

The park is often measured in river miles: 277 (456 km).

History Timeline

The Grand Canyon faced a long road to becoming a national icon. Benjamin Harrison tried three times to create a national park here. He succeeded in 1893, after he was president.

1906–08

Roosevelt establishes the Grand Canyon Game Preserve and the Grand Canyon National Monument, vowing to keep this natural treasure unspoiled.

2019

▽ Grand Canyon National Park, a UNESCO World Heritage Site, celebrates its centennial with a yearlong "100 Years of Grand" showcase of park highlights.

1901

▷ The first passengers arrive from Williams on the Grand Canyon Railway. The three-hour trip replaces the two-day stagecoach journey from Flagstaff, and costs $3.95.

1903

△ President Theodore Roosevelt visits the Grand Canyon and says it "fills me with awe." He declares it to be "the one great sight that every American should see."

1933–42

During the Depression, FDR's Civilian Conservation Corps of unemployed men carry out conservation duties, building trails and roads still in use today.

PARK PIONEERS
Mary Colter

At a time when there were few women architects, Mary Colter was the chief architect for the Fred Harvey Company from 1902 to 1948. Taking her inspiration from the surrounding landscape, she designed six distinctive buildings at the South Rim of the Grand Canyon: Hopi House, Hermit's Rest, Lookout Studio, Desert View Watchtower, Bright Angel Lodge, and, at the bottom of the canyon, Phantom Ranch. The first four of these are now National Historic Landmarks *(p23)*.

Right Lodgers stay in Park Service cabins, this one nestled in a perfect spot between the Colorado River and Bright Angel Creek

Few places on earth have the vastness and timelessness of the Grand Canyon. Try to spend a full day here, ideally an overnight, to experience it at different times of day—its colors and moods constantly in flux. In the crisp chill of dawn, thick clouds fill the canyon, and the rocky pinnacles poking out of the mist are tinged with soft-pink sunrise. Throughout the day, passing clouds may suddenly cast the brightly hued buttes into ominous shadow. And in late afternoon, the rainbow cliffs turn glowing orange, pink, and gold in the fiery rays of the setting sun.

Natural and human artistry

The South Rim is the most accessible and busiest section of the park. Grand Canyon Village, the hub of the South Rim, is where most people get their first breathtaking look into the chasm.

To reduce air pollution and maintain the pristine views, the road beyond is usually closed. A shuttle bus runs the 8-mile (13-km) route along Hermit Road, stopping at eight magnificent viewpoints. The last one, Hermit's Rest, is a popular place to see the sunset. A fabulous way to enjoy the canyon is to walk the trail along the South Rim between these viewpoints, taking playful photographs and lingering at secluded spots to watch eagles or California condors gliding effortlessly on the breeze.

In Grand Canyon Village, explore the amazing architecture, such as the rustic El Tovar hotel, Hopi House, or tiny Kolb Studio, clinging to the cliff's edge. These buildings were visionary for their time, using natural materials that blended with the landscape and evoked American Indian culture. Here, too, is the depot for the Grand Canyon Railway, a heritage railroad that takes you from Williams in restored vintage railcars.

Desert View Drive heads east to more spectacular viewpoints, such as Yaki Point and Grandview Point. At the Tusayan Ruin and Museum are remnants of an Ancestral Puebloan village. Their ancient architecture inspired Mary Colter's fantastic Desert View Watchtower, perched on the canyon's edge, which contains intricate design details and paintings of Hopi life and legends. Climb the winding stairs to the top for incredible panoramic canyon views.

Canyon Culture

Kolb Studio ▷ The historic home and photographic studio of Ellsworth and Emery Kolb is now a bookstore and art gallery, where many of their images from the early 1900s are on display *(p22)*.

Desert View Watchtower
Cultural demonstrations by tribal artisans from the Grand Canyon region, including Navajo weavers, Hopi kachina carvers, Zuni silversmiths, and more, take place here throughout the year.

Hopi House ▷ Shop for fine Southwestern arts and crafts at this striking Pueblo-style building, designed by Mary Colter in 1905 as an American Indian market. Hopi artisans once lived and worked here.

Grand Canyon Star Party
For eight days each June, around the time of the new moon, Arizona amateur astronomers come together to study the night sky at free public events held on the North and South rims.

California Condors

With a wingspan up to 10 ft (3 m), the California condor is North America's largest bird, but in the 1980s it became extinct in the wild. Saved through captive breeding, these vultures were released in Arizona in 1996; today, they number 500. From the South Rim, you might see them soaring over the canyon below.

Huge black wings hide white patches on the underside

Below Point Imperial looks down on the Painted Desert from a height of 8,803 ft (2,683 m)

Exhilarating exploration

As grand as the canyon appears from above, descending even a little way into its depths gives you an intimate connection to this remarkable place. Steep, rugged trails wind among the rocks down to the canyon floor, but these routes require backcountry camping. Even the fittest, most seasoned hiker cannot make it down and back in a day. There's an annual lottery for coveted overnight stays at Phantom Ranch at the bottom of the canyon.

Day hiking below the rim is an easier option. Bright Angel Trail is the most accessible, and even a brief trek from Grand Canyon Village is a thrill. As wonder and curiosity lure you deep in, keep in mind that it generally takes twice as long to hike back up. This route is also used for the park's famous mule rides along the rim and into the inner canyon.

Above Adventurers enjoy the thrill of rafting and kayaking on the Colorado, and become part of the scenery

The South Rim is more peaceful in winter, and you can witness the canyon covered in a magical frosting of powdery snow.

Hermit Road is open to cyclists year-round, and loops back to the village along the Greenway Trail. Float trips on the Colorado River give you icy highs through whitewater rapids, followed by tranquil views of the canyon from the bottom up.

Northern serenity

Although just 10 miles (16 km) away as the eagle flies, the North Rim is a five-hour drive from the South Rim. It's also 1,000 ft (300 m) higher—at over 8,000 ft (2,400 m)—and is closed in the winter. The North Rim is a cooler, quieter section of the park. Farther from the river, it is covered in alpine scenery, with thick forests of Douglas fir and ponderosa pine that are a haven for wildlife, as well as meadows and aspen trees that turn bright gold in the fall.

The winding Cape Royal Scenic Drive leads to the best overlooks. From Point Imperial, the highest point on the North Rim, survey the eastern Grand Canyon and see the distant wall of the Painted Desert and Marble Canyon. Vista Encantada affords more canyon views, and from the Walhalla Overlook, it's a short walk to Pueblo ruins.

Cape Royal, with its 180-degree vistas, is a wonderful spot to see the sun rise or set over the canyon. Here, Angel's Window,

a natural arch, artfully frames the Colorado River. Walk the short Cape Royal Trail to spy the silhouette of Desert View Watchtower across the chasm on the South Rim.

The North Rim has hiking trails that are less strenuous for day hikes than those on the South Rim: Bright Angel Point, with splendid views of Bright Angel Canyon and Roaring Springs, and the Transept Trail, along the rim between the park lodge and campground. Even a short walk on these easy trails delivers enough Grand Canyon magnificence to fill all your senses.

Three Hikes

Easy Uncle Jim Trail, 5 miles (8 km) round trip. This trail on the North Rim leads through old-growth forest to an overlook with fine views of the canyon and the switchbacks on the North Kaibab Trail.

Moderate ▷ South Kaibab Trail, 2–6 miles (3–10 km) round trip. Steep but relatively short, this hike on the South Rim offers spectacular views and the chance to spot California condors and bighorn sheep.

Challenging ▷ Rim-to-Rim Trail. This multiday trek joins the 14-mile (22-km) North Kaibab Trail from the North Rim to the South Kaibab or Bright Angel (9.5 miles/15 km) trail from the South Rim.

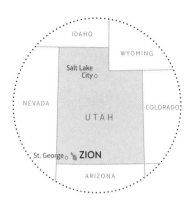

IDAHO
WYOMING
Salt Lake City
NEVADA
UTAH
COLORADO
St. George • **ZION**
ARIZONA

Utah

ZION

ESTABLISHED 1919

Zion is a magical and majestic wonderland cut from sandstone and sky. With towering walls, impossibly tight canyons, and adventures both great and small, this is Utah's most iconic national park.

Utah's first national park delivers big on beauty and grandeur. Everywhere you turn, you'll find narrow slot canyons, bulwarklike towers of sandstone, deep emerald pools, and canyons the color of fire—all, as the name suggests, in biblical proportions.

The natural balance of the desert ecosystem here is delicate, intricate, and marvelously complex. In the "low" elevations of 3,700 ft (1,127 m) up to the heady heights of 8,700 ft (2,651 m) lives a remarkable array of plant and animal life. Along the riverbanks of the Virgin River, find hanging gardens of ferns, carpets of humble mosses, and fields of wildflowers—with names like western wallflower, showy stoneseed, and shooting star. Giant cottonwoods stand tall amid lush wetlands, and above the valley floor, yucca, cactus, juniper, and desert grasses run riot.

Wondrous wildlife

The landscapes provide habitats for all kinds of wildlife, from top predators like mountain lions, to bighorn sheep, mule deer, and foxes. Some 291 species of bird are cataloged in the park. Look up to the bluebird-colored Utah skies to see the rare California condor. Saved from the brink of extinction and reintroduced into the wild, these superb gliders are massive, with wingspans stretching to 10 ft (3 m).

Above The agile, stealthy mountain lion is a solitary, carnivorous hunter

The Geology of Zion

This is the Colorado Plateau, just one step in the Grand Staircase that leads down to the Grand Canyon *(p90)*. At the heart of this mystical landscape are the towering Navajo sandstone formations, formed over millennia by wind, rain, continental uplift, and the powerful Virgin River. Upstream from the Temple of Sinawava, this fierce little river continues to gouge the landscape, carving its way through the hardened Navajo sandstone to the softer Kayenta Formation down below.

Diagonal patterns in the stone are called cross-beds.

Sandstone was sculpted from desert sand dunes created in the Jurassic period.

Cross-beds show which way ancient winds blew.

Left Hikers have to get their feet wet to see the 1,000-ft (300-m, neck-craning views of The Narrows—there are no trails on the route

Above Visitors can take in the kaleidoscopic colors of the canyon from the vertiginous heights of trails and overlooks

A world of adventure

Zion has no shortage of activities for adventurers of all skills and interests. For sightseers, there's an informative narrated bus tour that explains park history and ecology. Cyclists can pedal the 7-mile (11-km) Zion Canyon Scenic Drive instead. Once you hop off the park bus or your bike, that's when the real adventures begin.

Kids love taking part in the ranger-led activities and applying to become official Junior Rangers. Sunrise and sunset are truly bewitching hours. Find a spot to yourself and watch as canyon walls ignite in bursts of pink and orange. After the sun sets, the moon rises and the stars come out, and many head to the Pa'rus Trail for a night walk to see the Milky Way in all its glory.

The best shot is from Observation Point, where you'll see nearly all of the Grand Canyon's attractions.

Unrivalled canyoneering

Zion has some of the best canyoneering in the world. Nearly everyone starts their trip by tackling the celebrated Narrows, above the Temple of Sinawava. Wading through knee- to waist-deep waters in the Virgin River, with skyscraping 1,000 ft (300 m) walls on each side, you head deep into canyon country. More technical routes in The Subway (aptly named, as the canyon walls round up on all sides and feel like they were inspired by New York City subways) and Orderville Canyon give experienced hikers a chance to escape the crowds and visit farther into uncharted territory. There is also excellent rock climbing to be had—mostly big-wall climbs aimed at experts. It's always fun to scan the

rock face for parties making their way up the sheer cliffs of iconic routes like The Moonlight Buttress. On two established bouldering areas, the young (and young at heart) can play on the sandstone rocks.

The road to serenity

Of the myriad hikes here, some require permits and limit group size. From Zion Canyon, hikes match every ability and taste. You'll find short valley loops as well as all-day affairs that ascend clear to the tip of Angels Landing. In the Northwest corner, Kolob Canyon has a good selection of trails well away from the main canyon crowds. Beautiful backpacking trips take you into primitive wilderness, where the only noises you'll hear are the whispering of pines and the sweet sound of solitude.

Birding beauty

With a pair of binoculars and a keen eye on the horizon, you can spot a huge variety of birds in just a few short hours. The iconic species to be on the watch for are some of the top predators of the sky: the peregrine falcon, bald eagle, California condor, and Mexican spotted owl. Along with the California Condor, the peregrine falcon nests in the park, having found a safe haven to similarly recover their numbers after nearly being wiped out. The desert wildflowers and riparian habitats make this a good spot to see hummingbirds, too, including the black-chinned varieties.

Day Hikes

Popular ▷ Angels Landing, 5.4 miles (8.6 km) round trip. If you're going on just one hike during your visit, this is it. This is on a ridiculously steep trail that climbs several switchbacks before taking you to the top of Angels Landing, where the land spreads before you.

Family-friendly Emerald Pools, 3 miles (5 km) round trip. This hike is a perfect mix of ease and adventure, and leads to a series of pools and waterfalls. The delicate pools are off-limits for swimming.

Spectacular ▷ Canyon Overlook 1 mile (1.6 km) round trip. For remarkable views of Pine Creek Canyon and lower Zion Canyon, head to this super-short hour- long hike accessed near the east entrance of the Zion–Mount Carmel Tunnel. Views are best at sunrise and sunset.

Historic ▷ Kolob Canyon Trail, 1 mile (1.6 km) round trip. This trail takes you into a narrow box canyon with 1,700-ft (500-m) walls above to the Double Arch Alcove. There are fascinating geologic formations along the way, and you'll pass historic homestead cabins dating to the 1930s.

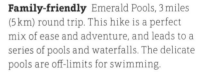

Above Overhangs on trails like Weeping Rock and Riverside Walk can provide shade from the sun

Maine

ACADIA

ESTABLISHED 1919

Nestled in the islands of coastal Maine, a romantic and charming natural oasis awaits. With serene boulder-filled lakes, granite mountains, hardwood forests, and dramatic coastal beaches, Acadia tees up countless outdoor adventures.

The Wabanaki people lived for thousands of years on what is now national parkland. They were blessed by plentiful fishing and easy gathering in the warm seasons. Over time, the land passed to others, and in the mid-19th century it became a retreat for "rusticators" (nature tourists) and artists who reimagined beautiful landscapes to share with the world. Classic painters like

Frederic Edwin Church (1826–1900) and Thomas Cole (1801–48) documented the region. Their work was found by John D. Rockefeller and George B. Dorr, who later donated thousands of acres of land to the government with the proviso that it be protected. Donations followed from locals who wanted the area preserved.

Today, Acadia remains the only national park that came about entirely through private funding. Forty-five miles (72 km) of historic carriage roads and bridges commissioned by Rockefeller meander through Mount Desert Island, allowing land passage without obstruction from cars, just as he envisioned. Stops along Ocean Drive bring cyclists, hikers, and visitors to Thunder Hole, Boulder Beach, and Jordan

BEST FOR

Painting and Photography

Acadia has a much revered artist-in-residence program. This initiative invites accomplished artists, in a variety of disciplines, to apply for a 14 day placement and during this time they create works to inspire the world to visit Acadia.

Above Bass Harbor Head Lighthouse is one of the most photographed lighthouses in the US

Far Right A hiker enjoys sunset near Schoodic Point, the only part of the park on the mainland

Ways to Explore

South Ridge Trail ▷ Hike the Cadillac Mountain South Ridge Trail, a 7-mile (11-km) out- and-back journey that leads you to and from Acadia National Park's highest peak, and the tallest mountain on the eastern seaboard. The peak is 1,530 ft (466 m) above sea level.

Park Loop Road ▷ Cycling is one of the most popular ways to experience the park. Cycle all or part of the 27-mile (43-km) winding, narrow Park Loop Road, where there are plenty of iconic stops along the route leading to inland lakes, historic sites, and rugged coastlines.

Jordan Pond Trail ▷ Take a leisurely wander along the Jordan Pond Trail and end with tea and popovers at the nearby Jordan Pond House, overlooking the water. Afternoon tea has been on the menu here since the 1890s.

Pond along a 27-mile (43-km) stretch of stone road. At the bottom of the island is the picture-perfect Bass Harbor Head Lighthouse. Other park areas sit on small islands accessible by boat. On the Schoodic Peninsula, you'll find a less-frequented area admired for its peaceful solitude.

The best time to visit is September and October, after the summer crowds thin and at the start of peak fall-foliage season.

Arkansas

HOT SPRINGS

ESTABLISHED 1921

With a burst of steam, the concept of American wellness was born in a tiny pocket of Arkansas. Hot Springs is an entirely different park from those with sprawling natural landscapes—and that's its beauty.

At one time, Hot Springs was a place utterly devoid of modernity. For millennia, American Indians came here to quarry novaculite from the Ouachita Mountains, which they used to make weapons and tools. They named the area "Valley of the Vapors," after the steam that billowed from the earth beneath.

In 1541, Spanish explorer Hernando de Soto happened upon the area and reported that America hid a fountain of youth. In time, word spread of its natural wonder. Seeing the value of the resource, President Andrew Jackson classified the Hot Springs Reservation area in 1832. It was the first national park unit founded.

Decades later, independent enterprises sprang up, turning Hot Springs into a sophisticated spa city that promoted wellness and served the elite and the ailing. Other businesses came—namely casinos and speakeasies—inviting in mobsters, athletes, and even presidents, who all sought the calming waters.

Rich in silica, the mineral water at Hot Springs continues to soothe aches and pains today. It originates in the Ouachita Mountains, another beloved park resource, which offers alternative forms of wellness along hiking trails through forests. Sunset Trail, a 15-mile (24-km) loop, is the longest and most popular, with ample opportunities for serene birdwatching.

20

In minutes, the average time in the soaking tub recommended for overall wellness.

10

The maximum number of minutes to be spent in a Sitz (sitting) tub to relieve back pain.

Right The Ozark Bathhouse was built in 1922 in the Spanish Colonial Revival style, a popular design of the time

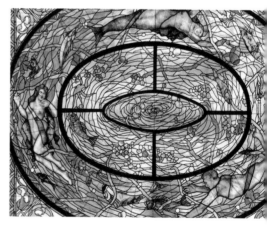

Above A beautiful stained-glass ceiling adorns the Men's Bath Hall in the Fordyce Bath House

History Timeline

The heart of Hot Springs is Bathhouse Row—where spas of the 19th and 20th centuries used thermal waters to fuel tubs, steam rooms, and other amenities to promote new-age wellness.

1915

▽ Fordyce was the most exquisite of the bathhouses, with wellness services, a gymnasium, and even bowling lanes. Today, it serves as the visitor center.

1893

▷ Hale was the first spa to offer modern amenities (a sunning porch, massage services, and a sweat room), making it contemporary and a favorite of refined visitors.

1912

△ Buckstaff is the only traditional bathhouse still in operation today. Enjoy a classic experience like those from Hot Springs' heyday at the turn of the 20th century.

1923

△ Lamar was centered around its grand marble lobby, and it was unique in offering a variety of tub lengths to accommodate clientele of different heights.

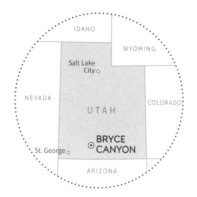

Utah

BRYCE CANYON

ESTABLISHED 1928

Cascading down from its highest point, at 9,105 ft (2,775 m), Bryce Canyon's series of amphitheaters will ignite your imagination as you marvel at the genius and wonder of this singular collection of limestone spires, slot canyons, and whimsical hoodoos.

The stars of this small-but-mighty national park are the ornate gothic rock formations carved from Utah's Paunsaugunt Plateau. This is the top layer of the famed Grand Staircase, a geologic masterpiece that descends to the Grand Canyon (p90).

Despite its name, Bryce Canyon is not a canyon at all. Rather, the geologic oddities found here were formed by years of erosion from wind and rain and cracking from freezes and thaws. Chiseled by time, these massive walls of corrugated rock, spires (called hoodoos), and other geographic forms take on the look of castles, ramparts, and citadels.

Unique microhabitats

This austere environment feels more mountainous than most of Utah's national parks. In this vertiginous biome, you'll find bristlecone and ponderosa pine, dry meadows of sagebrush, rabbitbrush, and other grasses, and, come springtime, an explosion of wildflowers bursting into life.

Animal life is different too: mountain animals like pronghorn deer and black bears, high-plains mammals such as the prairie dog, plus the desert regulars, lizards, and rattlesnakes, make their home here.

Bryce is at its best at sunrise or sunset, when the amphitheaters erupt in a resplendent symphony of reds, oranges, and yellows.

Did You Know?

The signature limestone hoodoos are carved by wind, snow, and rain, with more than 200 freeze-thaw events a year.

Infinite views

Adventures in Bryce Canyon start on the rim of the main amphitheater, Bryce, at the four main viewing points, namely Bryce Point, Inspiration Point, Sunset Point, and Sunrise Point. Find a quiet spot and ponder the wide-open landscape spread below you.

The best time of day to experience these views is either sunrise or sunset. As the sun cuts close to the horizon, the cliffs glow tungsten, rust, and bronze. The scene is so captivating that some people choose not to venture beyond the rim, opting instead to hop from viewpoint to viewpoint and explore the natural and human history through curated interactive exhibits.

Accessible to all

There are countless hikes for all levels and abilities across the park. Visitors who use wheelchairs or those with limited mobility

Left Stargazers get a front-row seat to the heavens, with unparalleled views of the Milky Way

will appreciate the excellent paved trails along the rim, including the straightforward route from Sunset Point to Sunrise Point. The Rim Trail, in fact, extends far beyond that, stretching a full 11 miles (18 km) round trip. Another easy trail takes you to Mossy Cave, a lush overhang with a small waterfall. Families love the super-easy Queens Garden Trail, which leads into the canyon, past many iconic, must-see formations, ending at the mesmerizing Queen Victoria hoodoo.

For slightly more challenging day trips, the Navajo Trail, Peekaboo Loop Trail, and Fairyland Loop are great hikes that can last anywhere from a few hours to a full day, depending on how you connect them. Along the way, you'll pass through narrow canyon passages carved into the rock that look straight out of an Indiana Jones movie, and alongside massive formations like the China Wall, Tower Bridge, and Wall of Windows. On the Riggs Springs Loop, leaving from Rainbow Point, you have the chance to experience the park's spruce, fir, and bristlecone forests.

High in the saddle

Bryce was once a cattle ranch owned by Mormon settlers Ebenezer and Mary Bryce. Ebenezer called it "a helluva place to lose a cow." In the 1900s, tourists started coming here by train, and horseback riding has been

a part of the park's tourist tradition ever since. Perched atop a mule or riding on a sure-footed horse, you'll embark on a steady tour that allows plenty of time to absorb the surrounding beauty as you descend via the 5.5-mile (9-km) Peekaboo Loop into the fantastical world of amphitheaters filled with hoodoos, spires, and canyons.

Above On winter walks at Bryce Canyon, hikers enjoy the park's stillness

Through the Seasons

Every season in the park has its special charms: whether it's the spring awakening, the magical mornings of summer, the fantastic hikes of fall, or the pull of winter sports. Take your pick:

▽ **Fall** Gone are the summer crowds. Fall is marked by solitude, optimum hiking weather, which is cool and dry, and a chance to make a closer connection with the wild flora and fauna of this remote corner of Utah.

▷ **Spring** While you may still get an errant snowstorm or two, spring is a wonderful time to visit. Wildflowers abound, such as blue flax, mountain death-camas, western iris, showy stoneseed, and Bryce Canyon paintbrush.

△ **Summer** Sunrise in the summer is pure bliss. Get up early to have the park to yourself and capture the vivid hues of the sun as it peeks over the horizon. The cooler temperatures also invite delightful long walks.

△ **Winter** The rock formations take on new forms, covered under a gentle coat of fresh snow. Winter offers its own joys. On the rim, snowshoe and cross-country ski. Visit the Winter Festival, usually held around Presidents' Day.

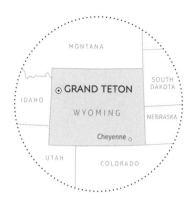

Wyoming

GRAND TETON

ESTABLISHED 1929

Whether they're rising regally over an icy blue glacial lake or acting as background to a bright summer meadow teeming with wildflowers and wildlife, the jagged peaks of the Grand Tetons are unforgettable.

The chiseled, silver granite peaks of the 40-mile-long (66-km) Teton Range are some of the most distinctive in the entire Rocky Mountains. Nineteenth-century French fur trappers christened them *les trois tétons* (the three teats), and the park is named after the loftiest peak, the 13,775-ft (4,200-m) Grand Teton. Together with its sisters, it looms over the broad valley of Jackson Hole, adding a backdrop of drama and mystery to a pristine open landscape of grassy meadows and sagebrush flats, where you're likely to come across bison, moose, elk, pronghorn deer, and perhaps even the fabled grizzly if you're lucky.

From mid- to late September, you'll find warm days, fewer crowds, and early displays of brilliant fall color.

Scenic drives wind through the park, leading to spectacular viewpoints. Teton Park Road skirts the base of the mountains, taking you to pull-offs and overlooks where you can see the mesmerizing Teton Glacier, access amazing hiking trails, and enjoy grand vistas of the Teton Range.

Picture perfect

Detour onto the Jenny Lake loop road, which runs along the eastern shore, for fabulous photographs of the peaks reflected in the crystal-clear waters of this pretty lake. The staging is so superb, there's no such thing as a bad angle. Then climb the narrow, winding Signal Mountain Summit Road for splendid panoramic views over the valley and Jackson Lake. You can then witness the wonders of Grand Teton from the John D. Rockefeller Memorial Parkway, which follows the Wild and Scenic Snake River all through the park, before it links to another iconic Rocky Mountain national park: Yellowstone (*p34*).

Three Hikes

Easy ▷ Taggert Lake Trail, 3.3 miles (5.3 km) round trip. This popular out-and-back hike offers stunning views of Grand Teton and passes through aspen groves, with great scenes of fall foliage.

Moderate Phelps Lake via the Lake Creek–Woodland Trail Loop, 3.4 miles (5.5 km) round trip. You'll have magnificent mountain views and a chance to see moose and osprey in the Laurance S. Rockefeller Preserve.

Challenging ▷ Lake Solitude, 15 miles (24 km) round trip. Inspiration Point and Hidden Falls are highlights on this strenuous all-day hike, with wildflower meadows and panoramic views of the mountains and lakes.

Above Friends make the leap into the clear waters of Phelps Lake

Left The youngest range in the Rockies, the Grand Tetons paint a vivid picture in fall

Historic homes

Scattered around Jackson Hole are the remains of pioneer settlements and early ranches dating from the 1890s. These rustic cabins are a romantic link to the past, surrounded by a virgin landscape that would have looked much like it does today. They're also a photographer's delight, adding a human scale to the grandeur of the Tetons. Head for Mormon Row, a cluster of 27 homesteads that include the picturesque, weathered Moulton Barns.

Menors Ferry Historic District is another evocative place that's a step into the past, with its general store, smokehouse, and storehouse. See early covered wagons and a replica bullboat covered in bison hide, which mountain men used to transport furs. The humble Maud Noble Cabin, nestled under the pines, was the launchpad for the creation of the national park. Other landmarks include the Murie Ranch and the Chapel of the Transfiguration, where, instead of stained glass, a clear window frames Grand Teton above the altar.

Outdoor adventures await

This park practically drags you out of your car to become part of its glorious landscape. From thrilling water sports to brisk snow

Right White-topped peaks and burnt orange trees provide an idyllic backdrop to an old barn house on Mormon Row

sports, you can enjoy outdoor recreation year round. Hiking trails lure you into backcountry beauty spots with tantalizing names like Paintbrush Canyon and Lake Solitude. Cyclists hit the paved pathway and pedal beneath the peaks to Jenny Lake or along the National Elk Refuge.

Here, the blue glacial lakes beckon: launch a boat into their idyllic waters from several locations, or steer a kayak between String and Leigh lakes, where the plunk of your paddle is all that interrupts the blissful calm. Sprawling Jackson Lake sees more action, but its 15 wooded islands, with backcountry campsites, provide solitary escape.

Ramp up your waterborne adventures by rafting on the Snake River, the fourth-largest in the nation. Its headwaters are in Yellowstone, and this part is a designated Wild and Scenic River. Guided float trips promise an exhilarating ride. The river is also famous for trout fishing, especially for snagging fine-spotted cutthroat trout. When winter blankets the park with snow and silence, explore the trails on skis or snowshoes and revel in its frosty beauty. No matter when you visit, the magnificent peaks and wonderful wildlife will be there to greet you.

FOCUS ON

Lichens

In contrast to the towering peaks are tiny lichens, among the oldest living organisms on our planet. A symbiotic marriage of fungi and algae, they grow just millimeters a year, yet they play an essential part in the park's ecosystem. Lichens thrive in harsh alpine environments, and secrete acids that break down the rocks they grow on, aiding soil formation.

The low, crusty green and brown growth is typical

There are 3,600 species of lichens in North America

Wildlife Hotspots

Grand Teton is a veritable Noah's Ark of Western wildlife. The swift deer and elk, the hulking bison, and the fierce grizzly bear and wolf all live here. Birders, too, are in for a rare treat.

▽ **Blacktail Pond** With its old beaver ponds and grassy meadows, this is a prime grazing spot for elk. Keep an eye out for moose munching on willows along the river. Several species of ducks come here to feed, too.

▷ **Oxbow Bend** This section of Snake River is a favorite fishing spot for bald eagles, osprey, and American white pelicans. Along the banks you might see playful river otters, moose, or even a grizzly bear.

△ **Antelope Flats Road** Herds of pronghorn and bison spend their time grazing on the grasslands of this spectacular route. You might even spot a coyote hunting small prey here.

△ **Moose-Wilson Road** In the south corner of the park, look for one of the park's approximately 800 moose in the willow marshes, and black bears feeding on the berry bushes along this road.

Left The Big Room has been dubbed the "Grand Canyon with a roof over it"

COLORADO

○ Santa Fe
Albuquerque ○

NEW MEXICO

ARIZONA

TEXAS

CARLSBAD
CAVERNS
⊙

Las Cruces ○

MEXICO

New Mexico

CARLSBAD CAVERNS

ESTABLISHED 1930

Explore a magical world of awe-inspiring underground rock formations, created over hundreds of thousands of years, in this remote national park that protects one of the largest cave systems in the world.

The rocky, shrub- and cactus-covered landscape in southeastern New Mexico conceals a phenomenal secret. Lying deep beneath the Chihuahuan Desert, Carlsbad Caverns is a fairy-tale setting of mysterious passageways leading into huge rooms filled with fantastical cave formations. Entering this subterranean world is a spine-tingling experience unlike anything above ground.

Jim White, a 16-year-old cowboy, discovered the caves in 1898 while tending cattle. He noticed a cloud of bats shooting up from the desert hills and found the cave entrance when he went to investigate. Using only a kerosene lantern and homemade ladder, he explored the caverns over several years and gave many of the formations their whimsical names. Ever since, visitors have marveled at the spectacular array of White's "sticky uppers" (stalagmites) and "hangy downers" (stalactites).

The bats still put on their nightly show, swirling in the thousand. Be ready, too, to explore the diverse plant life, birdlife, and desert terrain of this designated wilderness.

FOCUS ON
Forces of Nature

The spectacular cave formations, or speleothems, were created drop by drop as rain filtered through the limestone. As the water evaporated, it left deposits of crystallized calcite. Slow drips leave ceiling deposits, making stalactites, soda straws, and drapery formations. Faster drips hit the floor and build upward, as stalagmites, flowstone, and totem pole formations.

When you reach the canyon floor, set off on the path of amazement known as the Big Room Trail. This self-guided route, much of which is wheelchair accessible, is 1.25 miles (2 km) long. As the spotlighted features disappear into the darkness of the vast dome, you'll be welcomed into the largest single cave chamber by volume on the continent.

Each step brings you closer to astonishing cave formations. In the Hall of Giants, crane your neck at the fat, towering stalagmites known as Giant Dome and Twin Domes, soaring 62 ft (19 m) high. Along the trail you'll see the massive Rock of Ages, the slender Totem Pole reaching for the icicle-like Chandelier, and the chiseled column of the Temple of the Sun. Admire rippling flowstone draperies and miniature soda-straw wonderlands such as the Painted Grotto and Doll's Theater.

The ranger-led King's Palace Tour will take you into the cave's deep recesses. For a few magic moments, the lights are turned out, plunging the formations into their natural pitch blackness.

This extensive cave system runs for miles below the Guadalupe Mountains. Some 120 caves have now been found within the park, and there are likely more yet to be discovered. Some, including Lechuguilla Cave, the longest at over

Heading underground

Pictographs near the Natural Entrance imply that indigenous peoples visited the caves. But this magical world remained hidden until Jim White's discovery brought national attention. When tourists began arriving in the early 20th century, they had to be lowered into the rocky depths in a guano bucket, used to harvest bat droppings.

Entry options are more dignified today. An elevator now whisks you down 754 ft (230 m) to the Underground Lunchroom, a cafeteria built in the 1950s. It's much more exciting, though, to enter the Natural Entrance along the route White once used.

A steep switchback trail 1.25 miles (2 km) long has replaced White's handmade ladder, but the chill of anticipation stokes the same mood of discovery. You'll pass the bat cave, as well as evocative formations White christened the Devil's Den, Witch's Finger, Whale's Mouth, and Iceberg Rock.

The temperature underground is consistent year-round, but visit in winter (outside the holidays) to enjoy the main rooms in peace.

145 miles (233 km), are only open for research and exploration. Others, such as Spider Cave and Slaughter Canyon Cave, are undeveloped, but part of guided tours.

From late spring through fall, don't miss the Bat Flight, when thousands of Brazilian free-tailed bats emerge from the cave each evening to hunt for food. The soft purring of wings and the silhouettes of these tiny creatures filling the sky against the setting sun is unforgettable.

Glories above

Although it often takes second billing to the wonders underground, the surrounding landscape of the Chihuahuan Desert is quietly fascinating as well. Two-thirds of the park has been set aside as a wilderness area to protect the diverse plant and wildlife varieties that thrive here. Explore along an unpaved road and several hiking trails. One of the oustanding areas is the Rattlesnake Springs Historic District, where a natural oasis makes it a haven for more than 300 bird species and a prime birdwatching spot.

Below The fiery sunset skies over Rattlesnake Canyon look more like a movie set than reality

If you have...

An afternoon ▷ Walk down into the caverns via the Natural Entrance for an atmospheric hour-long descent. Then go on a self-guided tour of the magnificent cave formations along the 1.25-mile (2-km), largely flat, Big Room Trail.

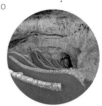

A day Join the King's Palace or Left Hand Tunnel ranger-led tour at noon to learn more about these amazing caverns. Then watch the Bat Flight at sunset from the Bat Flight Amphitheater. By late summer, the baby bats will have joined the flight.

Longer ▷ Take one of the lengthy ranger-led tours for more challenging cave explorations. Hike the trails in the Chihuahuan Desert or birdwatch at Rattlesnake Springs.

Did You Know?

The Chihuahuan Desert has 500 cacti species—more than any other desert.

2,200

At nearly 2,200 miles (3,540 km) long, the Appalachian Trail is the longest continuously marked footpath in the world.

Above A solitary hiker views the distant scenery through mountaintop cloud cover

FLORA AND FAUNA
Fireflies

From late May to mid-June, huge numbers of synchronous fireflies gather in the park, mostly around Elkmont in Tennessee, and they put on a spectacular display. As the sun starts to set, people line the roads and gaze into the woods. There in the trees, a few lights start to glow and flash, then more and more join in, until entire forest glades are illuminated by thousands of flashing green bulbs.

North Carolina • Tennessee

GREAT SMOKY MOUNTAINS

ESTABLISHED 1934

Spend a few hours in this magical place, with its mysteriously misty mountains, verdant forests, and incomparable hiking, and you'll understand why it's the most visited national park in the country.

5 to 7

The amount of time in months it takes the average person to hike the length of the Appalachian Trail.

41

The fastest time for walking the whole trail was 41 days, 7 hours, 39 minutes.

More than 12.5 million people come to Great Smoky Mountains National Park each year, and there are just as many reasons for why they are drawn here. Not least of which are those hazy and hauntingly beautiful mountains and the hiking trails that crisscross them—in particular, that giant among hikes, the Appalachian Trail. The thick forests, the scenic drives, the historic sites, and, of course, the mind-boggling variety of gorgeous plant and animal life all exert a magnetic pull. Although no one can give with certainty an exact number of all the plant and animal species in the region, it's estimated that as many as 100,000 different varieties live in these foggy wilds.

The park sprawls across two states; each side has its own unique attractions; both share those misty mountains. All peoples who have inhabited this region have been struck by its distinctive hue. The Cherokee called the mountains the "land of the blue smoke," and the first Europeans agreed, naming these the Great Smoky Mountains, along with the Blue Ridge Mountains, both part of the vast Appalachian mountain range.

The beaten path

The Appalachian Trail stretches from Maine to Georgia, passing through 14 states. Just 71 miles (114 km) is in the park, although the trail's highest point, Clingmans Dome (6,643 ft/2,025 m), is here, as well as its only dam crossing, Fontana Dam, which is where the trail exits the park.

Climb to the top

On the North Carolina side of the park, there are hundreds of miles of hiking trails, with almost boundless vistas of forests, streams, and waterfalls. Some trails straddle both states—one of the most popular being the Clingmans Dome, which starts in North Carolina and ends at the park's highest point, just inside Tennessee.

To embark on the trek, you need to drive to the Clingmans Dome trailhead, where you leave the car behind. The trail to the top is only 1.2 miles (2 km) and it's paved, but don't be fooled. It's steep, especially the last section. At the outset, views are partly obscured by trees, with occasional tantalizing glimpses of what lies ahead. Gradually, the trees thin and the mountains start to emerge, more and more of them, appearing on the horizon.

Pause and drink in this magnificent view before pressing on. As you cross the state line, a curved walkway takes you above the trees—if the walk didn't make you breathless, the panoramic, 360-degree views will. On a clear day, you can see 100 miles (160 km) over the peaks below.

The Clingmans Dome Observation Tower is easily the best spot in the park for photos, but you'll also get impressive shots at the Deep Creek Valley Overlook and the Newfound Gap Overlook.

Below Clouds roll over the Deep Creek area, which is renowned for its thick forests and streams

Right The Bradley Fork Trail shows itself at its finest when at the peak of its splashing fall glory

Lakes and trails

Fontana Lake—at 440 ft (130 m)—is the deepest lake in North Carolina and is easily viewed from Clingmans Dome. It also marks the spot where the park ends and the Nantahala National Forest begins. When it's at its highest levels in summer, the lake provides easy access by boat to more remote trailheads in the park. And if you walk across the gates of Fontana Dam, you'll have had a chance to walk part of the renowned Appalachian Trail. But don't stop there—keep walking into the lush woods until you get far enough away to look back and survey the lake surrounded by forests and mountains, its surface dotted with wooded islets. To call the scene picturesque doesn't begin to do it justice.

For some local sporting adventure, get out onto the park's waters at Deep Creek near Bryson City, where the tubing is superb. Choose from two areas—one for the adventurous, the other for the more laid-back. Rent your tube near the Deep Creek trailhead, a 20-minute walk from the put-in spot and right near a picture-perfect rushing waterfall. Then take the plunge and enjoy the thrill.

FAMILY FUN

Mountain Farm Museum

For a taste of what log-cabin life was like in isolated settlements, head 2 miles (3.2 km) north of Cherokee to the Mountain Farm Museum and Oconaluftee Visitor Center. They host activities for kids of all ages that illustrate the hardships faced by early settlers, despite the bounty of the mountains.

A watery wonderland

Tennessee more than holds its own when it comes to the wet and wonderful aspects of the park's natural splendor. To get up close—and wet—take the Trillium Gap Trail near Gatlinburg. This 2.6-mile (4-km) out-and-back trail leads you past bubbling streams, through a hemlock forest, past sweeping mountain views, and even behind the 25-ft (8-m) Grotto Falls. This is also one of the best places to spot the park's famous salamanders. You may be lucky enough to see one of the park's 1,500 black bears ambling through the neighborhood.

Much higher, at 80 ft (24 m), are Laurel Falls, and a 2.6-mile (4-km) trail gets you there and back. With rocks on one side and steep drops on the other, the paved trail is a sight in its own right, sporting dramatic views of the surrounding mountains. After walking about an hour, the sounds of Laurel Falls greet you, and a walkway takes you between the upper and lower sections of the falls and their thundering waters.

Green, green valley

If you prefer to experience the park by car, then the Smokies offer numerous spectacular drives. One of the best is undoubtedly Cades Cove—cove being the local word for a valley. The loop road is just 11 miles (18 km) long, but, even so, allow at least

FLORA AND FAUNA
Salamanders

The Great Smoky Mountains are known as the Salamander Capital of the World, and have 24 species of lungless salamanders, and four other families of salamanders. The lungless salamanders "breathe" through blood vessels that cover their skin, mouth and throat. Watch out for the vivid black-chinned red salamander, which definitely stands out.

A blunt snout is typical of salamanders

Thin skin is permeable to water

Four toes on the hind legs is highly common

half a day to accommodate the many stops along the way. Most of the park is thickly wooded but Cades Cove is open, so ideal for wildlife spotting. You might see deer grazing in the fields, hear the gobble of wild turkeys, or spy white-tailed deer. Bring binoculars to observe them from a distance. Cades Cove is also perfect for birdwatching. Flashes of color in the trees and bushes could be the the blue grosbeak, the pileated woodpecker, or the yellow-throated warbler.

Get a feel for the life of a pioneer at two historic buildings in the area. The John Oliver Cabin, one of the oldest structures in the park, was built without nails in the

History Timeline

The Great Smoky Mountains exude a timelessness, as if they have always been here and always will be. The oldest rocks in the park formed more than a billion years ago, and the constant change of nature ensures that the park will continue to evolve through the centuries.

2000 BC
◁ The Cherokee live for 4,000 years in the area that today makes up the national park, until they are forcibly relocated.

1830
▷ After president Jackson signs the Indian Removal Act, all tribes east of the Mississippi are made to walk to Oklahoma in the Trail of Tears.

1901
◁ Little River Railroad opens to export lumber from the Smokies (until 1939). Many oppose the park because of business interests.

1925
▷ The idea to make the area a national park is studied, including the ramifications for local people. It gets the go-ahead the next year.

1976
◁ The park is made an International Biosphere Reserve. The ecosystem is now studied in detail to ensure its sustainable development.

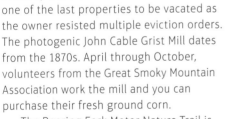

1820s by the first European settlers. It was one of the last properties to be vacated as the owner resisted multiple eviction orders. The photogenic John Cable Grist Mill dates from the 1870s. April through October, volunteers from the Great Smoky Mountain Association work the mill and you can purchase their fresh ground corn.

The Roaring Fork Motor Nature Trail is another notable drive. At just 5.5 miles (9 km) long, what it lacks in length it makes up for in beauty. The road winds through thick forests, alongside mountain streams that become noisy torrents after heavy rains, and past log cabins from days gone by.

Above The morning light shines through gauzelike clouds at Cades Cove, home to bears, elk, and deer

Left The cascading water of Doyle's River Falls in Shenandoah leaves a visitor transfixed

Virginia

SHENANDOAH

ESTABLISHED 1935

Even though the very name Shenandoah is evocative and harmonious, nothing prepares you for the simple but overwhelming beauty of the landscape, with its dense woods, rolling valleys, and gentle mountains.

Shenandoah is one of the iconic national parks whose well-known name conjures such breathtaking images you may wonder if the reality will disappoint. It doesn't, not by a country mile. The park's main draw, Skyline Drive, sounds an equally lyrical note, and it, too, exceeds expectations. As you travel the road, you'll want to pause to absorb the views or quietly witness the white-tailed deer—or bobcats or black bears—going about their daily routines. You may choose to set off on a woodland hike, visit some of the many waterfalls, or perhaps even follow parts of the legendary Appalachian Trail.

In the fall, the forest of trees is at its spectacular best, when greens turn to gold, to crimson, to yellow, to orange. Leaf-peeping is rightfully highly popular here, but you'll have to plan ahead and get an early start on the day if you're hoping to see nature dressed in all its breathtaking finery.

When fall turns to winter, Shenandoah is equally magical, and much less crowded. The views are enhanced when the distant peaks are tipped in white and a dusting of snow covers Skyline Drive.

Early evening is the perfect time to visit, when fewer cars are on the road. During a modest stroll in the woods, you're likely to come across some of its wild residents.

Three of the best spots for picture-taking are Hogback Mountain Overlook, Brown Mountain Overlook, and Crimora Lake Overlook.

Spring awakening

In spring, Shenandoah sheds its winter cloak, and the trees, day by day, put on their spring coats of many green colors. This is the time of year, too, when you're most likely to see black bears, as they emerge from their winter hibernation. Mother bears will be foraging for food, and if you're lucky, you may see a busy mama with her faithful cubs in tow. If you see a car parked on Skyline Drive at this time of year, there's every chance someone's spotted a bear nearby or stopped for one crossing the road. There's no need to fear bears—they will likely scamper away as soon as they're aware of your presence—but use caution and always follow park rules if you encounter one. Be on the lookout for bobcats, too, and coyotes, although you are far more likely to hear coyotes at night or in the early mornings—when packs howl like a canine choir—than to run across them.

You may see bats fluttering out from their roosts at sunset, or hear the hoots of owls calling to each other as they hunt. Some 190 species of bird live in the park, and these, too, are most active in the spring, which is when they nest and mate. Scan the skies for red-tailed hawks, golden eagles, and bald eagles, all of which are present here year-round.

A sight to behold

Although Skyline Drive is only 105 miles (170 km) of two-lane road, it will take you at least a day, or better yet, two or three, to explore in full. In part, that's due to the 35 mph (56 kph) speed limit and the frequency of cars idling to watch wildlife, but mostly it's because the road provides

Above The summit of Stony Man Mountain affords unbeatable views of the Shenandoah Valley

FLORA AND FAUNA
Black Bears

The American black bear is the smallest and most common bear in the United States, although when Shenandoah was established, there were thought to be just two bears living within its boundaries. Today, an estimated 200 to 1,000 bears can be found in the park at any one time, depending on their movements. Mothers give birth to between one and six cubs, with two to three being the norm. Cubs mature at around 18 months; until then they depend on Mom and stick close by.

access to numerous hikes and an impressive 75 named overlooks—which translates into a view worth stopping for every 1.4 miles (2 km). Most notably, the drive appeals because of its variety. At times you'll find yourself driving through tunnels of trees, then the road will curve and vistas will open up on both sides, or you'll see forest on one side and valley on the other. The route follows gentle, and sometimes not so gentle, twists and turns (which explains the reduced speed limit). In places, the road rises gradually, elsewhere it dips and weaves.

The walks are varied, too, and promise something for everyone: from easy hour-long strolls to challenging all-day treks. And so, too, are the above-mentioned overlooks, many of which have descriptive names like Signal Knob Overlook, Jenkins Gap, Range View, and Hogback Overlook— names and outlooks that are as delightful as Shenandoah itself.

Three Hikes

Easy ▷ 5.7 miles (9 km) round trip. The Lands Run Falls Trail is an easy hike along a wide fire road, which allows trucks access when needed. It leads through woods and across a stream to the Lands Run Falls.

Moderate 2.8 miles (4.5 km) loop trail. The Lewis Spring Falls Trail is a bit tough, with some rocks to negotiate, but the falls and views are worth the effort.

Challenging ▷ 9 miles (14 km) round trip. The hike to the top of the 3,284-ft (1,001-m) Old Rag Mountain is one of the most popular hikes in the park, but you'll have to tread with care and scramble over rocks to make it to the top.

Right This secluded beach is a tiny stretch of Olympic's 70 miles (113 km) of wild coastline

CANADA

Seattle
OLYMPIC
Spokane
WASHINGTON
IDAHO
Vancouver
OREGON

Washington

OLYMPIC

ESTABLISHED 1938

Home to the Lower 48's only rain forests, Olympic's stunning scenery runs an impressive gamut: beaches, glaciated mountains, crystal lakes, and bucolic woodland trails.

The nearby city of Seattle is infamous for its heavy rainfall, so it's not surprising that the USA's only rain forest is in the Pacific Northwest. The hot and humid conditions make it unique among the country's national parks, and provide dense and lush woodlands offering some wonderful hikes.

Tall trees abound, and wildlife is abundant. The topographical variety is unmatched: mountains, low-lying forests and lakes, and vast expanses of coastline. At the Olympic Coast National Marine Sanctuary, marine and birdlife flourish, and it's a hunting ground for orcas, sometimes seen from the shore.

The beaches are a marine wonderland, especially after high tide leaves behind fertile rock pools. The best of these can be explored at Kalaloch Beach 4 and Mora's Hole in the Wall, where park rangers are on hand to explain things to you, and you'll find more tide pools at Second Beach, Third Beach, and Ruby Beach.

FAMILY FUN
Tide Pools

Tide pools are nature's treasure hunts: see bright starfish clinging to rocks and anemones, like the giant green anemone. Look at, but don't touch these delicate beauties.

Diverse plant ecosystem

Rain forests, of course, mean rain. There's lots of it, so come prepared, although in some places you'll be protected by the canopy, which is so thick it acts like a giant umbrella. The trees, too, often soak up rainwater before it can get through to the ground. Even during showers, these are magical places, especially if you have the trails to yourself. In places, you wouldn't be at all surprised if Bilbo Baggins popped up from behind the thick ferns that carpet much of the woods.

More than 1,450 species of plant grow on the Olympic Peninsula, which is a truly phenomenal number. You'll also find some record-breakers among the tall trees, which popular hikes signpost you toward. One giant fir tree is the highest such tree in the park, standing at 246 ft (75 m). Meanwhile, a local western red cedar at 174 ft (53 m) is the largest one in the world, while a 1,000-year-old Sitka spruce has reached 191 ft (58 m), also the largest one of its kind.

Wildlife galore

Abundant water means abundant wildlife. You may get lucky and spot a black bear wandering its woodland home. Bobcats and lynx lurk here, too, although they are highly elusive creatures. In the early morning or evening, you're likely to hear the high-pitched barks and yips of coyotes. And you'll definitely see and hear the rich

FOCUS ON
The Quinault Indian Nation

Lake Quinault and Quinault River are named for the Quinault Indians, five tribes who have lived on the northwest of the Olympic Peninsula in family long-houses for centuries. If you fish here, it's with their permission. The main village of Taholah is on a reservation bordering the Pacific. Because of coastal erosion, the tribe is considering relocation.

Above Rain feeds the coniferous and deciduous trees, mosses, and ferns in mystical Hoh Rain Forest

birdlife—perhaps the melodious song of a wren, much louder than it ought to be for a bird this size, or the sudden screech of the blue jay. Listen out for true songbirds, warblers and thrushes, as well as the unmistakable hoots and screeches of owls.

Embrace your inner athlete

Much of the water that falls on the park ends up in its beautifully scenic lakes, including Lake Crescent and Lake Quinault, especially popular with visitors, and great places to swim, fish, and boat. Lake Crescent is the second-deepest lake in Washington state, at 624 ft (190 m). The low level of nitrogen in the water makes an unfavorable environment for algae to grow, resulting in some of the clearest water you'll ever see. The lake has several species of trout, as well as the Olympic mud minnow, found nowhere else.

Lake Quinault lies by Highway 101, on the stretch of the famous road that meanders through the park. A popular scenic drive takes you around the lake on its 30-mile (48-km) loop, though far better to leave the car behind and explore the loop by bike, with hiking trails providing many stopping-off points along the way.

Three Hikes

Easy ▷ Quinault Loop Trail, 4 miles (6.5 km) round trip. This leisurely trail is a popular option because it's mostly flat and passes through diverse scenery—along the shore of the lake, through rain forest, and past a waterfall.

Moderate ▷ Storm King Mountain Trail, 5.3 miles (8.5 km) round trip. Starting in Port Angeles, this hike takes you through montane forest, with views over Lake Crescent. The trail is steep in places, with the last section difficult, but it's possible to shorten the trek and omit this part.

Challenging ▷ Hoh River Trail, 33 miles (53 km) loop trail. Hike through rain forest, subalpine meadows, and montane forest. Starting out flat, this trail ends with a steep hike up to the Mount Olympus Blue Glacier.

Right Trails and bridges lead hikers into the deep serenity of the park's four rain forests

Mountains and meadows

Between the low-lying rain forest and the high-flying mountain peaks, Olympic National park boasts swaths of beautiful flower meadows, bursting into color once the blanket of winter snow recedes. There are several meadow loop trails to take you hiking around the meadows, starting from the parking lot at the top of Hurricane Ridge. You might see graceful tiger lilies in reds, oranges, and yellows, or the pretty blue harebell, also known as the bluebell of Scotland. There are vivid yellow fan-leaf cinquefoils, too, their color emphasized by the lush green grass. Tread quietly, and you might spot deer, as they like to graze in these thick grassy meadows.

Hurricane Ridge provides acres of color in summer, but at an elevation of 5,242 ft (1,598 m), in winter is covered in a coat of thick, white snow. It's a hub of the park's winter activities, which include skiing, snowboarding, snowshoeing, and snow tubing. From about the middle of December through late March, activities to suit all levels of ability are on offer. If you're a novice and want to try your hand at a new sport, lessons are available. Note, though, that in the winter Hurricane Ridge Road may be closed in poor weather.

Glacial beauty

Standing above all this beauty is the park's highest point, the 7,965-ft (2,428-m) Mount Olympus, in the western half of the park. Showing the extent of these mountain ranges, about 22 miles (35 km) to the east

Hiking at these elevations is yet another experience that contrasts with hiking in the rain forests far below. At these heights, the air is thinner and crisper, of course. You won't be sweating the humidity, but instead breathing more rapidly as your lungs work harder to take in oxygen. For the rough and ready, take the numerous trails that crisscross these mountains, some with haunting names like the Gray Wolf Pass Trail or the Lost Pass Trail.

Scaling to the top of Mount Olympus is recommended for very experienced mountaineers only, because of the difficulty of the terrain and the severe weather conditions. Fortunately, there's an easier way to see the best of the mountain scenery. From near the Hurricane Ridge Visitor Center, drive up the winding and rough Obstruction Point Road (open mid-July to mid-October). On one side is mountain, on the other a steep drop-off and an expansive horizon filled with snowcapped peaks. At Obstruction Peak Trailhead, take a final short hike to the top of Obstruction Peak, at 6,450 ft (1,970 m). Gaze around slowly, drink in the view—and the magnificent Olympic National Park unfolds in all its glory.

Above Climbers ascend the moraine for a heady view of Blue Glacier and Mount Olympus

is the next-highest point, Mount Deception, at 7,788 ft (2,374 m). Mount Olympus is home to features that, like the rain forests, make this park unique: the glaciers. There are several of these ice monsters, the longest being the Hoh Glacier, at more than 3 miles (4.8 km). Blue Glacier is the largest by volume and 2.6 miles (4 km) long. These mighty ice sculptors carved the landscape you see, and they comprise the most glaciated part of the States outside Alaska.

Through the Seasons

The park enjoys a temperate climate—regardless of season, temperatures are never wildly hot or cold. Summer days are long and winter days short, but each season has its charms.

▽ **Fall** This is elk rutting season, when the bugling calls of male elks bellow across the park. Now is when big-leaf maples get their fall colors and spawning salmon bring bobcats, bears, and eagles to hunt the rivers.

▷ **Spring** You're most likely to see black bears, a common inhabitant of the area, out and about. Now is when mothers emerge from their winter dens to forage for food, usually with two or three cubs trailing behind.

△ **Summer** The meadows are bedecked with wildflowers—glacier lilies, purple lupine, and magenta paintbrush put on a show. This is an ideal time to visit: rainfall is at a low and temperatures are perfect for enjoying outdoor pursuits.

△ **Winter** At storm-watching time along the coast in winter, the rain can be almost horizontal and huge waves come rolling and crashing into the shore. High tide is the best time, with Kalaloch Beach a prime viewpoint.

California

KINGS CANYON

ESTABLISHED 1940

Home to the deepest canyon in the United States, color-splashed alpine meadows, fast-flowing rivers, and vast groves of giant sequoias, Kings Canyon showcases nature at its most majestic.

Spanish explorers who came to this part of California christened the local river Rio de los Reyes (River of the Kings). Kings Canyon is its namesake, and it is indeed regal. Naturalist John Muir (*p18*), who campaigned to establish this park, thought it rivaled Yosemite in its wonders.

FOCUS ON
Soundscapes

Listen closely for the busy sounds of nature: birdsong, chatter, and hammering from the American robin, Steller's jay, or acorn woodpecker; the rustle of leaves made as a lizard or snake slithers by; or the rush of wind in the trees that signals a change in weather.

Winter wonderland

Carved out by an eons-old glacier active during the Ice Age, Kings Canyon is a breathtaking 8,200 ft (2,500 m) deep and just one of many canyons in the park. You'll be reminded of these icy beginnings if you visit in winter, which can be a magical (and long) period: winter here can run from late fall into late spring, due to its elevation—the highest point is 14,248 ft (4,343 m). One upside though, is the solitude. You'll have many viewpoints to yourself as you gaze out over white peaks, their lower slopes waves of snow-covered pines. It's bracing cold, so dress for it and throw yourself into skiing, snowshoeing, or other winter fun.

Above The views and burbling waters of Darwin Bench, at an elevation of 11,500 ft (3,500 m), make for a great photo

Winter Activities

Family fun ▷ Kids are catered to in winter, with designated snow-play areas just for them. Sled down hills blanketed in sparkling snow at the Big Stump area, or rent some skis here for gentle cross-country.

Snowshoeing ▷ Ranger-led snowshoe excursions are offered for adventurers of all ages and a range of fitness levels. Take in the scenery, too, on a guided walk.

Road trips ▷ Sightseeing by car can be spectacularly beautiful, but be prepared for the conditions. Drive past snow-filled meadows from Lodgepole to Grant Grove, and stop at the Redwood Mountain Overlook to admire the largest sequoia grove in the world dusted with swathes of white powder.

that 95 percent of the park is designated wilderness, in parts accessible only by foot or on horseback, there's always somewhere to go for a one-on-one with nature.

1,650

The age of the General Grant Tree, where Christmas morning services are held each year.

1890

The year the park was originally established, as the General Grant National Park. It was renamed and expanded in 1940.

Springtime glory

In spring and summer, the park sheds its winter coat and ushers in a renewed beauty. The valley floor erupts in shocks of intense colors in the wildflower meadows, especially the Zumwalt Meadow. The dense forests, where black bears and mountain lions roam, come alive, too. You're likely to witness one of the more than 200 species of bird here, or perhaps see deer with their fawn or a mother bear and her cubs. And, of course, there are the trees. The super-sized sequoia groves in Kings Canyon embrace some of the oldest and tallest trees in the world, and the park was founded to protect them. This time of year is busier, but given

Hiking happiness

Captivating hikes with the lure of stunning scenery await, from easy day walks to strenuous trails. The leisurely, paved General Grant Tree Trail is a portal into lush sequoia forest, and is named after the immense showstopper you'll meet along the way: the second-largest tree on Earth and the only living thing Congress has named a national shrine. For a long-distance trail that offers a challenge, tackle part of the iconic John Muir Trail for dramatic mountain scenery. It's worth steering off at mile 122 to the majestic Darwin Bench—the jewel in the crown of the Sierra Nevada range, with a stunning view across Evolution Lake.

ISLE ROYALE

Marquette

CANADA

WISCONSIN · MICHIGAN

Grand Rapids

Detroit

Michigan

ISLE ROYALE

ESTABLISHED 1940

From the frigid waters of Lake Superior rises a pristine island cradling untouched wilderness, where wolves and moose find refuge in boreal forests bound by freshwater that beats the shore with the wild energy of an ocean.

Born of volcanoes and sculpted by ancient glaciers, Isle Royale's mystique has enchanted modern explorers in the Midwest for more than 100 years. Sitting in the middle of the world's second largest freshwater body, Lake Superior, this relatively obscure park is a tousled world of lush trees, hidden lagoons, and stunning shoreline. The lack of communications signals offers solitude to all who seek it.

The island is 99 percent protected wilderness, so virtually anywhere you go, hiking opportunities overflow. Protected coves and bays shield paddlers from choppy waters, while inland lakes offer more tranquil experiences—however, you will have to portage (carry your watercraft). If underwater life piques your interest, cold-water scuba adventures will bring you to 10 shipwrecks while swimming among 40 fish species and diverse aquatic plants. For low-key adventure, there are ranger-led excursions from Rock Harbor, the park's hub, to historic places such as the Rock Harbor Light Head, a hop and a float away.

At the Bangsund Cabin near the Edisen Fishery, you can see specimens from decades of study on the moose and wolf populations and learn from the researchers about the historic grounds where these majestic creatures live.

BEST FOR

Skygazing

Early and late in the season, when the sky is at its darkest, astro-buffs get their fill when the enchanting Aurora Borealis can be seen dancing with green, red, and purple bands of color.

A Story of Wildlife Symbiosis

The world's longest predator-prey study examines the relationship between the wolf and moose populations on Isle Royale. The research has spurred recent efforts by the Park Service to reintroduce wolves here.

1900s

▷ In the early 20th century, moose arrive on the isle. It is unclear how they get there, but it is thought they swim from Canada.

1940s

Wolves cross an iced-over Lake Michigan from Canada, creating a dynamic wildlife environment where both flourish.

1958

Amid declining wolf numbers, the *Wolves and Moose study of Isle Royale* monitors animal populations, human impact, and plant life.

1960s

◁ Early work focuses on the plant-based food supply of prey, and how its health contributes to the sustainability of wolves.

1980

Wolf populations diminish after a canine-introduced virus reaches the island, showing the direct effects of human activity.

2005

Moose populations sink to the lowest recorded, 540, while wolf numbers are strong, at 30. In three years, the balance will shift: 700 to 23.

2018

▷ Only two wolves remain, alongside more than 1,500 moose. The National Park Service spearheads a reintroduction program.

Above A ranger shines a light to illuminate the chasm below

Left The classic Historic Tour, one of the most famous, has been trodden by humans for thousands of years

Kentucky

MAMMOTH CAVE

ESTABLISHED 1941

Winding hundreds of miles beneath the bluegrass of Kentucky, a subterranean underworld thrives among delicate blossoms of alienlike formations that fill the massive cave system. The hypnotizing songs of unseen dripping water greet you as you enter secret corridors.

Inside the longest cave system in the world, passages reaching deep into the earth fan out from vast chambers that drip with stalactites and cradle stalagmites, cave bacon, and coral formations. This giant underground sensation became a UNESCO World Heritage Site in 1941.

Lying above vertical ridges of rock is an umbrella of shale and sandstone, protecting airy pockets of empty space beneath it. Surface water finds its way through the soft ceiling, eroding limestone and carving an intricate interior.

American Indians first discovered the entrance to Mammoth Cave more than 4,000 years ago and mined for minerals within its walls. Their presence is still visible as cave art on the chamber ceilings— abstract impressions etched (or burnt) in charcoal overhead. In the early 19th century, enslaved people guiding wealthy tourists kept the tradition alive, immortalizing their work by signing their names to the walls.

Enslaved guides were vital in opening up the system for exploration, and their legacy continues to be celebrated. Today, rangers recount stories and legends of an era when the most notable explorers were enslaved people, sent underground to make many discoveries at the behest of their "owners."

Overground adventures

New finds and mapping still occur in the caves, where life-forms such as insects and bats enchant guests. Above ground, those who crave exploration in the sunshine hit cycling paths, hiking trails, and backcountry horse trails through the lush Kentucky setting. Running through the area are the Green and Nolan rivers, where paddlers of all experience levels kayak and canoe down more than 25 miles (40 km) of water. The park's astonishing terrain is a unique opportunity for adventurers to discover both subterranean wonders and wide open prairie—all in one day.

PARK PIONEERS

Stephen Bishop

The most legendary explorer of the cave, Bishop (p20) started life in slavery. Prolific in his findings and a skilled guide, he is buried at the park's Old Guide's Cemetery.

Texas

BIG BEND

ESTABLISHED 1944

Bright desert day fades to starry night at
Big Bend—where dusty roads lead to a wilderness
bisected by the mighty Rio Grande. Smack in
the middle of the Chihuahuan Desert, storybook
wildlife roams under endless sky.

Getting to Big Bend National Park requires
some grit—it is a long way from any airport
to the captivating wilds of Texas. Driving
south under the hot desert sun, on roads
that seem to stretch forever, suddenly you
hit a fertile oasis. With the dirt kicking up
from your wheels, the dry shrublands give
way to rugged mountainscapes.

FOCUS ON
Unique Desert Life

Low-elevation river corridors spanning
100 miles (160 km) transition to high
mountain forests. The varied
microclimates shelter an eclectic mix of
creatures: bobcats, badgers, and deer, as
well as diamondback rattlesnakes,
tarantulas, and 14 types of scorpions—
some found only here. This is also a
birding mecca, with 450 bird species.

A chequered history

The Americas have forever
been a land of migration,
as evidenced by the
geologic and human
timeline at Big Bend:
500-million-year-old rocks
preserve remnants of an ancient sea now
frozen in time. Artifacts from Paleo-Indians
living 10,000 years ago give clues to their
long-ago lives. For millennia, this was home
to the nomadic hunter-gatherer Chisos
Indians, who were largely undisturbed when
Spanish explorers came in the 16th century
searching for gold and silver. Some 200
years later, Comanche arrived, displacing
the Chisos and raiding neighboring villages
in Mexico along the infamous Comanche
Trail. The Mexican–American War would
alter the landscape forever, opening it to
homesteaders, ranchers, and miners, who
established and abandoned mines, such
as the now deserted Mariscal Mine.

Above Big Bend National Park contains the largest protected area of the Chihuahuan Desert

Right Paddling the river past 1,500-ft (457-m) cliffs provides shade from the sun

Far Right Walking trails cut through landscape filled with local vegetation: prickly pear cacti, yucca plants, and diverse desert scrub

Desert delights

Big Bend is expansive, remote, and in possession of an austere beauty. To describe it as merely a desert paints the picture of a barren wasteland, which it's anything but. Life is always on the move here. Black bears wander in high forests, mountain lions skulk elusively among craggy peaks, and reptiles slip into the slimmest of crevices. Close enough to make its presence felt flows the Rio Grande, coolly drifting in some areas and raging in class IV rapids in others—a natural border between two countries that share a wild ecosystem.

Visitors bring movement to the land, too. With more than 100 miles (160 km) of paved roadway weaving through the park, anyone with a car can get a taste of what makes the Chihuahuan Desert special. Morning drives are met by coyotes hunting breakfast, javelina (which look like wild pigs, but aren't), and roadrunners darting to safety. Hikers follow trails leading to unexpected water features, rock formations, and historic mining relics. Fossils can be unearthed from clay and limestone sediment and mounds of volcanic-ash tuff.

If you've ever fantasized of finding tranquility in the vast desert quietness,

BEST FOR
Backcountry Off-Roading

It's nearly impossible to explore this enormous park fully by foot, kayak, or paved scenic roadway. Venture beyond the easily accessible in an off-road adventure. Take the wheel of a high-clearance vehicle, lay in supplies, and head out across the rough and rugged land, through bedrock washes brimming with wildlife. Check at the visitor center in advance, as these areas are infrequently patrolled.

you've come to the right place. Landscape photographers are also well served. Iconic shots abound—for instance, Balanced Rock at sunrise, when the stone is dressed to perfection in golden light. Off-roaders find adventure on River Road, a 50-mile (80-km) glorified dirt track that cuts through stark desert formations.

Nighttime nirvana

The evening is a special time in Big Bend—as the rangers say, "half the park is after dark." Beautifully undimmed by light pollution, brilliant stars blanketing the cosmos are in full view. This starriest park in the contiguous US rates Gold-Tier status from the International Dark-Sky Association. While camping in the backcountry, you will fall asleep beneath the impossibly starry skies, your only lullaby sung by fellow creatures of the night.

Below The muddy river water matches the colors of the surrounding soil

Rio Grande Butterflies

Big Bend is well known for its unique desert wildlife and must-see birdlife. It is also home to more than 180 species of butterfly. October and November provide the liveliest activity and best viewing, although you can spot butterflies in the Lower Rio Grande valley all year long, particularly in these spots:

Davis Mountains ▷
High peaks and dense ponderosa pine forests, along with adjacent arid flatlands, are home to beautiful juniper hairstreaks, which flit from flower to flower.

◁ **Green Gulch** The drainage basin runs from mountain woodlands to desert lowlands; you'll see many species, such as Big Bend favorite, Chisos "Nais" metalmarks.

Blue Creek Canyon ▷
This deep canyon west of the Chisos Mountains is a haven for both highland and lowland butterflies, including colorful sleepy oranges.

◁ **Lower Chisos Basin**
Here's one of the best places in the park to spot butterflies, including the giant swallowtail butterfly, the largest species in North America.

Rio Grande Village and Dugout Wells ▷
Situated next to the Rio Grande, this area is home to the western pygmy blue, the smallest butterfly on the continent.

Florida

EVERGLADES

ESTABLISHED 1947

Forming one of the most enduring images of Florida is a broad expanse of wetland dotted with tree islands. With a peculiar beauty that is a paradise for its prolific wildlife, this is one of the world's most precious places.

On the southern tip of the peninsula, the vast wilderness of the Everglades acts as a fascinating natural counterpoint to the beach and city focus in the rest of the state of Florida. Comprising swamps and marshes, forests and islands, and an endless supply of water, Everglades National Park is the ideal place to explore this famous natural wonder and the many rare and endangered species that call it home.

Despite being bigger than Delaware, at 1.5 million acres (0.61 million ha), only a few hundred people live here. The rest of the inhabitants fly, walk, swim, or slither their way around. In this unique ecosystem, you're guaranteed to sight thrilling creatures including alligators, the more reclusive crocodile, and the strange beast that is the manatee. Best of all, this open expanse offers myriad ways to get up close to these inhabitants and the dense landscape, with hiking trails, inviting waterways, and even one long, winding road.

Walk the Mahogany Hammock Trail for great wildlife photos, especially of the barred owls that make their home here.

Did You Know?

The Florida Everglades is the only place in the world where you will see alligators and crocodiles living side by side.

On the water

Although it's thought of as a wetlands, the Everglades is actually an enormous and slow-moving river, some 200 miles (322 km) long. It begins life at the Kissimmee River, from where it makes its lazy way south, passing through several lakes until it finally reaches Lake Okeechobee. The name Okeechobee, a Seminole word meaning "River of Grass," aptly describes this unique landscape where water and land merge.

The river gathers the waters of the lake in its arms and together they continue to flow slowly south toward Florida Bay. As the land narrows and the water widens, they eventually form a river that's over 100 miles (160 km) long and up to 60 miles (97 km) wide, stretching from the Atlantic Ocean to the Gulf of Mexico. This slow flow is the result of the very gradual slope of the land from north to south, as well as the marsh vegetation that the water seeps through.

Take to the open waters by renting a canoe or kayak, breathing in the tropical air, and immersing yourself in mangrove forests. Wherever you choose to set off from, you would swear the water wasn't moving at all. Its slothlike speed is close to 0.25 miles (0.4 km) per day, making for a leisurely trip that ensures you're truly at one with the river.

With trails through the waters that last only an hour, to routes that take up most of the day or even a week, the

Below On a thrilling airboat ride above the swamps, groups are treated to the park's untamed environments

wetlands at Everglades National Park are calling out to be explored by all. The more adventurous can take on multi-day backcountry excursions that feel like a behind-the-scenes glimpse of nature, and stay overnight at elevated camping areas, or "chickees," though you'll need a permit. If you'd rather stay solely on the languid river, board an organized boat trip from the settlement of Flamingo or take an airboat ride above the swamps for a unique perspective.

Moving in your own canoe, though, and at your own pace, adds a frisson of nervous excitement as you glide through the water, looking for the next marker to ensure you don't get lost in this tangle of trees and mangrove tunnels. A chorus of croaking from the various species of frog and toad that live here will be one of the few sounds that pierce through the idyllic solitude as you paddle along—this, and the peculiar noise made by the gulf toadfish, which gets its name from the toadlike call that's a cross between a grunt, a whistle, and a low boom. There's the thrill, too, of getting close—but not too close—to the park's incredible crocodiles and alligators. The waters of the everglades are truly magical.

On the land

Away from the famed waters, the park has plenty to offer in the way of scenic walking and cycling trails, from those that offer expansive views over the Everglades to lesser-known trails through wooded areas.

Despite its vast size, the park has only one main road, called simply the Main Park Road (Route 9336)—but what a road it is.

With various boardwalk trails that lead off the highway and a handful of minor side roads on the route, a journey down this stretch easily turns into a full-day adventure. The most beautiful and less-visited of these trails lies between Mahogany Hammock, where bromeliads live and junglelike vegetation is especially dense, and Flamingo, where birdwatching is at its best and highly rewarding in the early morning and late afternoon.

Above Kayaking through the mangrove forest canopy is the best way to explore the watery trails

River Trails

Easy ▷ Nine Mile Pond Trail, 3.5 miles (5.6 km). Take this easy trail for a rewarding introduction to the park, with clear signposts and a narrow mangrove tunnel to navigate.

Moderate West Lake Kayak Trail, 15 miles (24 km) round trip. Paddle through a series of lakes connected by narrow mangrove-lined creeks.

Challenging ▷ Wilderness Waterway, 99 miles (159 km). The ultimate adventure, this trail leads through lush creeks, lakes, and rivers and takes even the most intrepid 7–10 days to complete. You'll need to camp, and will require a permit plus a lift back to the start.

Florida Panther

At one point, this distinct subspecies of mountain lion ranged from Florida to Louisiana and even Arkansas. By the mid-1950s it was almost extinct due to poaching and human encroachment on its habitat. Today there are around 120 living in the wild, making it critically endangered. The park is one of the few places it inhabits.

Before embarking on the park's labyrinth of trails, the highly informative visitor centers are excellent places to learn more about the unique landscapes you'll traverse. At the main park entrance, the Ernest F. Coe Visitor Center offers orientation films and educational displays, as well as the chance to converse with the rangers who live and breathe the park.

A few minutes farther on, a side road takes you to the Royal Palm Visitor Center, the setting-off point for two of the most popular—and best—little trails in the park. The wheelchair-accessible Anhinga Trail passes over Taylor Slough, which contains slightly deeper water than the surrounding terrain; in the dry winter months it attracts wildlife to drink. On this route, you are guaranteed to see alligators congregating and sunning themselves. You'll also sight some of the 16 species of wading bird that live in the park, such as the white ibis, the wood stork, and several species of herons.

The Gumbo Limbo Trail also starts here, named after the gumbo limbo trees along the way that attract a host of birds, especially in the winter months. Embark on this rough trail through woodland, watching out for poison ivy, before emerging for panoramic views over the Everglades, where you'll be sure to spot cormorants eying the water, or spreading their wings to dry them after their pursuit of a fish.

Dozens more trails await as you make your way further into the park. At the end of the Main Park Road is the Flamingo Visitor Center, from where you can embark on the Coastal Prairie Trail, a round trip of 15 miles (24 km) where the smell of sea air and the screaming calls of sea birds fill the landscape. The trail leads to Clubhouse

Below The popular Anhinga Trail winds through sawgrass marsh

Above The American crocodile, which lives in these waters, is a shy species

Through the Seasons

Spring ▷ This is prime dry season, and the animals get more active as the temperatures warm up. Wildlife is at its most diverse and visible, so pack your binoculars and your best camera gear. This is also the best time to take on lengthy hikes in the pleasant climate.

Summer ▷ The Everglades become intense at the start of the wet season, when both heat and rain increase. With the humidity and swarms of biting insects, this is a quiet time, so welcome the solitude on scenic kayak trips. It's also when you'll have the best chance to see baby alligators.

Fall ▷ The wet season has its charms: more migratory birds, warm weather, and a park that's practically all yours. On an airboat ride, an enjoyable breeze will keep you cool and the lower water levels make spotting wildlife a lot easier.

Winter ▷ Florida draws the birds escaping the harsher winters of more northerly climes in the winter, making the park prime birdwatching territory. As the dry season approaches, the mosquitoes also decline, and the park throngs with visitors.

Beach, right on Florida Bay, where the land ends and the ocean begins. Not even the Everglades go on forever: it just seems so, sometimes, when you're in the heart of them.

Endangered in the Everglades

The Everglades' ecosystem and Florida's human population are in direct competition for this priceless commodity: roads and irrigation canals disrupt the natural through-flow of water from Lake Okeechobee, and the drainage of land for development has also had detrimental effects on wildlife.

All is not lost, though: the state and federal governments are studying how best to protect the area, and a host of wildlife still manages to make a home here. Place names like Bear Lake, Snake Bight, Trout Cove, and Alligator Creek emphasize what some of those creatures are. This is one of the last refuges for the Florida panther, and the West Indian manatee is another threatened species. These huge but endearing creatures, with their gentle ways and graceful movements, are mesmerizing. The seemingly ubiquitous American alligator has been on the endangered species list, as has the more reclusive American crocodile. Whether you drive, hike, or kayak through the Everglades, don't be deceived by the seeming abundance of wildlife, but savor the privilege of seeing it.

St. John, US Virgin Islands

VIRGIN ISLANDS

ESTABLISHED 1956

On the island of St. John, teal-blue waters dotted with vibrant coral reefs lap against powdery beaches, while farther inland, lush rain forests flourish under the tropical sun. Nestled among all this beauty are historic sites that tell the centuries-old stories of those who have called this idyll home.

Beautiful, blissful scenes of Eden-like beaches are everywhere you look on the island of St. John, where the only thing more magical than the views is the luxurious feeling of slipping into the blue warmth of the Caribbean Sea. Swimming and snorkeling off fine-sand beaches, hiking forested mountainsides, and immersing in the unique culture that is the US Virgin Islands are just a few of the pleasures of this island park.

Storied past

For more than 3,000 years, humans have lived on St. John—for centuries, they clustered in small villages, practicing local customs and looking to their gods to bless the harvests. Christopher Columbus's arrival in 1493 put a swift end to that way of life. His tales of the fabled "emerald isles" sparked the interest of European

FLORA AND FAUNA

Sea Turtles

Green, hawksbill, and leatherback sea turtles inhabit the waters of St. John. The green turtle is the most common, and they nest between June and September.

Paddlelike flippers help the turtle move swiftly through water

Despite its name, the green sea turtle isn't always green

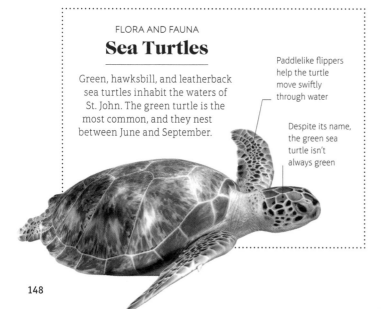

Did You Know?

Cars drive on the left-hand side of the road in the US Virgin Islands.

Ways to Explore

Scuba dive ▷ Head to Eagles Shoals, between Ram Head and Luduck Island, to explore underwater tunnels, caves, and arches—the habitat of coral, sea sponge, and schools of colorful fish, such as the French angelfish.

Hike ▷ The Ram's Head Trail, a craggy 1-mile (1.6-km) path, leads you to a mountaintop that offers panoramic views of Santa Cruz Bay. Along the trail, you'll pass through landscape teeming with curious-looking insects and small wildlife.

Investigate ▷ The ruins at the Annaberg Plantation tell the story of plantation life, with a windmill tower, factory, and slave quarters. The buildings stand facing out to sea on what is the highest point on the island.

colonizers, changing the island forever. The land would pass hands between many nations, all eager to profit from sugarcane and cotton, lucrative cash crops that grew readily on the island. St. John eventually became part of the Danish West Indies. Native vegetation was wiped out to make way for sugar plantations, with enslaved Africans and their descendants laboring on the land. After emancipation, plantation farming waned. Reforestation, with native and non-native plants, began, and today vegetation is largely secondary forest. The US purchased St. John in 1917.

Left With its pure azure waters, Trunk Bay is a favorite of visitors to the island park

Sporting life

Today, tourism is the main industry on St. John. The island is just 9 miles (14 km) long and is the smallest and most unspoiled of the three best-known US Virgin Islands. About two-thirds of the land is federally protected, not counting the thousands of acres beneath the sea.

Like many island chains near coastal mainlands, St. John is a haven for mariners and island hoppers who find respite on the tranquil utopia. Basking in the sun, lying on the sand, and swimming in the sea are everyday pastimes here. Beyond the water, multisport activities lure visitors who want to break a sweat before splashing in water that's so warm it feels like bathwater. Bays are brimming with watersports—sailing, windsurfing, kayaking, and stand-up paddle boarding. Scuba divers and snorkelers enter the magical undersea world, sometimes passing by preserved shipwrecks from generations past. Majestic sea turtles glide up to the surface as sunlight pierces the blue, illuminating the graceful creatures to the delight of underwater explorers.

Above Trunk Bay looks serene and peaceful as the rising sun backlights cloud cover

> BEST FOR
> # Snorkeling
> The island of St. John is world-renowned for snorkeling, and the best spots fall within the park. At Salt Pond, powdered sandy shores give way to pristine coral reefs where tropical fish and stingrays make their home.

Winding trails

With the island containing just a few roads, it is very hard to get lost here. Twenty hiking trails in the park traverse the hillsides, ascending to viewpoints overlooking Santa Cruz Bay, with its coral and pristine beaches. Along the way, tropical insects and lizards may well skitter alongside you. The life-affirming combination of bewitching scenery, the caws of soaring birds, and year-round sunshine make trail-wandering a euphoric experience.

Above Diverse plant life includes seagrass beds, algal plains, and, seen in the distance, forests

History Timeline

Today, travelers to the US Virgin Islands are drawn in by the lush tropics, bluest-blue waters, and island tranquility, but there's more history here than first meets the eye.

710 BC

▷ Humans land on St. John, canoeing from the southern hemisphere. Their agriculture is based on crops such as cassava, a root vegetable native to South America.

AD 500

△ The earliest petroglyphs and carvings are made by the Pre-Columbian Taino Indians on Cinnamon and Trunk bays. Their art has fascinated archeologists for decades.

1492

▽ Searching for a route to India, Christopher Columbus arrives. He names the islands after St. Ursula and her 11,000 virgins. He calls the people he meets "Indians."

1500s

△ Spain, France, England, the Netherlands, and the Knights of Malta battle to lay claim to the islands, while the original Carib inhabitants are exterminated.

A step back in time

In the midst of this abundant nature are artworks and architectural ruins that speak to us of those who came before. The Petroglyph Trail displays rock carvings by the pre-Columbian Taino people. South of Mary Point lie the ruins of Annaberg Sugar Plantation. Visitors learn about 18th- and 19th-century plantation life on a self-guided tour that includes a sampling of "Dumb Bread"—a rich round loaf named for the way it's made. "Dumb" is derived from the Indian word "dum," a style of baking brought here by the indentured workers who replaced freed slaves. Even the food on the island is flavored with history.

Eventually, all roads lead back to the water—too beckoning to ignore. Seagrape trees and coconut plants adorn popular beaches like Trunk Bay and Scott's Beach. However you slice your adventure, a historic past will meet a dreamy present.

1717

▽ The Danish colonize St. John, making it part of the Danish West Indies. Enslaved Africans are forced to grow sugar cane, cotton, and other crops on the island.

1848

▽ Slavery on the island is abolished by the Danish after rebellion on the nearby island of St. Croix, while revolutions foment in other parts of the world.

1950s

▽ Laurance Rockefeller, who thought St. John was one of the most beautiful places he'd ever seen, acquires 5,000 acres (2,000 ha) of land and donates it to the US.

1779

△ The Annaberg Sugar Plantation, centered on a hill overlooking Leinster Bay, becomes the largest industrialized plantation on the island.

1917

△ During World War I, the US purchases St. John for $25 million under the Treaty of the Danish West Indies. The US immediately establishes a naval base.

HAWAII
Honolulu ○
Kahului ○
HALEAKALĀ ◎

Pacific Ocean

Hawaii

HALEAKALĀ

ESTABLISHED 1961

Few volcanic craters are as awe-inspiring as the vast expanse of Haleakalā on the Hawaiian island of Maui, a landscape so primitive you almost expect to see dinosaurs lumbering across the desolate sands before disappearing into the lush rain forests below.

Reminiscent of a film set from *Game of Thrones*, Haleakalā sounds like the name of an ancient kingdom. In fact, it means "house of the sun," and if you reach the highest point in the park, Pu'u 'Ula'ula ("Red Hill") at 10,023 ft (3,055 m), it feels as if you could reach up and touch the sun.

Legend has it that the first Hawaiians chose the name after their chief, Māui, climbed the peak and lassoed the sun as it rose in the morning sky. He released the sun only after it agreed to make the days longer in summer so that his mother, Hani, could dry her laundry.

Join other adventurers at sunrise when the crater is at its most spectacular, backlit by blazing coral skies.

Scientists estimate Haleakalā is about one million years old. They believe that what's commonly referred to as the crater isn't the result of a volcanic eruption at all, but was caused by two valleys slowly merging on either side of the peak.

Haleakalā last erupted in 1790. As you gaze into the 7-mile-wide (11-km-) crater, it's easy to imagine the rumble of molten lava under the surface and the dormant volcano coming to life again like a mythic beast woken from its slumber.

One real creature you might see—which is among the 103 endangered species living in the park—is the nēnē, or Hawaiian goose and the state bird. More than 200 of them survive in Haleakalā, as does the Hawaiian petrel, which nests in colonies at the volcano's summit. As you pick your way over the lunar landscape on top, or push through dense forests farther down, stop and watch for wildlife… or listen for the growling of the earth deep beneath your feet.

Left The rising sun peeks through the clouds over Haleakalā

BEST FOR
Stargazing

To see the sunset from the summit is a spectacular thrill, but more awaits after dark. Take a telescope or binoculars with you and stay on for the stargazing. On a clear night, the heavens spread before you in all their glory. If you prefer to admire the cosmos with other stargazers, the park offers plenty of organized tours led by experts.

UTAH

NEVADA

PETRIFIED
FOREST

Flagstaff ○

NEW
MEXICO

CALIFORNIA

ARIZONA

Phoenix ○

Tucson ○

MEXICO

Arizona

PETRIFIED FOREST

ESTABLISHED 1962

The badlands of the Painted Desert spread across the northern portion of the park, while trees that have turned to stone—trees that once shaded dinosaurs—lie tumbled amid the gnawed hills and hoodoos of the southern half. Welcome to Triassic Park.

Never has the toppling of a forest ended in such colorful elegance. Sheltering the largest concentration of petrified wood on the planet, Petrified Forest National Park delivers scenic and scientific wonders in equal measure. The plant and animal fossils unearthed tell the story of a time when the world was young.

Forest to fossil

Imagine if the landscape were the exact opposite of what it is today. Instead of high, dry grasslands, picture a humid forested basin slashed by winding rivers and streams—such was the terrain of northeastern Arizona 200 million years ago during the Late Triassic epoch. In this subtropical lowland, crocodilelike reptiles, giant amphibians, and small dinosaurs roamed among towering conifers and leafy ferns. As the trees died, they washed into swamps and were buried beneath mud and volcanic ash. Entombed in the sediment layer known as the Chinle Formation, the wood absorbed silica from minerals in the groundwater. Over time, these crystallized within the wood's cellular structure, forming a stonelike material.

Human history at Petrified Forest is but a blink of an eye in geological terms, yet it, too, is fascinating, The first people

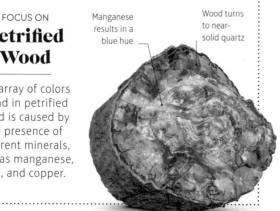

FOCUS ON

Petrified Wood

Manganese results in a blue hue

Wood turns to near-solid quartz

The array of colors found in petrified wood is caused by the presence of different minerals, such as manganese, iron, and copper.

here 10,000 years ago were nomadic hunter-gatherers who later settled in agricultural villages. They left behind petroglyphs, pottery, and dwellings, such as the 100-room Puerco Pueblo from 1250.

Take the trail

The best way to take in these wonders is via the 28-mile (45-km) scenic drive that

Prime your camera before and after sunset for "golden hour" and "blue hour."

cuts north to south through the park. The drive connects highlights, from roadside vistas to historic sites to hiking trails. Don't miss Blue Mesa, a short loop road skirting a dazzling display of badlands. Some of the best examples of petrified logs can be seen along the three-quarter-mile (1.2-km) Crystal Forest Trail. Combine the trails to Long Logs and Agate House (2.6 miles/ 4.2 km) to explore a collection of fallen trees, as well as a pueblo of petrified wood. The intrepid will want to explore the backcountry of Petrified Forest on trail-less routes. Some are relatively easy, such as Martha's Butte. Others, like the journey to fossil-rich Red Basin Clam Beds, require navigation skills.

Above Blue Mesa's layers of rock chronicle millions of years of history

Nature's Sculptor

Some 300 million years ago, when the Canyonlands stood at sea level, sand and rock from distant mountain ranges were carried here by water and wind. Over time, they solidified into geologic layers that built up across massive plains. Then, some 20 million years ago, an uplift in the Earth created the Colorado Plateau. The Colorado and Green rivers now reversed the process, eroding down through the layers to create the canyons.

Left Winding desert roads inside the park afford stunning views

Utah

CANYONLANDS

ESTABLISHED 1964

In this vast, rugged wilderness, carved out by two mighty rivers, you'll find dramatic desert landscapes and blissful solitude.

"The most weird, wonderful, magical place on Earth"... is how Edward Abbey, author, environmentalist, and desert lover, described the Canyonlands. After visiting this vast national park, carved from the Colorado Plateau by the relentless force of the Colorado and Green rivers, you will no doubt have fallen under its spell, too.

Quiet repose

The high, flat-topped mesas afford magnificent views over the rivers below, as they twist, turn, and plow their way across the red-rock landscape, plunging into deep warrens of hidden canyons. Hiking trails wind through pristine deserts punctuated by massive buttes and phenomenal rock formations. At night, the pitch blackness of the skies reveals a space-scape so dense you feel swallowed by the stars.

The park is divided into four districts: Island in the Sky, The Needles, The Maze, and the rivers themselves. Each has separate access points. There is also the remote Horseshoe Canyon, a rock-art "museum" of American Indian petroglyphs.

This wilderness park is a desert jewel for backcountry adventurers seeking peace, solitude, and a deep bond with nature.

7,120
The highest point in ft (2,170 m) is Cathedral Point, in The Needles District.

50
Different mammal species living here.

273
Number of bird species in the park.

3,700
The lowest point in ft (1,128 m) is Big Drop Rapids on the Colorado River.

Endless views

True to its name, Island in the Sky is a majestic mesa rising up more than 1,000 ft (300 m) in the air, with sheer sandstone cliffs that cut down through rugged canyons to the desert floor. The vistas are spectacular in every direction: east to the goosenecks of the Colorado River, west to the meandering Green River, and south toward the rivers' dramatic confluence in the distant Needles.

Early risers will be rewarded with spectacular photos of the morning sun lighting up Mesa Arch.

This northern triangle is the most easily accessed section of the park. A paved scenic drive runs south for 12 miles (19 km) from the visitor center, with lofty overlooks such as the vertigo-inducing Shafer Canyon Overlook, where the cool breeze and warm sunlight enhance the sweeping views. A short loop trail leads to the enormous Mesa Arch on the edge of a cliff, its sandstone curve framing the layered canyons below snowcapped mountains.

At the Green River Overlook, the deeply gouged terrain following this waterway into the distance is a dramatic sight. The panorama from Grand View Point at the southern tip of the mesa sweeps across the Canyonlands, giving you one of the best views in the park.

There are easy walking trails for casual day hikes here, as well as more strenuous routes that take you down into the canyons.

Below As it rises in the sky, the sun glints off the rocks at Mesa Arch

White Rim Road, a rough four-wheel-drive road that loops for 100 miles (160 km) around and below the mesa top, is a favorite with mountain bikers.

Reaching for the skies

The Needles district is famous for its orange- and white-banded spires, visible for miles. You'll have to hike to see these sandstone giants up close, through a landscape festooned with red-rock arches, monoliths, and other amazing formations.

This southeastern section of the park is much less visited, and you'll know you are in the backcountry here. The only paved road runs 10 miles (16 km) in, offering tantalizing views of the Needles in the distance before ending at the Big Spring Canyon Overlook. From here, you can hike to a viewpoint that looks down on the two mighty rivers hundreds of feet below.

The Needles is lower in elevation than other areas, but what it lacks in scenic viewpoints, it makes up for in glorious hiking trails and four-wheel-drive roads. There are short, easy walks to Cave Spring and Pothole Point, where rainwater shimmers in natural wells in the rock. Longer, sometimes overnight, hikes take you along rugged ridges and canyons, across sandy washes, and through narrow slickrock passes culminating in stunning natural arches and the Needles themselves.

The Needles district is also rich in archeological sites, especially in Salt Creek Canyon, where many Ancestral Puebloan and Fremont structures have been preserved. At Roadside Ruin, you'll find a fine example of a prehistoric granary.

Three Hikes

Easy ▷ Grand View Point Trail, Island in the Sky, 2 miles (3 km) round trip. Walk along the clifftop to the tip of the mesa, where a stupendous view of Canyonlands stretches before you.

Moderate Slickrock Foot Trail, The Needles, 2.4 miles (4 km) round trip. Look for bighorn sheep on this open, unshaded, rocky trail that ends in panoramic views.

Challenging ▷ Maze Overlook Trail, The Maze, 8 miles (13 km) round trip. Among the highlights of this tough trail are pictograph panels and views of the Chocolate Drops rock formation.

Left A canoer paddles down the tranquil and scenic Green River

Backcountry challenge

Only the most determined travelers see the wilderness landscape of The Maze. This remote southwestern district of the Canyonlands is only reached along rough four-wheel-drive tracks or from the river. Its hiking trails are strenuous, if not downright dangerous in places. Anyone who ventures here must be self-sufficient.

And yet, for experienced backpackers, the challenges of The Maze are exhilarating and its desert solitude is sublime. Given the slow, difficult journey to simply get here, most stay for at least three days (permits are required). Their scenic trophies are worth every bone-rattling mile. There are the towering orange walls of organ shale, called the Chocolate Drops, rising from a ridge. And the remarkable Chimney Rock, defying gravity in the Land of Standing Rocks. From there, a trail drops down into Pictograph Fork, an isolated canyon that shelters amazing panels of prehistoric rock art known as the Harvest Scene. And from the hoodoo spires of the Doll House, hikers descend to the Colorado River at Spanish Bottom and continue along its banks to a series of rapids.

Hunter-gatherer artistry

Horseshoe Canyon, an isolated unit west of the main park, contains some of the most important rock art on the continent. Its finest panel, the Great Gallery, depicts life-size figures in evocative detail. They hover on the canyon wall, the ethereal, ancient guardians of this sacred place.

The figures are painted in the Barrier Canyon style, which dates to the period from 2000 BC to AD 500, a time when nomadic hunter-gatherers lived seasonally

BEST FOR
Stargazing

Remote national parks like Canyonlands offer some of the darkest skies in the country. Away from urban light pollution, you can see up to 30 times the number of stars you would see in a city setting. The pristine night skies at Canyonlands are so superb that the park was designated a Gold-Tier International Dark Sky Park in 2015. When conditions are right, you may even be able to sight the rings of Saturn through your binoculars.

in the canyon. The site features both painted figures (pictographs) and artistic symbols etched into the rock (petroglyphs). Later panels were added by Ancestral Puebloan and Fremont cultures.

In the early 20th century, ranchers established trails into Horseshoe Canyon so that their livestock could graze and find water. Today, the old cattle path makes a beautiful, if long—7 miles (11 km) round trip—hiking trail, leading you down between the sandstone walls to the cottonwood groves and bubbling stream on the canyon floor, a timeless entry to this incredible display of prehistoric art.

Take to the water

The final district of Canyonlands National Park is the great rivers themselves. Above the confluence, the waters are calm and you can paddle lazily in kayaks and canoes, or simply float on a raft, gazing up in bliss at the surrounding desert beauty. But after the Green and the Colorado merge into one mighty river, they plunge into a torrent of whitewater that blasts through rapids in the 14-mile (22-km) Cataract Canyon.

Whether you ride the waves on a raft adventure, hike the desert trails, or admire the vistas from above, the Canyonlands are truly one of Earth's magical places.

Below This view from afar shows clearly just why The Maze district is such challenging terrain

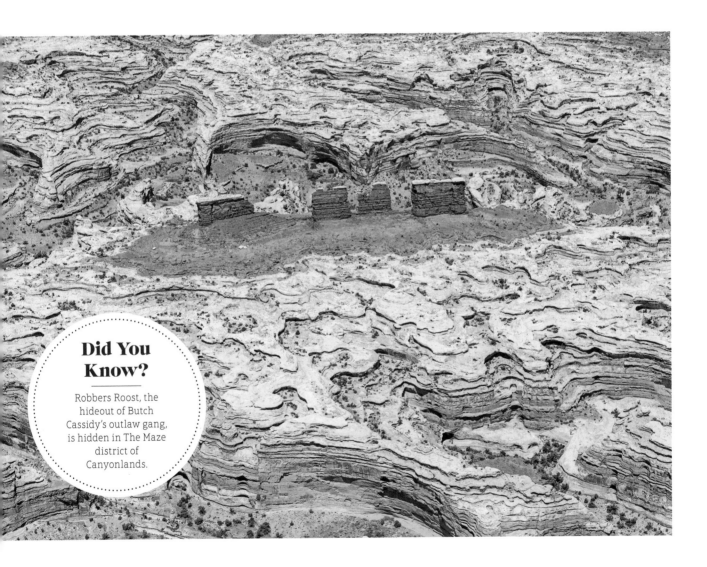

Did You Know?

Robbers Roost, the hideout of Butch Cassidy's outlaw gang, is hidden in The Maze district of Canyonlands.

Washington

NORTH CASCADES

ESTABLISHED 1968

In the untouched wilderness of the North Cascades, it's easy to imagine you've traveled back to a time before human civilization, when the loudest sounds are made by the waterfalls, the stars send out the brightest lights, and only the trees and mountains hem you in.

The jagged peaks of the North Cascade Range are home to more biodiverse plant life than any other national park. Outside Alaska, it's also where you'll find the most glaciers—a third of those in the Lower 48. As you'd expect in such a wild landscape, there are endless backcountry adventures to be had, with hundreds of miles of trails finding their way to unspoiled meadows and lakes, which you may well have to yourself.

A last bastion of untamed wilderness, this barely developed park is a fantastic place to escape the modern world. Here is an unmediated experience of nature: rugged backcountry hikes, awesome scenery, and primitive camping in remote places—like the Desolation Peak fire lookout, which inspired Beatnik writer Jack Kerouac to spend 63 days here in 1956. The hiking trails deliver sonnet-worthy views of spiny mountain peaks, alpine lakes, fields of wildflowers, and the iconic larch trees that turn brilliant red-gold in the fall.

Campgrounds are hike-in only, and just one paved road gives access. If you're up for adventure, the park's two sections are divided by the Skagit River and form part of a complex that includes the Lake Chelan recreation area. From the town of Chelan, head to trails in the southern section by taking a foot-passenger-only ferry, *Lady of the Lake*, across Lake Chelan to the tiny, otherwise inaccessible Stehekin village, sited on an old Salish trade route.

Below The North Cascades Lodge at Stehekin houses a small shop, a restaurant, and several rooms for rent

Best Hikes

Cascade Pass ▷ 3.5 miles (5.5 km) round trip. This popular route has the only trailhead you can drive to. Enjoy a day hike with views in all directions along an easy path that starts near Marblemount. Follow the route used for generations by indigenous peoples, early traders, and prospectors. For a more arduous hike, extend the trip to Sahale Glacier—12 miles (19 km) in total.

Easy Pass 7.5 miles (12 km) round trip. The name may be deceptive, but, even so, this trek makes for a gorgeous day hike, with spectacular views of glaciers off Mount Logan, and a great place for viewing fall colors.

Maple Pass ▷ 7 miles (11 km) loop trail. From the Rainy Lake trailhead off Highway 20, this is particularly pleasing when fall foliage is in full swing. The trailhead offers options for shorter trails.

Rainy Lake 1.8 miles (3 km) round trip. This rare wheelchair-accessible hike in the Cascades is on paved path through forest. It ends at a picnic-perfect lake flanked by cliffs and waterfalls.

Left The Excelsior Ridge Trail is one of the best places to stop and marvel at Mount Shucksan, in the north of the park

Did You Know?

The name "Stehekin" comes from a Salish word meaning "the way through."

California

REDWOOD

ESTABLISHED 1968

On California's magnificent Pacific coast stand vast numbers of majestic giant redwood trees, some of the oldest and biggest trees on Earth, inspiring respect and awe.

To see and touch trees that have lived on the Earth for over 2,000 years is magical. In Redwood, you can walk among whole groves of these ancient behemoths, in both the national park and in nearby state parks. The stately forests are also a refuge for wildlife, home to black bears, Roosevelt elk, cougars, bobcats, coyotes, and even flying squirrels.

FOCUS ON
Indigenous Peoples

American Indian history is older than the trees, as tribes have inhabited this area for 3,000 years. Some still live here, and four distinct languages survive: Tolowa, Yurok, Hupa, and Karuk. In the past, people lived in huts made of redwoods, which they also used to build boats. They regarded the trees as sacred Spirit Beings, here before humankind.

Long and winding road

If traveling by car, take the beautiful but challenging Bald Hills Road, which is a thrilling 36-mile (58-km) round trip filled with hairpin turns and steep inclines winding up a 15 percent grade. These roads are too tricky for motorhomes and RV, so it's cars only.

Favorite hiking trails, such as Lady Bird Johnson Grove and the Tall Trees Grove, are accessible just off the road, and scenic overlooks abound. Stop at the Redwood Creek Overlook, which looks out over much more than a creek—from here, you're treated to an unimpeded view stretching all the way to the Pacific Ocean.

Hiking and biking are equally wonderful ways to explore the parks. On foot, you may come across a fallen giant lying over a quiet trail. There's no better way to appreciate the trees' vast scale than walking a length of the colossus. The state parks offer bike trails, too, where your only company will be those esteemed redwoods.

Three Bike Rides

Easy ▷ Gold Bluffs Beach is a 3-mile (4.8-km) stretch of the California Coastal Trail, where you are very likely to run across elk herds and meander past waterfalls and the mostly deserted beach.

Moderate The Ossagon Trail Loop includes Gold Bluffs Beach, then extends inland for a 19-mile (31-km) loop with a few steep sections and plenty of giant redwoods on display.

Challenging ▷ The Little Bald Hills Trail offers a demanding climb up out of the redwood groves onto pine-covered mountain slopes. Out and back, the trail runs a rugged 18 miles (29 km) in total.

Above The ironic signposts state the obvious: big trees are everywhere you turn

Left Hikers seem small and insignificant passing among the giants

Timeless trees

The Coast Redwood (*Sequoia sempervirens*) is the world's tallest tree, reaching heights of up to 380 ft (116 m). Now protected, about 5 percent of the old-growth forest survives after voracious logging in the 19th and early 20th centuries. They don't grow directly on the coast but thrive in lush valleys and plains sheltered by beaches, dunes, and scrub. Their thick bark is bright red-brown when freshly exposed—hence the name.

The semantics don't really matter when you're walking among groves of these lanky monsters, marveling at their size and scale, and respecting them as the American Indians do. It's almost impossible when

With low rainfall and comfortable temperatures, summer is the ideal time to hike in Redwood.

you're up close not to be compelled to show that respect by touching them, as if feeling for a heartbeat and life pulse, knowing that some of these beauties have been here since a time when the Roman Empire flourished, before the era of Confucius, before the empire of Alexander the Great, since before the Bible.

Below A hiker balances gingerly on a fallen log in Redwood forest

The tallest tree in the park—and the world—is the Hyperion, and it stands 379.1 ft (115.55 m) tall. Don't expect to see it, though, as its location is kept secret to protect it. Other venerated trees are also protected from visitors. Unfortunately, even park rangers can't save them from the wild inhabitants. The Hyperion is not expected to grow any taller due to woodpecker damage at its very top.

Walk on the wild side

As you hike or bike, you'll likely be greeted by the sound of woodpeckers drilling into trees. Woodpeckers are common, and owls, too, including the park's largest owl species, the great horned owl. While it's true that owls are mainly active at night, you'll occasionally see—and hear—them during the day. The local northern pygmy owl is diurnal, so listen for its call, which is more of a toot than the traditional owl hoot.

You may witness the splendid sight of a regal bald eagle soaring on the thermals, or even spot a California condor, the largest land bird on the continent. This vulture with its turkeylike face, is being reintroduced to the park thanks to the efforts of the Yurok tribe, who want the birds restored in their Ancestral Territory.

Of the mammals, coyotes are common throughout the area, although they are mainly nocturnal hunters—the eerie sound of their packs howling in chorus is unmistakable. It's thought, too, that between 50 and 200 black bears live in Redwood. Sightings, though rare, do happen and are always exciting, especially in spring, when mother bears plod through the woods with their little ones in tow.

Above Coast redwoods, the biggest of the big boys, grow thick along Stout Grove Trail

Did You Know?

Redwoods live an average of 500 to 700 years, but some survive for 2,000.

FLORA AND FAUNA
Mighty Elk

Named for President Theodore Roosevelt, Roosevelt elk are common sights here, as they have come back from the brink of extinction and now roam in large herds. Weighing 1,200 lb (544 kg), they're hard to miss and are the largest of the six species of elks in North America. The biggest herd in the park numbers about 250 animals and they inhabit the Bald Hills, while others can be seen in, not surprisingly, Elk Valley.

Utah

CAPITOL REEF

ESTABLISHED 1971

Giant domes, rainbow-colored cliffs and buttes, remarkable geologic features, and spectacular desert solitude await on the scenic drives and hiking trails of this remote national park.

Imagine a colossal geologic wrinkle rising thousands of feet out of the desert and running a hundred miles through the middle of Utah's red rock country. It's known as the Waterpocket Fold, and it lies at the heart of this stunning national park. Over the eons, erosion chiseled away at the rock layers of this remarkable region, creating a wonderland of sculpted spires, imposing monoliths, awe-inspiring arches, winding canyons, and colorful sandstone cliffs that turn fiery red and gold in the setting sun. It also dented the sandstone with potholes, or "pockets," which capture seasonal rains and help the desert creatures survive in the arid climate.

The road less traveled

The park takes its name from a string of huge white domes that reminded early settlers of the United States Capitol. They used the nautical term "reefs" to describe the layered ridges that formed land barriers. Capitol Reef is more isolated than Utah's other parks, and the journey through this unpopulated, otherworldly landscape to get to the park is rewarding in itself. When at last you do arrive, you'll be greeted by miles of open gravel roads and unspoiled trails to explore.

Above A lone car winds its way north along Scenic Drive toward Waterpocket Fold and the Mormon settlement of Fruita

Above Cathedral Valley is so named because its rock formations resemble Gothic cathedrals

Highway 24, a designated scenic byway, runs through the park, and from here you can see landmarks such as the sculpted red tower of Chimney Rock and the massive white bulk of Capitol Dome. The Capitol Reef Scenic Drive takes you deeper into the park, revealing the towering cliffs of Capitol Gorge. Some of the most spectacular areas, such as the Waterpocket District, can only be reached by unpaved roads and hiking trails. Cathedral Valley, the rugged northern section, is marked by impressive desert landscapes and rock formations.

The park may seem untouched, but it has a long human footprint. Petroglyphs by the Fremont Culture Indians have adorned the cliffsides for a thousand years. Showing animals and people, the art serves as a record of their hunter-gatherer way of life.

If you have...

An hour ▷ Drive through the park on Highway 24, stopping at the overlooks to see natural landmarks and petroglyphs.

A day Follow the Capitol Reef Scenic Drive and the dirt roads leading to Grand Wash and Capitol Gorge. Take a short hike, and visit the pioneer village at Fruita.

2–3 days ▷ Explore deep in the park on a backcountry hike, such as Cathedral Valley or the Waterpocket District, with stunning views of the Fold.

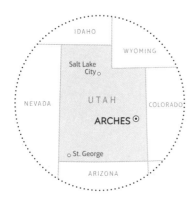

Utah

ARCHES

ESTABLISHED 1971

Beloved for its otherworldly rock formations and the brilliant hues of the landscape, Arches is one place everyone should visit at least once in their lives.

Justifiably famous, the spectacular rock formations and vivid colors at Arches make it an artists' and photographers' dream. The landscape can be harsh and forbidding, especially in the midday sun, but it rewards exploration as long as you're prepared with the essentials of hats and lots of water. The park is surprisingly accessible, too, with hiking trails for all abilities. Many of the 2,000 natural arches are easily viewed from the park's roadside pull-offs. And those who want to get out have their pick of rock climbing, canyoneering, backpacking, cycling, stargazing, and camping.

Delicate Arch is always a draw. Try Garden of Eden or the Windows at sunset and Three Gossips at sunrise.

Nature's workshop

The scenery here is world-renowned: improbable sandstone arches and rock formations in almost supernaturally intense colors. So far, around 2,000 arches have been catalogued, each eons in the making.

Arches National Park lies on a massive salt bed, deposited about 300 million years ago, when this whole area was part of an inland sea that slowly evaporated. Over centuries, strata of debris collected on the salt layer. The debris solidified into rock, and the weight of the rock liquefied the salt deposits beneath, causing them to bulge upward into domes. Erosion did the

Above The arches in North Window were sculpted by sandy winds

Far Right Balanced Rock is a park icon, the 128-ft (39-m) formation looking like it will teeter over at any moment

If you have...

Half a day ▷ The key is to start early. The light is better at sunrise, and the temperature is not too hot for exploring. Do the entire scenic drive, stopping at several viewpoints. Hike to Delicate Arch from Wolfe Ranch or, for a shorter option, to Balanced Rock.

A full day ▷ Keep going after your half-day trek with a hike into the Devils Garden area to see Landscape Arch, the longest arch in North America, as well as Broken Arch. Make a brief stop at the Fiery Furnace viewpoint.

A weekend ▷ Building on the above, camp overnight at Devils Garden for epic stargazing. Early the next day, explore the Windows Section; short trails go to Double Arch, North and South windows, and Turret Arch. Tackle the Courthouse Towers area on your way out, hiking 1 mile (1.6 km) between Park Avenue Viewpoint and Courthouse Towers Viewpoint, then stopping at the paved La Salle Mountain Viewpoint.

rest, wind and rain whittling away rock and salt at different speeds and leaving the sculpted landscape that remains. A million years ago, all these formations were buried under a mile of rock and dirt. When you gaze at them now—Delicate Arch, Balanced Rock, Landscape Arch, the Devils Garden— imagine the millennia of slow-motion chaos that created them, and what they might look like in another few thousand years. Change here is constant. Balanced Rock, for instance—the gravity-defying sandstone boulder atop a mudstone pedestal—will eventually topple; its smaller sibling, "Chip off the Old Block," already has.

Artist in the Park

The Park Service runs the Artist in the Park program, in which an artist from the community is selected each year to showcase their talents. The artist sets up shop in prominent locations to share how surrounding nature influences their work. Visitors are encouraged to bring a sketchpad or easel, slow down, and absorb the landscape. The best light in early morning is at Double Arch and Landscape Arch; in late afternoon, it's at Courthouse Towers, Balanced Rock, and North and South windows.

A pretty picture

The area surrounding Arches National Park is richly adorned in rock wall art, both petroglyphs—images cut, carved, ground, or scratched into rock—and pictographs, paintings made with mineral- and plant-based dye. The park contains a classic example of the former: the Wolfe Ranch panel of petroglyphs at the end of a spur trail off the route to Delicate Arch. The panel shows people on horseback, bighorn sheep, and wolves or dogs. These were likely made by the Ute Indians, who have lived in what is now southeast Utah since the 1200s. No two examples of rock art are the same, but these are typical of the Ute style of the time and contain imagery of horses, which weren't depicted until after Spanish explorers brought them to North America in 1540. It's estimated the unique, impressive art was carved between 1650 and 1850.

Another set of rock art is at Courthouse Wash. A panel on the cliff face consisting of both petroglyphs and pictographs follows a style typical of the much older Barrier Canyon Archaic civilization, as seen in the ghostly, elongated human forms and abstract shapes. The white circular shields were probably added later by Ancestral Puebloans or Utes. The forms can be faint and hard to see, but look for them on the surfaces tinted a shiny dark red or black—called "desert varnish," this darkening of the rock, caused by mineral deposits, made a good painting surface and served as background to the main scene.

Below Petroglyphs that graffiti the walls of Courthouse Wash convey the local history in images

Rock art is often found in places like this, where waterways or travel routes meet. Many archeologists believe these images served a purpose beyond the merely decorative—the rock art may have been meant to communicate knowledge and practical wisdom to those who followed in the path of early inhabitants.

Hidden history

The Courthouse Wash panel was vandalized in the 1980s, and while restoring it, scientists found there were more layers of older work hidden beneath the art visible to the naked eye. Infrared photos of the panel revealed previously unseen detail in the hidden layers and added to the mystery surrounding how prehistoric people made the pigments for this artwork. The National Park Service continues to study rock art throughout the area.

Above The red sandstone walls stand out in relief against a cotton-cloud sky

History Timeline

Human history dates back at least 2,000 years at Arches, when ancestral Puebloans called the area home. It wasn't until the 20th century that the beauty of the rock formations and the surrounding area was brought to the attention of the National Park Service.

AD 20
▷ Ancestral Puebloans establish agricultural villages in and near Arches where they cultivate plants and create rock art panels.

1200s
Early American Indians like the nomadic Shoshoneans (Utes and Paiutes) arrive, leaving petroglyphs at Wolfe Ranch.

1844
French-American fur trapper Denis Julien chisels his name and June 9, 1844, into the rock, the first marker of European contact.

1880s–90s
◁ White farmers and ranchers, including John Wolfe of the Wolfe Ranch, found permanent settlements in the area.

1911
Moab newspaper editor Loren Taylor spearheads efforts to preserve the landscape by designating it as a national park.

1929
On April 12, 1929, President Herbert Hoover sets aside land in Windows and Devils Garden for Arches National Monument.

1973
▷ Geography professor Dale Stevens devises a scientific method for cataloguing the natural arches; about 2,000 have been identified so far.

Left Red sandstone cliffs and rock formations line the trails leading to Devils Garden trailhead

Best Hikes

Double Arch ▷ 0.5 miles (1 km) round trip. A family favorite, this short, flat gravel trail ends in a picture-perfect view of two giant arches.

Balanced Rock 0.3 miles (0.5 km) round trip. This easy hike takes in one of the park's many famous visual delights. The wheelchair-accessible part is paved and leads to a viewpoint of the Windows.

The Windows ▷ 1 mile (1.6 km) round trip. Embark on a gentle climb, mostly on gravel, and take in North Window, South Window, and Turret Arch.

Landscape Arch 1.6 miles (2.5 km) round trip. From Devils Garden trailhead, there's an hour-long trail to the mighty Landscape Arch, with short spur trails to other formations. For the intrepid, there's a rougher trail through Devils Garden.

Fiery Furnace 2 miles (3 km) round trip. Explore this otherworldly part of the park, a trail-free labyrinth that involves scrambling over rocks and squeezing through tight sandstone canyons.

Delicate Arch ▷ 3 miles (5 km) round trip. Journey along an undefined trail, over slick rock and up a steep incline, ending in the improbable beauty of Delicate Arch.

Into the wilderness

Although you can see much of what's spectacular about the park from roadside overlooks and short hikes, there are plenty of opportunities to venture farther into the landscape and seek peace and quiet. The Devils Garden area has a primitive trail that makes a 7-mile (11-km) loop between Landscape Arch and Double O Arch, which involves some difficult terrain and wayfinding with cairns, but the trade-off is a well-earned sense of solitude. There is one designated backcountry campsite off the Devils Garden primitive trail (permit required). Those with good navigation skills can also travel to allocated overnight sites in the Courthouse Wash area, and it's possible to backpack in most of the land adjacent to the national park.

Night sky

The chief appeal of spending the night in the backcountry is, of course, those billions of stars above—which, in this remote place, seem close enough to touch. Those who aren't the rural type can still get a front-row seat by camping overnight at Devils Garden campground or in one of the appointed sites just outside the park.

Camping is not required to appreciate the night sky. Arches National Park was designated an International Dark Sky Park in 2019. Officials make a point of keeping artificial light within the park to a minimum, so light pollution doesn't block out the incredible blanket of stars. You may be surprised by how many you can see with the naked eye; rangers say that under the right conditions, a pair of binoculars is all you need to see the rings of Saturn. It's so rare to be in a place without artificial light that you might find yourself as affected by the pure night sky as you were by the spectacular daytime landscape. Beyond the sheer "wow factor," Arches' dark sky is especially delightful for night-sky photographers, who can capture that silhouette of eerie rock formations set off by an impossibly vivid Milky Way.

For the best stargazing, plan to visit when there's a new moon, bring a star map, and use only a red light to find your way around rather than a regular flashlight. The farther north into the park you drive, the darker the sky will be. Panorama Point, the Windows section, the Balanced Rock picnic area, and the Garden of Eden are all great places to stop and stare. In summer, the park offers ranger-led stargazing events, too.

Above Imagine standing under Double Arch and looking upward into the vastness of the starry Milky Way

FLORA AND FAUNA

Kangaroo Rats

Their name doesn't immediately say "adorable," but these tiny nocturnal mammals are quite cute, as well as impressively well adapted to their harsh desert environment. The seeds they eat provide enough hydration that the rats never need to drink water. Their ears are good enough to hear an owl's silent approach. And they can leap eight times their body length to escape predators, which include snakes, coyotes, and the aforementioned owls.

Texas

GUADALUPE MOUNTAINS

ESTABLISHED 1972

In the sprawls of Texas, at the base of the state's highest peak, lies a kaleidoscope of prehistoric relics. At the top, a sweeping panorama awaits, revealing white gypsum dunes, and pine forests.

Deep within a 40-mile (65-km) mountain range straddling Texas and New Mexico lie treasures from the ancient past. Rocks, fossils, and minerals from a prehistoric sea are buried here, while human artifacts tell stories spanning millennia, giving a glimpse into early human life. Spear tips, rock art, baskets, and pottery remain from the hunter-gatherer tribes who lived in the Guadalupe Mountains 12,000 years ago. Learn more about this fascinating past at the Pine Springs Visitor Center.

Spaniards searching for gold arrived in the 16th century and introduced the Mescalero Apache to horses. After the Civil War, homesteaders and miners came and took up ranching. The Apache tried to fend off the invasion, but were either killed or forced onto reservations. Later, petroleum geologist Wallace Pratt, smitten by the richness of the landscape, purchased 6,000 acres of land and gifted it to the federal government—and a national park was born.

Above The mountain forests are home to 300-plus bird species

Above Hikers can ascend the naturally formed staircases in Dry Creek

260

In millions of years, the age of the reefs.

10,000

Length of time in years of human habitation.

Did You Know?

At 8,749 ft (2,667 m), Guadalupe (or Signal) Peak is the highest in Texas.

High-rise hikes

While driving across the landscape, you'll see monolithic towers looming ahead—with the right timing, you'll catch them bathed in the warm colors of the full desert sun. Explore on foot via one of the 80 hiking trails that cut through desert lowlands before giving way to high-elevation conifer forests, with its rich wildlife and varied plant life. From the base of Guadalupe Mountain to the top, the adventurous can climb 3,000 ft (900 m) in 4 miles (6.5 km). At the summit, make sure to record your journey by signing the park logbook.

FOCUS ON
Fossils

More than 300 million years ago, primitive organisms, fish, and insects lived on Pangea. When the supercontinent broke up, the Permian Basin formed, capturing life-forms in a 400-mile (650-km) fossil bed.

Fossils like this were once creatures living on the seabed

Cephalopods with chambered shells were common

Voyageur People

In the 18th and 19th centuries, the *Voyageurs*—French-Canadian fur traders who traveled by canoe—navigated the waters between Quebec, the Great Lakes, and the US interior, opening trade routes and forming ties with the Ojibwe. They came in search of beavers, both plentiful and highly sought after, as their fur was prized by European fashion houses. The Ojibwe provided them food, clothing, medicine, and guidance. In return, the *Voyageurs* traded goods, technologies, and knowledge of European ways.

Above Hiking paths follow the park road into the woods and among rocky outcrops

Right The sun sets over an island opposite Rudder Bay, in Lake Kabetogama

Minnesota

VOYAGEURS

ESTABLISHED 1975

As you venture into the park on foot or by boat
you will be greeted by hidden pockets of wilderness;
calm, reflective waters; and statuesque outcrops of
the oldest rock on Earth. Traveling the waterways
that guided early explorers, you are steeped in
a groundbreaking era of history.

With more than one-third of Voyageurs made up of lakes, this is a haven for those seeking restorative time on the water. Passages wind among 900 islands, giving access by boat to the unforgettable landscape of Minnesota's North Country. The islands comprise forested uplands, marshes, bogs, and ponds—all perfect for hiking and exploring. Just beyond the rocky shorelines lie excellent spots for camping. The glassy waters reflect glacier-formed rock, intriguing to the eye and even more so to geologists researching three-billion-year-old specimens of Earth.

An angler's heaven

Unsurprisingly, in a land of endless water, you'll find world-class fishing, with the chance to snag 50 different species—lake sturgeon, northern pike, and smallmouth bass among them. Also angling for fish amid the serene beauty are black bears, gray wolves, and bald eagles. The plant-eating moose roams here, too, while in the distance is the ever-present call of the loon.

A journey back in time

This raw wilderness is matched by an intriguing history of the indigenous peoples and the intrepid *Voyageurs*. You will need to travel by boat to retrace the historic route the fur traders took.

FOCUS ON
Rock of Ages

Voyageurs is one of the few national parks where you can hold rocks half the age of Earth in the palm of your hand. Part of the Canadian Shield, the rocks cradling Voyageurs formed two billion years before the dinosaurs appeared.

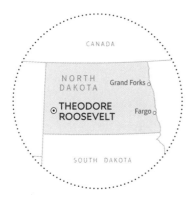

North Dakota

THEODORE ROOSEVELT

ESTABLISHED 1978

Tucked away on the prairie grasslands of western North Dakota are some of Earth's great natural treasures. Colorful badlands follow the bends of a crooked river, while fabled Great Plains animals such as bison, cougars, more than 186 types of bird, and even wild horses, thrive in diverse microclimates, from dry slopes to wet woodlands.

"It was here that the romance of my life began." So said Theodore Roosevelt, "the conservation president," when musing on the restorative time he spent in the Dakota Territory. Spend time here, and it's easy to share the love. The Little Missouri River, which began life as several small streams 65 million years ago, carves colorful stripes into a rolling landscape that looks like it's been brushed onto canvas by a master painter. Welcome to one of the best-kept secrets in the national park system.

The park's South Unit is the most widely visited and accessible, thanks to a 36-mile (58-km) scenic loop drive, with overlooks of iconic sites like the Painted Canyon.

A national heritage species

Herds of wild (technically, feral) horses with windswept manes roam the park's grassy expanses. Their impact on the culture of the West cannot be overstated, particularly for the Plains Indians, who became mounted hunters after the Spanish reintroduced horses to North America. Today's herd, which numbers between 70 and 120 animals, is one of the few running free in the national parks. This area is also the best bet for spotting the big game wildlife that made the region famous.

Off the beaten path

The North Unit offers picturesque views of the Little Missouri, and the surrounding trees provide a nutrient-rich diet for medium-sized animals. Here you'll find great camping and backcountry trails, as

Above The free-roaming feral herds are considered part of the historic landscape

well as the odd Cannonball Concretions, smooth, mostly round geologic formations that look like cannonballs.

Elkhorn Ranch makes up the third unit. Markers outline the grounds of the old cattle ranch, while walking paths follow the perimeter of the homestead. Fittingly, the man who preserved more federal parkland than any other president gave his name to the only park named for one person.

Above The craggy, rugged landscape of the badlands stretches for miles

Early summer is prime time for wildflower viewing, with the peak season hitting in June and July.

If you have...

An hour ▷ The Elkhorn Unit is the most off-the-beaten-path of the park's three units, with its unspoiled, wide-open landscape, just what drew Roosevelt here in the first place. With no visitor center, you're left to your own devices to plot your path amid this peaceful countryside.

A day ▷ The scenic drive in the South Unit is a trip in itself, with wildlife-watching often best done from the car. Here, too, you'll find easy self-guided hikes that can be just a half-mile or a mile long. Ranger-led tours include full-moon walks.

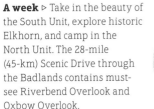

A week ▷ Take in the beauty of the South Unit, explore historic Elkhorn, and camp in the North Unit. The 28-mile (45-km) Scenic Drive through the Badlands contains must-see Riverbend Overlook and Oxbow Overlook.

Oglala

The Badlands have been American Indian hunting grounds for thousands of years. In 1890, many tribes joined the Ghost Dance movement, hoping to drive white settlers from their lands. One of the last Ghost Dances was at Stronghold Table, in the South Unit. The Oglala Lakota now co-manage this district, teaching visitors about their cultural heritage.

Left The layered rock formations in the Badlands stretch on for miles

NORTH DAKOTA

SOUTH DAKOTA

Rapid City

Sioux Falls

BADLANDS

NEBRASKA

South Dakota

BADLANDS

ESTABLISHED 1978

The vast expanse of weathered rock canyons may seem desolate and forbidding, but the park's striking sawtooth ridges and surrounding prairie lands are a haven for bighorn sheep, bison, and prairie dogs.

Its very name stirs excitement and even a bit of trepidation as you approach this rugged and starkly beautiful park. Barren, battered buttes, hills, cliffs, and canyons stretch before you in a sweeping expanse all the way to the horizon.

The Badlands are more than an evocative name. They also define a specific type of geologic formation, consisting of sedimentary rock that has been eroded by wind and water. It looks as if someone painted neat orange bands across the gray mounds of rough-faced rock. Each stripe is a stratum of rock revealing layers of geological time stretching back eons. The eternal winds have also unearthed rich fossil beds with the remains of prehistoric animals that roamed these lands more than 30 million years ago. The South Dakota Badlands are still eroding, wearing away at a rate of about one inch (2.5 cm) each year. There's another side to the Badlands, too.

In contrast to its alien landscape, the park also contains the largest tract of mixed-prairie grassland in the United States. It's the last vestige of the vast prairie that once stretched across the heartland of America. This complex ecosystem of plants and grasses supports an array of wildlife—from burrowing prairie dogs to shaggy bison—including rare and endangered species. It remains the homeland of the Oglala Lakota.

In early morning and late afternoon, the low angle of the sun brings out colorful bands of soft pink, orange, and deep red in the canyons.

Black-Footed Ferrets

Badlands National Park is home to around 120 black-footed ferrets, one of the world's only self-sustaining populations. Saved from extinction through a careful breeding program, it remains one of the continent's most endangered animals. You're unlikely to see this cute nocturnal creature, which lives underground. Its main diet? The prairie dog—one ferret can eat 100 a year.

Below Herds of hulking American bison run across the open Midwestern plains

Venture into this otherworldly landscape on the Badlands Loop Road, the only paved road through the park. It winds for 30 miles (48 km) among the spires and buttes of the Badlands Wall, the rugged escarpment that divides the upper and lower prairie lands. Pause at one of the many overlooks to drink in the view, clamber onto the rocks, and take the perfect photograph of the scenic surroundings. You'll also find stunning vistas over the Buffalo Gap National Grassland.

Wilderness and wildlife

West of the Pinnacles entrance, drive the dirt and gravel Sage Creek Rim Road, which borders the Badlands Wilderness Area. This is a great place to see wildlife. The park's bison herd is often spotted in this area, and you can get a rare glimpse of how this land once looked when vast herds of these majestic animals filled the plains barely more than a century ago.

The pristine prairie is also home to elk, pronghorn, mule deer, bobcats, coyotes, and foxes. Keep your eyes peeled for bighorn sheep, which seem to defy gravity on the sheer rock ledges, and rattlesnakes, which are prevalent here. You may also see eagles, hawks, or peregrine falcons circling overhead. One Badlands resident you won't want to miss is the black-tailed prairie dog. These chubby, highly social rodents greet each other with nuzzles and kisses, and the frisky pups romp together in play. A large colony lives at Roberts Prairie Dog Town, where you can watch their antics up close.

Exploring on foot

One of the best ways to enjoy the Badlands is to lace up your hiking boots and set off on some of the park's many trails. Meander through rolling prairie and a natural garden of wildflowers on the Medicine Root Loop. Or climb a log ladder and navigate a narrow ledge on the Notch Trail for an awesome view over the White River Valley.

Two of the trails, the Window Trail and the Door Trail, are wheelchair accessible along a raised boardwalk. Both lead to gaps in the Badlands Wall, with views of the sweeping grasslands and colorful rock formations.

A favorite hike takes you along the Fossil Exhibit Trail, an easy boardwalk lined with replica fossils and exhibits. The Badlands fossil beds are among the richest in the world, and the list of prehistoric animals that once lived here is jaw-dropping: aquatic and running rhinos, alligators, miniature camels, saber-toothed cats, three-toed horses, and extinct mammals called oreodonts among them. You might even find fossils yourself when exploring the park.

The Stronghold Unit, the southern area of the park, lies within the Pine Ridge Indian Reservation. Fewer roads are open to visitors here, but it's still worth experiencing—you can catch some incredible sunsets from the Sheep Mountain Table and Red Shirt Table viewpoints.

Above Surveying the scene—a prairie dog pops up from a hole in the intricate network of its tunnel home

Best Bike Rides

Easy ▷ Sage Creek Loop, 23 miles (37 km). You'll have good chances to spot wildlife on this relatively easy ride through rolling grasslands on paved and unpaved roads.

Moderate Northeast–Big Foot Loop, 27 miles (43 km). After a hill climb from the Ben Reifel Visitor Center, this long but moderately easy ride takes you through classic Badlands scenery and adjoining ranchland.

Challenging ▷ Sheep Mountain Table Road, 14 miles (23 km). This out-and-back dirt road climbs to a lookout with striking views over the park's South Unit and the distant Black Hills to the west.

California

CHANNEL ISLANDS

ESTABLISHED 1980

California's answer to the Galápagos in Ecuador, the Channel Islands are inhabited by a staggering number of unique plants and animals living in a verdant playground. In this wildlife-spotters' utopia, you'll love the hiking, paddling, and diving adventures, too.

At the edge of the North American continent sits a wild group of primitive islands that provide a rare glimpse into California at its most raw and untamed. Not far from here, you have the bustle, bright lights, and big city of Los Angeles. But in these wild environs of the Pacific, life couldn't be more different. Visitors head out for hikes across bucolic bluffs, camp under the stars—reveling in remarkable ocean views on all sides—kayak to the edge of lost coves, and spend afternoons sprawled on rocky beaches having a picnic.

Five distinct habitats

Discover a unique world of wildlife and nature on each island. Closest in, Anacapa encompasses three tiny islets, where birds caw and clamor for space in springtime. Farther out into the winds and wilds of the Pacific Ocean is Santa Cruz Island, topped by the menacingly named but beautiful 2,450-ft (747-m) Diablo Peak, with the huge striped Painted Cave in the sea below. You can explore archeological sites and other treasures on this most-visited spot. California's second-largest island, Santa Rosa, is home to just three terrestrial mammals: the island fox, island spotted skunk, and island deer mouse, whereas San Miguel Island hosts one of the oldest American Indian archeological sites, dating back 11,600 years. On Santa Barbara Island, 38 miles (61 km) out to sea, amateur botanists can learn about endemic plant species, including unique forms of dudleya buckwheat, and cream cups, along with the native and threatened island night lizard.

Above Three rocky islands make up Anacapa, whose name derives from the Chumash "Anypakh," meaning "mirage island"

Did You Know?

The islands are home to 2,000 plant and animal species, 145 of which are found nowhere else.

Wildlife at a Glance

The islands have been inhabited, in turn, by American Indians, traders, and ranchers, and this delicate habitat is still recovering from human excesses. In and around the water is a tapestry of native animals seldom seen elsewhere.

▽ **California brown pelican**
On the rebound, this once endangered species has breeding colonies on Anacapa and Santa Barbara Island. At sunset, watch them dive for dinner with keen precision and speed.

▷ **Northern elephant seal**
Brought back from the brink of extinction, these barking, mighty sea mammals mate and have their babies here in the winter months. Adult males can weigh more than 5,000 lb (2,270 kg).

△ **California sea lion**
Playful pinnipeds abound. These sea lions—one of six species worldwide—love to frolic. Watching them dash in and out of the water (or just sun themselves) provides hours of entertainment.

△ **Island fox** One of only three native land mammals to call this habitat home, this petite fox lives on six of the eight islands. Each island's population is considered its own separate and endemic subspecies.

Diving

Advanced divers will love exploring the sea caves, kelp forests, and wild underwater habitats found here. There are dives off every island, and some of the world's most unique sites can be found at the park. In the harbor, you can dive to the remains of the USS *John C. Butler*. Seals and giant bat rays are among the bigger animals you will see on the wall, reef, and cavern dives found here.

California coast. Erosion and changing sea levels eventually split the island apart, creating the chain you see today, comprised of eight islands in total, although people often refer to the three islets of Anacapa as one. The individual islands were formed just 2,000 years ago, a mere blink of an eye when looking at geologic time. Evolving in isolation, the islands each nurtured the rare, unique flora and fauna that exist today.

Human footprint

People have made their mark here for the past 12,000 years. The native Chumash were the first to call these islands home, and they largely lived in balance with the islands' natural ecosystems. Ongoing sociological research into these early

Below Gregarious sea lions gather in crowds at a rocky rookery on Anacapa

The natural history of these singular islands dates back 14 million years, when volcanic activity and tectonic shifts formed a large 724-sq-miles (1,875-km) island just off the

Above A scuba diver squeezes through tight crevices filled with Californian hydrocorals

inhabitants is shedding light on the migration patterns of early American Indian tribes. Interestingly, the Chumash did not live in isolation. Rather, they crafted plank canoes, called *tomols*, from drifting redwoods and likely had contact with the mainland and engaged in commerce with the people there.

The first European to reach the islands was Juan Rodriguez Cabrillo, who arrived on San Miguel in 1542. Explorers and traders followed, hunting otters, seals, and sea lions for their pelts and oil. By the 19th century, settlers had set up large-scale sheep and cattle ranches. The United States military took over in the 20th century, building lighthouses on Anacapa and Santa Barbara Island and establishing army, navy, and air force bases on Santa Rosa and San Miguel. The human imprint is still felt today: on East Anacapa, there are a cluster of historic buildings and a scenic lighthouse to visit, and the navy retains a small post on Santa Cruz.

The park was first established as a National Monument in 1938, protecting only Anacapa and Santa Barbara Island. In 1980, the Channel Islands National Park was formed, bringing in the remaining three Northern Channel Islands.

Through the Seasons

Spring ▷ Wildlife watching is plentiful in spring, when migratory birds and western gulls nest here. The island fox pups are also born at this time, and California sea lions and northern fur seals gather in their rookeries. Look to the horizon for the last of the season's gray whales.

Summer ▷ The summer months bring long days, warmer temperatures, and less rain. It's a great time to go camping on a serene backcountry beach or take on some of the longer day-hike excursions offered in the park.

Fall ▷ Kayaking is a wonderful way to explore the lost coves of the Channel Islands. In fall, blue and humpback whales pass through, along with a number of migratory birds, and the northern elephant seals begin to gather in their rookeries. Ocean temperatures reach 70°F (21°C).

Winter ▷ The park is home to more than 800 plant species. In late winter and early spring, the bluffs come to life. You won't want to miss the bright yellow coreopsis flowers, which peak between January and March.

Florida

BISCAYNE

ESTABLISHED 1980

Dip your toes into the sublime waters of Biscayne Bay, and the hectic world slips away. Shimmering sun lights up the land and glints off the sea—here in this time capsule full of secrets of a rich, sometimes dark past.

On the northernmost point of the Florida Keys, a vibrant preserve nestles in the paradise waters of Biscayne Bay. Inhale the salty sea air and take in the boldly hued seascape, where the world's third-longest coral-reef tract dances beneath the surface. Scattered across the water is Stiltville, a cluster of raised houses where Prohibition bootleggers once conducted their shady

dealings and threw raucous gambling parties. Beneath the stilts, sunken ships tell hundreds of years of maritime tales— of Spanish Conquistadors, pirates, and unlucky sailors taken by turbulent seas.

It is a minor miracle Biscayne Bay National Park even exists. Adjacent to the rapidly developing coastline of Miami, this fragile ecosystem could easily have been swallowed up. Environmentalists and locals fought to save it, and today, it's the longest undeveloped coastline in Florida.

Beauty by boat

With 95 percent of the park underwater, exploring by boat is the only way to go. Start at shoreside areas where manatee sightings are fairly common, and row through dense, junglelike forests of protected mangroves. Head farther out for snorkeling and scuba diving at their best. At Boca Chita Key, from the 65-foot (20-m) ornamental lighthouse, cast your eyes over the islands, bay, ocean, and Miami skyline.

Above At the lagoon, canoe through the mangroves to see birds, crabs, and manatees

FOCUS ON

Pirates

Elliot Key is the largest island in Biscayne Bay, and the surrounding waters have long been one of its key attractions. Historically, it was home to Pioneer communities of the Florida Keys, and was also a pirate strong-hold. Legend goes that, in the 18th century, pirate Black Caesar joined forces with Blackbeard's crew to loot treasure from passing ships. They posed as castaways along the shoreline to trick sailors into picking them up.

Above The lighthouse sits at the entrance to Boca Chita Key, where boats dock at the island

Left The islands are home to a variety of subtropical plants and lush mangroves

Marine Life

Biscayne Bay is one of the largest marine preserves in the nation, and its reef teems with aquatic mammals, dolphins, sea turtles, precious corals, and more than 600 native fish varieties.

▽ **Manatee** Also called a "sea cow," the manatee is Florida's official marine mammal and is a mainstay in local folklore. It is federally endangered and protected, although sightings are relatively common.

Coral colonies Reefs created by coral colonies provide vital nutrients for all living things beneath the surface. Distinct shapes of fans and flowers sway with the currents, inviting marine life into the fortresslike nursery.

Seaweed-eating parrotfish These creatures clean coral reefs with their sharp front teeth, exposing rich food sources for other aquatic creatures to feed on. They are protected, as they are key to a healthy bio-network.

△ **Sharks** Florida coastal waters host one of the world's most diverse shark populations—lemon, nurse, bull, tiger, and more. Apex predators, sharks aid aquatic diversity and are vital to the health of marine ecosystems.

△ **Mangrove hammocks** By connecting land and sea, mangrove hammocks provide a safe habitat to birds, and aquatic and land species. They erode pollutants caught in their twisted branches, cleaning the waters.

Alaska

KATMAI
ESTABLISHED 1980

This remote national park on the Alaskan Peninsula offers a front-row seat to one of nature's most storied hunting events. Each year, hulking brown bears converge here to feast on the running salmon.

Katmai National Park and Preserve offers a classic image of wild Alaska. In the middle of Brooks River stands a massive brown bear, poised at the waterfall's edge. Just as a sockeye salmon leaps, the bear pounces, and "click"—the photo (if not the fish) is yours.

Brooks Camp is the heart of the salmon run, where as many as 30 brown bears may show up in a day. And, while this is the mainstay attraction of this remote 6,400-sq-mile (16,575-sq-km) national park,

it's by no means the only draw. From Brooks Camp, set out on the 5-mile (8-km) established trail into a forest that sings with the chirping of birds and provides cover for scurrying martens, porcupines, and weasels. Forty-two mammal species live here, and you stand a good chance of running across many on the trails. The bears, too, aren't the only ones in for some great fishing—trout, salmon, and char are plentiful.

Into the wild

Exploring this remote and wild park isn't easy. Intrepid travelers with good wilderness skills will be rewarded, however, with canoe or kayak trips that take you through mile after mile of river and lake. For ocean kayak adventures, extend the trip to look for sea lions, seals, and sea otters, or stay closer

---

July is the time to visit when the salmon are running, the wildflowers are at their perfect peak, and the bears at Brooks Falls are hungry.

700

The number of unique plant species that thrive in the park.

9,000

Years since the first human inhabitants moved here. People of Alutiiq descent still call this land home.

Above A pack of Alaska brown bears gather at McNeil River; 2,200 roam the park

to home with an overnight paddle to Fure Cabin on Naknek Lake's Bay of Islands. A rustic frontier experience in a 1926 spruce log cabin awaits.

From Brooks Camp, you can take a short, doable hike to the top of Dumpling Mountain, which offers magnificent views of this land of lakes, forest, streams, and marsh. Ranger-led treks reveal the mysterious and ethereal Valley of Ten Thousand Smokes, the site of the largest volcanic eruption in the 20th century. The blast formed the bizarre-looking, ash-covered moonscape you see today, as well as the crumpled summit of Mount Katmai, which collapsed in the 1912 eruption.

Above Sea lions lounge on rocks on the Pacific side of Katmai National Park and Preserve

ALASKA

CANADA

Anchorage ○

GLACIER BAY

Alaska

GLACIER BAY

ESTABLISHED 1980

Glacier Bay is just how you imagine Alaska to look—
with cliff faces of sheer ice rising from a crystal-blue
sea, all set against an uninterrupted backdrop of wild
and unspoiled nature.

Little compares to seeing a house-sized block of ice crashing into the water or a huge humpback whale seemingly defying gravity as it breaks the water's surface, but these scenes are common in Glacier Bay National Park and Preserve. In this ever-changing landscape, there is also abundant wildlife.

On a good day, you might see the spouting of breaching whales, hear the cries of seabirds, spy bald eagles wheeling overhead, or watch a raft of sea otters floating lazily on their backs while balancing a meal of clams on their tabletop bellies. You may even spot a brown bear plodding along the shore or catching salmon for its supper. But the real thrill is in watching a massive block of ice dislodge from the glacier face and slide silently into the sea. A second later comes the thunderous crack, followed by swells that cause your boat to bob up and down like a cork. This is nature at its most sublime. You may be so cold your that cheeks start to tingle, and you may be waddling around in multiple layers of clothing, but nothing will dampen the experience.

FAMILY FUN

Whale Watching

June through September is ideal for whale watching. The sight of a humpback whale leaping from the water will be a memory forever. You may see pods on the hunt— herding schools of fish into tight balls, before racing in and swallowing them.

Long and winding journey

Just getting to Glacier Bay is an adventure. First, you have to fly or take a ferry to the city of Juneau, which isn't directly accessible by road. From Juneau, another flight over islands and inlets, or a ferry weaving a meandering route, takes you to the tiny town of Gustavus. The few hundred people who make this remote place their home are mostly the descendants of settlers, and they prefer the isolated life.

At Gustavus, you've still not made it to the park, although you can join one of the boat tours here. From Gustavus, it's a 15-minute drive or 3-hour hike along one of the few roads in this wilderness. You travel through pine forests to Bartlett Cove, and, at last, you've made it into the park. The scattering of buildings—a lone hotel, park headquarters, the Huna Tribal House, a dock—is the only sign of civilization in the park's 3,223,384 acres (1,304,457 ha).

In addition to getting out on the water, by boat or kayak, to experience the park

15,325
The height in ft (4,670 m) of Mount Fairweather, the highest point in the park.

—

200
The average age of the ice that has broken off the park's glaciers.

1,410
The deepest part in ft (430 m) of Glacier Bay.

—

5,037
The area in square miles (13,045 sq km) of Glacier Bay, which is almost as large as the state of Connecticut.

fully you need to set out on foot. For this, be prepared, as in all that wilderness there are only a handful of marked hiking trails, radiating from Bartlett Cove, and the backcountry hikes require a permit. Even the marked trails give a sense of the wildness and make you feel like a tiny speck in a giant landscape.

The trails take you past rivers, ponds, and lakes, through forests where bears and bald eagles live. On some, you'll see trees carrying ancient carvings made by the Tlingit. This people created tools, even clothing, from the roots and bark of trees, such as the Sitka spruce and the western red cedar. The wood-carving tradition remains strong today, and Tlingit carvers continue to favor a traditional style that incorporates stylized creatures from the natural world and expresses spirituality through art.

In the distance, from a pond or lake, you may hear the wailing of a loon, or one of its other calls, which can sound eerily like the howling of a wolf. Or you might hear the real thing, for wolves, too, live in this seemingly enchanted forest. The journey to get here may be round-about, but it's worth it to feel the release from the modern crush and to experience the genuinely remote.

FOCUS ON
Tlingit

The indigenous people who first lived around Glacier Bay were the Tlingit, and an estimated 15,000–16,000 still live in the region. The Tlingit divide themselves into two moieties, or groups—Ravens and Eagles—and then into smaller clans. Their society is matrilineal, so children belong to their mother's clan.

Above Campers enjoy the pristine surroundings of Glacier Bay

Left A Tlingit totem pole is a work of art that tells the story of a person or a clan

Did You Know?

Potlatches—lavish, days-long feasts—were held to mark major life events.

Alaska

GATES OF THE ARCTIC

ESTABLISHED 1980

For raw, remote wilderness, nothing beats this park—no roads, no trails, no permanent population, and landscape straight out of a Jack London tale.

It's the lucky few who get to savor this beauty. Only 10,000 people visit Gates of the Arctic National Park and Preserve each year, mainly because of the challenge in reaching it—effort rewarded tenfold. The six rivers coursing through the terrain make the park surprisingly lush in summer.

> PARK PIONEERS
> ## Bob Marshall
>
> Scientist and early explorer Bob Marshall coined the name "Gates of the Arctic" in 1929, after observing the twin peaks of Frigid Crags and Boreal Mountain faced off across the Koyukuk River. Sadly, he died at age 38, but his book about his exploits was published posthumously and was influential in the park's creation.

By contrast, winters are extremely harsh. Yet this part of northern Alaska has been home to nomadic peoples for 11,000 years. Nunamiut Eskimo roamed the land now covered by the national park, gathering food and following the migrations of the caribou, which they depended on for survival. These massive deer were the local lifeblood: providing meat and hides for clothes, snowshoes, and sleds; bones that were fashioned into hunting tools; and sinews that became fishing nets.

Great migration

The people have now moved to a nearby village, but the caribou remain, some half a million of them, and they still migrate

Above In the summer months, the Koyukuk River flows calmly through the landscape beside the Brooks Range

Best River Activities

Fishing ▷ The Alatna River runs for 83 miles (134 km) through what is traditional hunting territory for the nomadic peoples of the region. Its gentle pace and prime fishing make it popular.

Scenic float The Kobuk River, at 110 miles (177 km), is one of the most scenic rivers, winding through forests and mountains, making it good for an easy float on a kayak or raft, although there are a few tricky rapids to negotiate.

Arctic trip ▷ The Noatak River is 425 miles (684 km) long, all of it within the Arctic Circle, but not all of it in the park. The park section, navigated in a canoe, leads through a glacial valley below snowcapped peaks.

Rapids rafting The North Fork of the Koyukuk River offers the challenge of whitewater rapids along parts of its 102-mile (164-km) length, as it flows through glacial valleys in the Endicott Mountains.

north in the summer and south in the winter. Witnesses to the migration are seeing one of the world's great wildlife spectacles. Other animals live here, too: brown and black bears, moose, and the beautiful Arctic foxes, which, like the land, turn snow white in the winter. In the skies, you may spot golden eagles, bald eagles, red-tailed hawks, goshawks, or perhaps a fearsome osprey stretching out its talons to pluck a fish from a river.

Such moments make the effort of getting here—an adventure in itself—worth it: from Fairbanks, hop on a flight to one of the gateway settlements near the park, then take an air taxi or hike into the park, where the rest of the adventure unfolds.

Above A musher drives a dog team through Anaktuvuk Pass; this mode of transportation has been around 9,000 years in the Arctic

ALASKA

CANADA

Anchorage ○

⊙ KENAI FJORDS

Alaska

KENAI FJORDS

ESTABLISHED 1980

This magnificent park is a Tolkien-like land of deep, narrow fjords, crashing glaciers, teeming wildlife, and adventures aplenty. Whether you are standing atop a glacier or paddling through a maze of icebergs, Kenai Fjords never fails to surprise.

Here, on the leeward edge of Alaska's rugged Kenai Peninsula, sits one of the best arctic maritime parks in the world. The easiest way to explore the watery delights is aboard a guided boat tour. As you cut your way across the icy waters of Resurrection Bay, setting out from the charming fishing village of Seward, you'll encounter the locals going about their day: porpoises, orca, Stellar sea lions, and humpback whales trolling the rich waters.

To extend the adventure—and really investigate the nooks and crannies of this expansive tract of wilderness—set out on a multiday kayak trip, stopping at public-use cabins or camping on remote beaches, with nothing but the sound of lapping waves and the occasional crash of calving glaciers to keep you company.

Landscape architect

Harding Icefield is another star draw. The fjords were forged 23,000 years ago, give or take, by glacial ice extending down from the 700-sq-mile (1,813-sq-km) ice field. The 40 glaciers here today continue to hew a mix of coves, fjords, and emerald bays bedazzled with ice and bright ocean life.

Take a trip in September, when the weather is still mild, boat tours are running, and the park is quiet and serene.

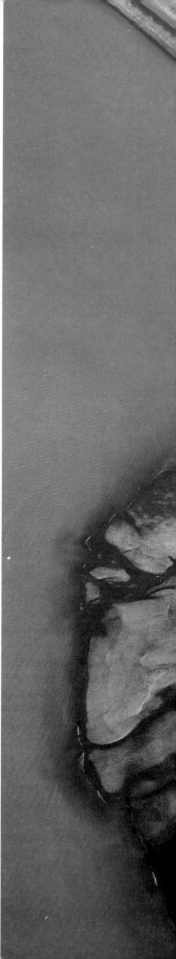

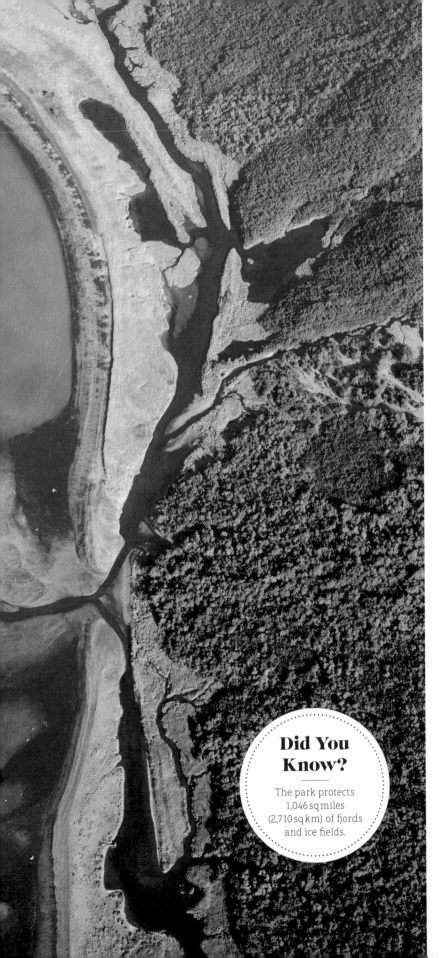

Wild on Kenai

By land or by sea, there is a remarkable diversity of wildlife on display. Aboard tour boats, naturalist guides point out the myriad sea mammals in the fjords: playful seals, clicking porpoises, and the fearsome orca. On land, take a gander at mountain goats, bears, martens, and moose.

Orca ▷ These mighty predators patrol Prince William Sound during the summer and are best spotted in May and early June. About 250 in 15 pods reside in the waters of the sound.

Puffins ◁ Horned and tufted puffins live in the rookeries here. They are excellent swimmers, but also able fliers— surprising, given their robust bodies. Mating season begins mid-May.

Mountain goats ▷ These climbers are out in spring and summer, seen from boat tours in Resurrection Bay or along Harding Icefield Trail. About 4,000 range across the peninsula.

Birds ◁ Find a seaside café in Seward and let the birds come to you: you'll likely spy bald eagles, gulls, black oystercatchers, marbled murrelets, peregrines, and the fabled puffins.

Moose ▷ Alaska is the land of the moose, and these majestic animals set up home in the park's vegetated areas in the summer. Head to the Exit Glacier area and you might spot a calf.

Did You Know?

The park protects 1,046 sq miles (2,710 sq km) of fjords and ice fields.

For landlubbers

The wilds of the Kenai Peninsula await—
and half the fun is the journey there. From
Anchorage, the Alaska Railroad carries you
through beautiful stretches of wilderness
to the seaside village of Seward. You'll
want to spend at least a day checking out
the murals, quirky art galleries, and seaside
restaurants in this picturesque little town
perched on the edge of Resurrection Bay.

Most visitors start the adventure with a
stop at the Exit Glacier Nature Center,
where you learn about ranger-led tours.
Exit Glacier, the only area of the park
reached by car, is the starting-off point for
inland tours. From here, there's a very easy,
accessible 1-mile (1.6-km) loop trail that
winds through forest. A small detour on the

Below The fjords are a
spectacular sight on a
bright summer's day, with
Exit Glacier, as always,
an imposing presence
in the background

545

In miles (877 km),
the extent of
coastline, with
every channel
offering new
perspectives.

191

The number of
bird species that
call this arctic
parkland home,
including the
lovable puffin.

more strenuous side trail of Glacier
Overlook Trail ends at Exit Glacier Overlook
and the stunning sight of the glacier and
the valley below—the exertion well repaid.

A land of plenty

Along the way, cast your eyes up toward the
moraines—masses of rock and sediment
left in the glaciers' wake—and the talus

Left The alpine huts
of Harding Icefield
overlook a gray, rocky,
almost lunar landscape

fields, which sport even heartier rocks and boulders. In this landscape, you may spot marmots, martens, mink, short-tailed weasels, and the other small creatures that live in the neighborhood. Trek farther into the wilds to see mountain goats, brown and black bears, lynx, moose, gray wolves, and wolverines, along with playfully named creatures like the northern bog lemming and the meadow jumping mouse.

The view from above

For an adventure you won't forget, hike to the top of the world on the Harding Icefield. This spectacular, exacting trail is just 4 miles (6.5 km) long, starting from the valley and passing through meadows and blooming wildflower fields. Don't underestimate it though—the trail can take a full eight hours round trip to complete, because of its quick rise in elevation and technical scree areas. Once at the top, you'll be rewarded with views of an ice field that stretches to the edge of forever.

A number of tour companies offer glacier tours, where you strap on a pair of crampons, grab an ice axe, and rope in to explore the crevasses, crystal-blue caves, and the wild moonscape of nearby glaciers.

If you have...

One day ▷ You'll want to hit the water right away. Start the tour early in the morning for the flattest water and good wildlife watching. From there, take a quick hop up to Exit Glacier or just explore around Seward, taking in the plentiful local fauna of this rustic fishing village.

Three days ▷ Hike to the top of Harding Icefield or take on a longer sea kayak and venture farther afield. An unforgettable stay at Kenai Fjords Glacier Lodge gets you closer to the icebergs, wildlife, and top-of-the-world nature near Pedersen Glacier.

A week ▷ This is where real adventure begins. Plan to go for a multiday kayak through Aialik Bay and out to the Holgate Arm. Reserve one or even two nights in a remote public-use cabin, and relax on a private beach looking over Resurrection Bay at the charming Alaska Paddle Inn.

Most visitors will have time to see just a small corner of Kenai Fjords National Park, but that "corner" will be something else. Take your pick of natural highs: climb steep mountains, kayak remote coves, fish on river or sea, backpack to the edge of the peninsula, or simply get lost in the solitude, beauty, and bounty of this majestic wilderness.

Alaska

KOBUK VALLEY

ESTABLISHED 1980

One of North America's greatest land-mammal migrations takes place each spring and fall, when thousands of caribou pass through the park. Bold adventurers can also paddle along remote rivers or take to the air for a bird's-eye view of the show below.

At the edge of beyond, you'll find the solitude and majesty of Kobuk Valley. Framed by the Baird and Waring mountains, it comprises 2,736 sq miles (7,085 sq km) of river, meadow, forest, and even sand dunes.

The park is famous as the staging area for one of the greatest migrations on earth, when each spring a quarter million caribou embark on a 600-mile (950-km) journey to their summer grounds up north. In the fall, when 24-hour days begin to fade to dark, the herd returns. Witnessing the migration from the air or on a multiday river trip is on a par with any safari in the Serengeti, Tanzania—only more challenging and a lot colder.

For the brave souls who make it here, the rewards are rich: some of North America's boldest predators, including gray wolves and grizzly bears, live in the park, along with fun big animals like Dall sheep and moose. This is the summer home of millions of migrating birds. Expect to see Arctic terns—coming from Antarctica on the world's longest bird migration—along with ducks, cranes, loons, geese, and swans.

Human history here dates back 12,000 years, and one Arctic dig turned up evidence of nine unique cultures. Native Alaskans still gather at their ancestral grounds of Onion Portages to hunt caribou and get ready for a long winter under the Northern Lights.

Above Caribou bulls, with their distinctive antlers, swim across the Kobuk River

Ways to Explore

Camping ▷ This park is only accessible by plane, so be prepared to forgo creature comforts. A singular experience is a night in the Great Kobuk Sand Dunes or the Onion Portage, where you can ascend the nearby bluffs for views of the Jade Mountains and the migrating herds of caribou.

Kayaking ▷ One of Alaska's best river trips runs through here. From Walter Lake in the Gates of the Arctic National Preserve, you can paddle for five to eight days down 115 miles (185 km) of river. Along the way, you will meet subsistence hunters and fishers camped along the riverbank and encounter any number of natural delights.

Flight-seeing ▷ This roadless wilderness takes on a whole new dimension from the air. During the migration, a bird's-eye view is the best way to witness the movement of the great caribou herd in all its grandeur. Along the way, you'll see countless lakes, technicolor sand dunes at Little Kobuk and Hunt River, and many wild animals going about their business.

Lodge stays ▷ At the Kobuk River Lodge and Bettles Lodge, warm up with a hot shower and a steaming cup of coffee before venturing out on day trips into the wilderness. For the ultimate in adventure, come in winter for dog-sledding and cloud-free night views of the Aurora Borealis.

Left There's no better way to grasp the glory of the Great Kobuk Sand Dunes than from the air

ALASKA

CANADA

LAKE CLARK 🐾   ○ Anchorage

Alaska

LAKE CLARK

ESTABLISHED 1980

Astounding in its grandeur and remoteness, this is Alaska at its wildest, untamed and uncharted. Intrepid explorers will find a patchwork of towering peaks to explore, mountains and volcanoes to be climbed, and salmon-filled lakes to be fished.

Above Mount Redoubt Volcano, part of the Aleutian Range, erupted as recently as 2009

Left Kayakers ply the icy, changeable water of Twin Lakes

Far Left A brown bear sow and her cubs stick together in the long grass

Alaska is often called The Great Land, and there's nothing greater than Lake Clark National Park and Preserve, a wilderness of more than 6,000 sq miles (15,540 sq km) of volcanoes, rivers, and turquoise lakes.

There are no roads into Lake Clark, so you arrive by floatplane, an adventure in and of itself, with incredible bird's-eye views of the vast Neacola and Chigmit mountains, Lake Clark, and the 130-mile (209-km) coastline on Cook Inlet.

Adventures are limited only by time and cost. Many come to fish for the plentiful salmon—almost 150,000 migrate to the lake annually. All those salmon draw bears, making this a prime spot for sightings. Alaska is home to three subspecies of brown bears: the coastal brown bear found here, the inland grizzly, and the Kodiak, a subspecies due to its isolation on Kodiak, Afognak, and Shuyak islands. Roaming the landscape, too, are black bears, caribou, Dall sheep, moose, and wolves.

For those looking for creature comforts, the Redoubt Mountain Lodge and Silver Salmon Creek Lodge offer great fishing and wildlife watching. Explore remote corners of the 42-mile-long (68-km) lake by kayak, or head into backcountry for hikes up Tanalian Mountain and between Turquoise and Twin lakes, or simply walk the beach between Silver Salmon Creek and Chinitna Bay and revel in the glory of Alaska's wilderness.

FOCUS ON
Athabascan Indians

For 12,000 years, the Dena'ina Athabascan have fished Lake Clark, or *Qizhjeh Vena* (place where people gather). In the early 20th century, the tribe abandoned the 1,000-year-old Kijik village. This ghost town is the largest Athabascan archeological site in Alaska.

Left The Wrangell Range is a dramatic contrast between snow-covered peaks and lush grasses

ALASKA CANADA

WRANGELL – ST. ELIAS

Anchorage ○

Alaska

WRANGELL– ST. ELIAS

ESTABLISHED 1980

Where the roads end and the snowcapped peaks scud to the sky, the wilds of Wrangell–St. Elias begin. Bigger than Yellowstone, Yosemite, and the state of Maryland combined, this is the nation's largest national park.

There is nothing bigger, wilder, or more untamed on the planet. Sitting at the convergence of four mountain ranges—the Wrangells to the north, the Chugach to the southwest, the St. Elias mountains toward to coast, and the Alaska Range to the east—this huge national park encompasses a breathtaking variety of mountain and alpine landscapes. This is also the world's largest international protected wilderness, which has been designated as a World Heritage Site, and combines Glacier Bay National Park and Preserve, and Canadian neighbors Kluane National Park Reserve and Tatshenshini-Alsek National Park.

The claims to fame don't stop there. Here you will find some of the highest peaks in the United States, including the awe-inspiring Mount St. Elias. A few of the largest glaciers on Earth also flow through the park, such as the Nabesna Glacier, which is the longest nonpolar valley glacier in the world, stretching for 80 miles (129 km).

FOCUS ON

The First Ascent of Mount St. Elias

Climbing Mount St. Elias is not for the faint of heart or spirit. The first ascent of this 18,008-ft (5,488-m) peak was made by Luigi Amedeo di Savoia-Aosta, the Duke of Abruzzi. Using siege tactics, the Abruzzi expedition took several months to make it to the top. On July 31, 1897, they successfully summited.

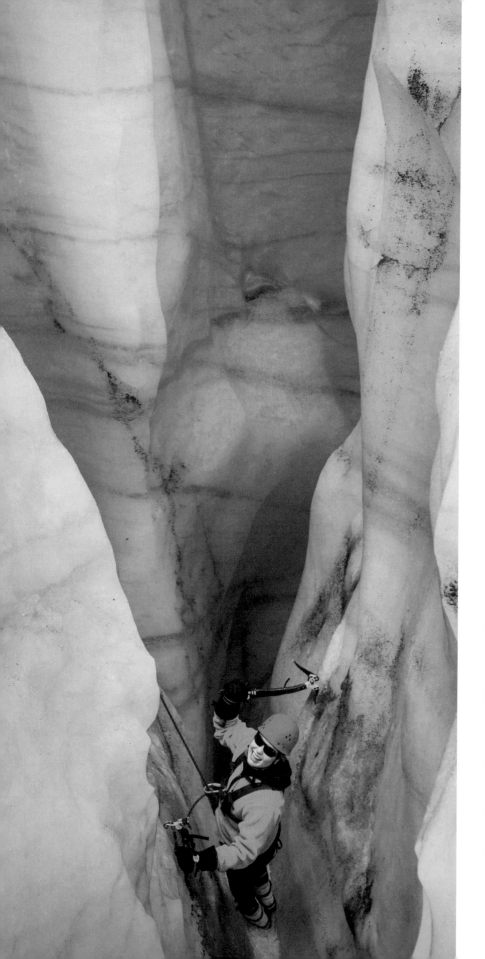

Left Ice-climbing on
the Root Glacier is a
breathtaking way to get
up close to the formations

There's even a volcano, too. Dominating
the landscape at 14,163 ft (4,316 m), Mount
Wrangell is one of the largest active
volcanoes in the United States.

While the higher peaks of the park are
buried beneath a perennial coat of snow
and ice, there are spruce forests, mountain
slopes covered by dwarf shrubs and grasses,
and coastal areas where sea lions and
harbor seals play in the arctic waters.

Wilderness adventures

Thanks to its diverse topography, there
are adventures big and small to be had
in Wrangell–St. Elias National Park and

Best Day Hikes

Root Glacier Trail ▷ 8 miles
(13 km) round trip. Marvel at
the grandeur of the glowing
blue-and-white edges of the
Root Glacier on this classic
hike from Kennecott.

Bonanza Trail 9 miles (14.5 km)
round trip. It's a steep one, with 3,800 ft
(1,158 m) of vertical gain, but the reward
is a spectacular view over the confluence
of the Root and Kennecott glaciers. Have
your camera at the ready.

Skookum Volcano Trail ▷
2.5 miles (4 km) round trip.
Accessed via the Nabesna
Road in the north, this short
trail along an eroded volcanic
system leads to a high alpine
pass where you're guaranteed
to spot Dall sheep.

Preserve. From the historic mining village of McCarthy, embark on epic glacier hikes or unwind with a fishing trip in nearby rivers. To the north, the Nabesna Road is a 42-mile (67-km) dirt route where you can camp and hike to remote crystalline lakes.

These road systems cover only a minuscule fraction of the park, and thrillseekers can engage in a bolder means of exploration. It all starts with a floatplane trip out to the middle of nowhere. From there, you can raft, backpack, or climb in some of Alaska's most remote wilderness. If you'd rather not take on a big expedition, opt for a quick flight-seeing tour: the immensity of the park takes on whole new proportions from the air.

A day spent hiking around a glacier is an unbeatable experience. With crampons on your feet, an ice axe in your hand, and a guide who really knows their way around these dangerous ice environments, you'll descend into magical ice caves, come face to face with vertical ice-climbing routes, or simply walk across these enigmatic natural features that have their own unique movement, sound, and energy.

Some of Alaska's best rafting is found within the park, too. Whether you take on a four to eight-day expedition on the Copper, Tana, or Chitina rivers, or just keep it simple with a day trip out of McCarthy, rivers offer an easy way to explore deep into this wilderness and experience nature at her most pure.

A wealth of wildlife

The unspoiled lands in the park provide a sublime home for myriad species. On the ground, scan the lakes and willow bogs for moose, or if you're up in the mountains there's a good change of spotting Dall sheep. Look for black and brown bears in the fall, or smaller species, such as lynx, coyotes, and the lovable pikas and voles.

The Copper River valley offers the most awe-inspiring birding opportunities. Here you'll sight migrating and nesting birds, including trumpeter swans, Canada geese, and rock ptarmigan. Expect to see species you've never seen before in the Lower 48, plus at least one or two bald eagles. Wherever you set up a watching station, Wrangell–St. Elias is a wildlife haven.

Above Taking a floatplane to one of the park's creeks is a thrilling start to a rafting trip

FOCUS ON
The First Guardians

The park is inhabited to this day by the descendants of its original settlers. The Ahtna and Upper Tanana Athabascans live in the interior of the park, while the Eyak and the Tlingit inhabit the coastal areas. Connecting with these Alaskan Natives and learning about their affinity with the land and unique way of life are an essential part of any journey into The Great Land.

Nevada

GREAT BASIN

ESTABLISHED 1986

Great Basin National Park is Nevada's wild jewel—
its many facets coming together to create one exquisite
gem. Wander caves deep underground before coming
into the light to ascend a mountain covered in some of
the world's oldest known living trees.

This park presents a Nevada that most wouldn't recognize—worlds away from the bright lights of Vegas and the "Biggest Little City in the World," Reno. On the eastern state line lives a Nevada that is savage wilderness, where the world's oldest tree species survives in a vital ecosystem rarely seen elsewhere on the continent.

Above The fantastic limestone formations inside the Lehman Caves can be seen on various tours

Basin life

The ancient Great Basin is made up of 90 small basins, which feed into the system, rather than out of it, as most bodies of water do. Along its slow march, the water collects in salt lakes, marshes, and mudflats, which support an array of animal and plant species. The geologic dynamics that formed the basins also created the most mountainous area in the contiguous United States, as old as the Ice Age. Rising to the top is Wheeler Peak, at 13,063 ft (3,982 m), where the Fremont and later Shoshone Indians once hunted high in the hills. It is here that you'll find bristlecone pines, with their thick, twisted trunks rooted in the harsh land.

Seas to sediment

Another prized feature in the park are the Lehman Caves, their grand marble caverns filled with limestone stalactites and

Above A splash of orange and yellow aspen trees contrast with the stark Wheeler Peak in the background

The Bristlecone Pine Tree

Atop glacial moraines at subalpine altitudes live ancient bristlecone pines. In a frigid climate with little oxygen, the trees grow at a snail's pace. Their density shields them from infection and rot, aiding longevity.

▷ Nearly 5,000 years ago, a tree that would later be given the moniker Prometheus by Great Basin mountaineers began to form on top of Wheeler Peak.

◁ In 1964, a geographer named Donald R. Currey was conducting research on ice-age glaciology and received permission by the US Forest Service to sample the 4,862-year-old tree.

▷ It is believed that the sampling, which involved boring into the tree to extract rings, caused it to die, and Currey was given permission to cut Prometheus down.

◁ The stump of Prometheus is all that's left, that and a ringed slice in the visitor center. In 2012, a bristlecone pine in the same area proved to be older still—age 5,065.

▷ Today, what is believed to be the second-oldest living tree, Methuselah, stands in California's White Mountain Range. Also a bristlecone pine, it is over 4,800 years old.

📷

Capture a great long-road shot on Highway 50, which runs from California to Maryland. The road is surrounded by sprawling mountain views as it courses through Nevada.

stalagmites, drapes, cave popcorn, and a collection of rare "shields." Known as limestone solution caverns, they began forming around 600 million years ago when shallow seas covered what is now Nevada. Tucked inside the Snake Range, the caves were discovered in the mid-1880s by a miner-turned-rancher named Absalom Lehman. He became a passionate advocate for the park and inspired the first set of laws protecting it in 1922.

Great Basin offers year-round pleasures. Trout fishing is popular during the spring snowmelt, while in summer thunderstorms swirl in the wild skies above. In fall, gather delicious pinyon pine cones, and when winter comes, don snowshoes or skis to explore a peaceful landscape cloaked in snow.

Samoan Culture

Created in part to conserve the rich Samoan culture—one of the oldest in Polynesia—the park is a real partnership with the indigenous peoples who inhabit the landscape, and whose traditions intertwine with modern lifestyles.

▽ Many traditional crafts still color American Samoa, such as artfully painted bark on mulberry trees, handwoven mats, and traditional tattoos that are punched into the skin with ink-tipped sticks.

▷ American Samoans hold island tradition (called *fa'a*) very close. To Samoans, faith, family, and music are key to daily life. Communities are made up of extended families, Christianity is widely practiced, and song is ever-present.

△ Fishing is both a popular pastime and a way of life for Samoans. Age-old methods still practiced include spear-fishing and "gleaning," where fish are pulled directly from reefs.

△ Fruit bats, which are found only in the Samoan Islands and Fiji, are one of the main reasons for national park protection. Locals hunt and eat them, and say their flavor changes depending on what fruit they most recently ate.

HAWAII

NATIONAL PARK OF AMERICAN SAMOA
⊙

FIJI

AUSTRALIA

Pacific Ocean

NEW ZEALAND

American Samoa

NATIONAL PARK OF AMERICAN SAMOA

ESTABLISHED 1988

In the heart of the Pacific Ocean, Samoan culture and natural treasures converge, creating a completely distinct national park experience, where islands born of volcanoes preserve immaculate coral reefs in the shadow of tropical cloud forests.

FOCUS ON
Traditional Umu Feast

An *umu* is an above ground oven common across Polynesia, used on special occasions, when food is caught, prepared laboriously by hand, and cooked.

South of the equator in the world's largest ocean lies a national park cradling secret treasures that many have never heard of, let alone experienced. From the lush island wilderness emerges the Samoan culture which, despite the gravitation toward popular culture on the US mainland, holds true to its 3,000-year traditions in the secluded villages that dot the land.

The remote park resides on three gorgeous, verdant islands. Ta'ū and Ofu are both part of the Manu'a Islands chain. Ta'ū, regarded as the most traditional island in American Samoa, is an unparalleled spot from which to enjoy panoramic views over rugged cliffs and cloud forest. Ofu sees the most tourist activity because of its perfect shorelines, especially Ofu Beach—the most coveted stop in the park. Tutuila, the third island, is where you will find the capital city of Pago, home to the National Park Service headquarters. Pago (or "Pongo" as locals call it) offers the best understanding of modern American Samoa with the highest concentration of services. Wherever you start or finish in this national park, though, you will in some way find yourself being immersed in the rich culture of Samoa.

"Samoa" means "sacred Earth," and it is in motion at all times. Fruit bats (also known as flying foxes) glide from branch to branch in tropical canopies like tree monkeys. Sharks and brightly colored fish weave through unbleached coral reefs, all clearly visible through transparent waters. To Samoans, the ocean is their earthscape. It is here that they fish, travel from island to island, and connect with the volcanic islands that bore their home. And you too might feel yourself irresistibly drawn into this magical, glistening world.

Explorer's spirit

With three areas of parkland to journey through, adventurers are spoiled for choice. On Ta'ū, you are likely to thrash through overgrown rain forest with a local guide on the hunt for blue crabs, before making your way to the ragged coastline where aquamarine waters crash against black rocks.

Once a week you can board the small aircraft to Ofu-Olosega. Some stay on Ofu;

FLORA AND FAUNA

Flying Foxes

The fabled fruit bat has a wingspan that can measure up to 3 ft (0.9 m), which is large for a bat. They can be easily spotted in the daytime as they fly through the trees, playing and looking for food like mangoes and avocados. Three species inhabit the island: two large-sized ones that eat fruit, and one smaller one that lives on insects.

Above Lush mountains overlook the pristine waters and traditional Samoan beach houses (fales) at Pago on Tutuila

Ways to Explore

Hike ▷ Mount 'Alava Trail, 6 miles (10 km) round trip. This challenging hike passes through lush rain forest and muddy paths before reaching the summit. The reward is a spectacular viewpoint at a height of 1,611 ft (491 m), overlooking Pago Harbor and the island of Tutuila, where deep blue ocean is seemingly endless.

Snorkel Home to more than 250 species of coral, the waters that surround the national park are unparalleled when it comes to snorkeling. The 4-mile (6-km) stretch of paradise beach on Ofu is often ranked among the top ten most beautiful beaches in the world.

Fish ▷ Tutuila and the Manu'a Islands are prime fishing territory. Try out traditional Samoan techniques such as spearfishing and hand collection, or go modern with rod and reel for cast fishing.

some go to the neighboring island of Olosega. Connecting the two is a bridge from where you can jump into the sparkling waters surrounding the Manu'a Islands chain.

After the short island flight, one of two park visitor centers greets you from the runway, ready to impart their wisdom on why Ofu is so special. On the walk between Ofu beach and the visitor center there is total seclusion and an unmistakable scent of salty sea air and plumeria wafting through the crackling branches. The underwater marine life and the coral nurseries it lives in are unique to the park, and to the world, providing habitat to immensely diverse marine systems that have earned it designation as a National Marine Sanctuary, one of only 13 in the US. Every five to ten years, cyclones disturb the nurseries, yet they have shown a remarkable ability to regenerate. Luckily, because there are so few visitors, snorkeling is allowed in this delicate environment. This is a rare privilege, and an unforgettable experience for those fortunate enough to make it here.

On Tutuila, verdant mountains hover over the bay and invite intrepid hikers to lace up their walking boots. To reach the trailheads, you will need some smart advice from the rangers at the visitor center before navigating your way through the capital city by rental car, cab, or bus before walking the rest of the way. Often, the adventure starts before the hike even begins. One of the most rewarding trails in the park is Mount 'Alava, which attracts hikers from across the globe. As you wind through dense tropical rain forest to reach the peak, look out for fruit bats, native birds, and lizards that make their home here. It's a challenge, but after climbing 56 ladders and 783 steps, you'll reach the top of the island, gaining an impressive 1,300 ft (396 m) in elevation.

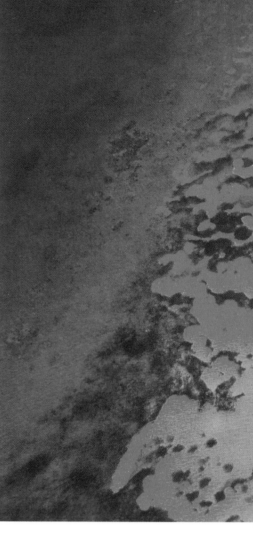

Florida

DRY TORTUGAS

ESTABLISHED 1992

Accessible only by boat or seaplane, this group of seven small islands off the Florida coast is well worth the effort it takes to reach it—you'll be greeted by coral reefs teeming with marine life, rich birdlife, and the magnificent, historic Fort Jefferson.

In the Dry Tortugas, the coral reefs are pristine—even without donning a snorkel and flippers, you'll be treated to the dazzling sight of technicolor fish skimming just below the water's surface. If you're adventurous enough to get into scuba gear, other worlds await, including the remains of long-ago shipwrecks. The waters are also home to several turtle species and fish ranging from angelfish to barracuda. Birders, too, will have a field day identifying the more than 300 species of island bird.

A mighty fortress

Nothing quite prepares you for the sheer imposing size of the park's most famous landmark, Fort Jefferson. With more than 16 million bricks, it's one of the largest brick buildings in the world, although it remains unfinished. Work began in 1846 with the aim of protecting these desirable waters from pirates and military foes. The builders took no chances: the fort is protected by a moat, even though it's on an island in the middle of the ocean.

Wandering the deserted rooms, it's easy to imagine the long-gone soldiers who were

Above Dressed in its harlequin-like coat, the ruddy turnstone winters on the islands

---

FLORA AND FAUNA

Turtles

You're sure to see turtles during your stay—it's always an exceptional thrill, whether you're sharing the sea with them or spying them from a boat while sailing among the islands. There's a mysterious, primeval quality to these creatures, with their bodies so ungainly on land, but totally at ease in water.

stationed here, as well as the ghosts of infamous inhabitants past. In 1861, President Abraham Lincoln made imprisonment at Fort Jefferson an alternative to capital punishment. After his assassination in 1865, four accomplices of his assassin, John Wilkes Booth, were sentenced to life imprisonment at the fort.

One famous guest who didn't arrive in shackles was author Ernest Hemingway. When he lived on Key West, this was a favorite place to indulge his passion for sportfishing. He and his fishing buddies were once marooned for two weeks at the fort after a storm. The islands are still a fishing hot spot, and anglers and other visitors can reach them from Key West, 70 miles (113 km) due east, by hopping aboard a ferry, seaplane, or private boat.

Best Dive Sites

Little Africa ▷ Off Loggerhead Key, this is perfect snorkeling and is family-friendly.

The Windjammer A ship sank here in 1901. Divers follow a map of the site, which reveals its treasures, some of which you can also see when snorkeling.

The Moat Wall ▷ Fort Jefferson is for experienced divers only. Night diving is a real thrill, but make sure to explore first during daylight.

Above Fort Jefferson is part of a chain of coastal forts that stretches from Maine to Texas

California • Nevada

DEATH VALLEY

ESTABLISHED 1994

Hottest, driest, lowest—Death Valley earns a stream of superlatives. Yet none fully captures the geologic drama, radiant textures, and soothing solitude found amid this scenic swath of the untamed West.

Death Valley is as far removed from everyday life as most of us can get. This feels like the edge of the world, where the terrain is scraped to the bone, the sun snarls like a beast, and silence wraps around everything and holds on tight.

282
Depth of Badwater Basin below sea level in ft (86 m).

18
The actual number of mules in a 20-mule team.

11,043
Height of Telescope Peak in ft (3,366 m), the highest point in the park.

2
Average yearly rainfall in inches (5 cm), the driest place in North America.

Dazzling salt flats stretch to the flanks of cloud-spearing mountains. Twisting canyons, colorful badlands, and silken sand dunes interrupt the expanse. And dotting the backcountry are the sun-bleached ruins of nearly forgotten boomtowns.

Yet beneath the stark exterior beats a vibrant heart. The most hauntingly named national park proves to be a remarkably diverse landscape, bristling with life. Death Valley supports more than 400 animal species and 1,000 types of plant—some, like the Panamint monkeyflower and Devils Hole pupfish, exist nowhere else.

A few paved roads slice across the land, connecting aptly named highlights such as Badwater Basin and Devil's Golf Course, making Death Valley surprisingly accessible to all. The largest national park outside Alaska is more than 90 percent wilderness, sprawling and unspoiled—a defiant frontier. How nice to know those still exist.

Left Death Valley brims with photogenic vistas, including Manly Beacon, best viewed from Zabriskie Point

Through the Seasons

Spring ▷ Visitation peaks with the hope of sunny days and a carpet of gold, pink, and white wildflowers across the park. They germinate after winter rain, then flower and seed quickly to avoid the harsh summer heat, but even when sparse these ethereal beauties soften the seemingly barren land.

Summer ▷ This is your chance to dance with the devil, as the park becomes the hottest area in North America. Sample the blast furnace of the flats, stay on paved roads, and then cool off in mountain meadows.

Fall ▷ Warm temperatures and clear skies make perfect camping and hiking weather, so pitch your tent, lace up your boots, and get exploring. For adventurous spirits, the craggy mountains and desert terrain that make up the expansive backcountry beg for a little exploration.

Winter ▷ Cool days and chilly nights come to the valley floor while snow blankets mountain summits in the winter months. The dazzling sight of the low-angled sun streaking the rough hills with long velvet shadows makes for an outstanding photo opportunity.

134

Highest temperature in Fahrenheit (56.7 °C) recorded on Earth at Furnace Creek in 1913.

A rich history

It was the impatience of fortune-seeking pioneers that put Death Valley on the map. When gold was discovered in California in 1848, thousands streamed west. One wagon train set out from Salt Lake City, but several families broke off, seeking a shorter route. The migrants reached Death Valley and wandered through on the brink of starvation. When one group struggled to go on, two men trekked 250 miles (402 km), secured provisions, and returned to rescue the others. Legend has it that as they crossed the mountains, one party member turned back and said, "Goodbye Death Valley."

While pioneers saw hardship and death, this was a valley of life for the Timbisha Shoshone people who had occupied these lands for centuries. Traversing the valley floor to the mountain ridges offers a glimpse into the seasonal migrations that the Timbisha undertook, hunting game and harvesting pinyon pine nuts between varying elevations. As gold fever continued to spread, mining activity sprang up in Death Valley, forever changing how the Timbisha lived. They did not attain federal recognition until 1983, and received a permanent parcel of land near Furnace Creek only in 2000. The Timbisha now have an active role in making decisions affecting some of their traditional land.

FOCUS ON
Hollywood Comes to Death Valley

The otherworldly terrain of Death Valley has provided backgrounds for hundreds of movies filmed here—often pinch-hitting for other worlds. *Star Wars* fans make pilgrimages to Tatooine and other distant planets that were actually Death Valley, a galaxy not so far away. Epics like *Spartacus* and *The Greatest Story Ever Told* were shot in and around the park, as well as dozens of Westerns including *The Professionals*, *Django Unchained*, and *Three Godfathers*.

Industrial heritage

Gold and silver lured prospectors back to Death Valley. With each new discovery, towns sprang up. None lasted for long, but in keeping with the park's haunting name are abandoned ghost towns. If traveling by car, head to Rhyolite, once the largest town in the area and still home to alluring ruins such as a train depot and a jail. Panamint City is as mysterious as it gets, with a chimney of the smelter its most arresting wreckage.

The real wealth of Death Valley lay in the borax deposits on the salt flats. One of the earliest operations was the Harmony Borax Works, which became most famous for their 20-mule team wagons used to transport ore. A ranger-led tour here is a fascinating window into borax history.

A man named Walter Scott worked as a swamper on the 20-mule teams. He later found fame as a con man known as Death Valley Scotty, coaxing investors to sink money into his fictitious gold mine so he could embark on extravagant spending sprees. Businessman Albert Johnson found he was being swindled but didn't care; he bought a lavish home in Grapevine Canyon, which Scotty then declared as his own. Scotty's Castle is a highlight of the park, preserving as it does the life and times of the early 20th century.

Below Badwater Basin takes the title as the lowest point in North America, proudly marked on its entry point

The Legendary 20-Mule Teams

The discovery of borax was significant, but the largest obstacle was transporting it to a distant railroad. The solution became iconic. From 1883 to 1888, 20-mule teams hauled massive wagons across the terrain.

▷ The 20-mule teams actually consisted of 18 mules and two horses at the rear. The horses' greater strength helped in starting the wagons.

◁ Three specially built wagons were hitched behind the mules. The first two each held 9 metric tons of borax, and the third hauled water and feed for a load of 33.2 metric tons.

The muleskinner controlled the team by a jerkline running through the collar of each left-hand mule to the leader 80 ft (24 m) away. He guided the team with pulls.

To prevent wagons from overturning on a sharp curve, a few mules in the rear were trained to jump over the chain and pull at an opposite angle. The swamper fed the mules and cooked.

◁ The man who had the idea to market a cleaning product as 20 Mule Team Borax was Stephen Mather. He would later become the first director of the National Park Service.

▷ *Death Valley Days*, sponsored by 20 Mule Team Borax, was a long-running television program featuring true accounts of the Old West. Past hosts included Ronald Reagan.

FOCUS ON

A Traditional Harvest

Saguaros have long been an important food source for the Tohono O'odham and other indigenous peoples. April through June, mature saguaros produce white flowers that become ripe, red fruit in midsummer. Using long poles made of dead saguaro "ribs," tribe members harvest the fruit, which they eat fresh or make into syrup and saguaro wine to be drunk during religious rain ceremonies. The saguaro harvest marks the beginning of the new year.

Left The cactus forest is bathed in soft pastels each evening at sunset

Left The cactus forest is bathed in soft pastels each evening at sunset

Arizona

SAGUARO

ESTABLISHED 1994

The giant, multi-armed saguaro cactus is a much-loved symbol of the Old West, and these spiked giants show off in all their stern glory in the sprawling national park.

The silhouette of a towering saguaro, stretching its enormous arms skyward against a blazing pink-and-orange sunset is as iconic a Southwestern image as it gets. Surprisingly though, this regal cactus, the largest in the US, grows only in the Sonoran Desert of southern Arizona and northern Mexico. Saguaro National Park, comprising two areas on the eastern and western edges of Tucson, was established to protect these one-of-a-kind plants.

The fascinating saguaro grows to 60 ft (18 m) tall. Beneath its thick, spiny skin is a reservoir of water that it drinks in during the rainy season. When the larder is full, a mature cactus can weigh up to 4,800 pounds (2,175 kg). These cacti are incredibly slow growers, with their first fledgling arms appearing when the plant is 75 to 100 years old. Under the right conditions, the mighty saguaro can live for two centuries.

Forest of cacti

The park preserves some of the world's last saguaro "forests," which once covered this desert. Encroaching human development has, sadly, hit their numbers hard.

The park's scenic roadways and the many hiking, biking, and horseback trails wending through the desert scape make it easy for visitors to explore this exceptional biome and discover the curious plants and elusive animals that thrive in this harsh but intriguing desert wonderland.

In April, temperatures are cooler, and colorful cactus flowers bloom throughout the park.

Sonoran plant life is fascinating up close. As you walk the trails, you'll encounter a mind-boggling array of cacti, including fuzzy teddy-bear cholla, with their deceptively soft-looking branches; short, spiny hedgehogs and tiny round pincushion cacti; and dense clumps of prickly pear. All bloom together in a magnificent display of bright pink, yellow, red, and purple flowers in the spring and early summer. There are shady pockets of mesquite and green-barked palo verde trees, and, of course, saguaros everywhere, as individual as humans in shape and character.

Heat-loving animals

This hot, parched landscape supports a surprising variety of wildlife. Many animals

Three Hikes

Easy ▷ Wild Dog Trail, 1.8 miles (3 km) round trip. This peaceful trail in Saguaro West leads through cacti and wildflowers to a low ridge with splendid views over a saguaro-filled valley.

Moderate Cactus Forest Trail, 10 miles (16 km) round trip. The mostly flat route in Saguaro East is a showcase for many cacti, with views of the Rincon Mountains.

Challenging ▷ Wasson Peak, 8 miles (13 km) round trip. In Saguaro West, climb to the highest point in the Tucson Mountains via the Sendero-Esperanza and Hugh Norris trails for panoramic views that make for incredible photographs.

Javelina

One of the more unusual desert animals in this park is the javelina, or collared peccary. Although they resemble wild boars—with their flat snouts, short legs, bristly salt-and-pepper coats, and sharp canine teeth—these hoofed mammals are not pigs. Javelina live in saguaro forests and desert washes, eating prickly pear, agave, and other desert plants and roots. They rest in the shade during the heat of the day.

Above Ancient petroglyphs, like this spiral at Signal Hill, were etched in stones

are elusive or nocturnal, but on quiet trails you may spot coyotes, javelina, mule deer, or jackrabbits. Watch for the sharp-beaked, greater roadrunners and plumed, black-faced Gambel's quail scurrying through the underbrush. Tiny hummingbirds hover over cactus flowers, and red-tailed hawks and huge ravens soar above. Listen for the scolding of the cactus wrens and the tapping of Gila woodpeckers, who carve out nests in the saguaros. And keep an eye out everywhere for the creature that commands the greatest respect: the rattlesnake.

Trails and hikes

The eastern Rincon Mountain District is the largest section of the park. Cactus Forest Loop Drive is an 8-mile (13-km) paved road that takes you to picnic areas and overlooks with fantastic views of the army of saguaros spreading across the valley. It's all near a short, accessible ecology trail that starts at the visitor center.

Cyclists can ride along the hilly loop drive, or on two of the park's many hiking trails, which pass the ruins of old ranches and mines. Longer backcountry trails guide you on foot or horseback into remote wilderness and up into a mountain landscape of woodlands and pine forest.

In the western Tucson Mountain District, the 5-mile (8-km) dirt-and-gravel Bajada Loop Drive follows more stunning desert scenery. A highlight is the Signal Hill picnic area, where a short walk leads to dozens of ancient Hohokam Indian petroglyphs carved into the rocks.

Above An alert greater roadrunner looks poised to take off at any minute

California

JOSHUA TREE

ESTABLISHED 1994

Joshua Tree National Park is a botanical marvel. Meander through whimsical cactus gardens, explore boulder-strewn canyons, and gaze at starry night skies: this is a desert wonder you don't want to miss.

A unique ecosystem where the Mojave and the Colorado deserts meet, Joshua Tree is known for its striking, fanciful flora. Prickly Joshua trees and spiny cacti shoot up from gravel and sand, and ancient boulders dot the landscape. Though deserts may appear to be barren, Joshua Tree is a reminder that life persists in the harshest environments.

With dagger-sharp leaves and fibrous bark, the park's namesake Joshua tree isn't actually a tree, but a variety of yucca plant and a member of the cactus family. Legend has it that the name was bestowed by Mormon settlers traveling through the Mojave Desert in the mid-19th century. Its distinct shape reminded them of a biblical story where Joshua raises his hands to pray.

Botanical enthusiasts will delight in the variety of other native flora such as the fuzzy teddy bear cholla and the jumping cholla, named for the ease with which thorny segments detach and cling to unsuspecting passersby. For a stunning wildflower display, visit in the early spring, when the California barrel cactus and ocotillo erupt in pink and scarlet flowers, and the air is tinged with the distinct aroma of Joshua tree blooms.

This unique desert ecosystem is also a climber's and hiker's paradise. An array of walking trails winds through remote canyons and interesting rock formations such as Skull Rock, a naturally formed oddity carved out of the sandstone by wind and water, and a popular spot for photographers.

Into the night

The clear, cool nights are perfect for stargazing, and afford a shimmering respite from California's light pollution. Established campgrounds offer privacy with spots nestled between boulders, so you can explore by day and retire to camp in the evening under the twinkling sky.

FLORA AND FAUNA

Joshua Trees

The park's most iconic plant species co-evolved over millions of years with the tiny, unassuming yucca moth, a type of dung beetle. Lacking the ability to produce nectar, Joshua trees rely solely on the yucca moth for pollination. The yucca moth in turn pollinates only Joshua tree flowers, using its nimble mandibles to collect pollen, thus ensuring the survival of this cactus.

Above Namesake Joshua trees thrive in the park's stark desert landscape beside rugged boulders such as Jumbo Rocks

PARK PIONEERS
Minerva Hoyt

Celebrated as the first desert conservationist, Hoyt is considered the founder of Joshua Tree National Park and was a pioneer in the movement to protect the United States' wild places. A wealthy socialite from Pasadena, Hoyt eschewed high society in favor of the beauty of the desert. She founded the International Desert Conservation League in 1910, and in 1936 she convinced President Franklin D. Roosevelt to designate 1,250 sq miles (3,237 sq km) of the California desert as Joshua Tree National Monument.

Colorado

BLACK CANYON OF THE GUNNISON
ESTABLISHED 1999

A startlingly deep chasm cut with knifelike precision into the land, the Black Canyon emerges as if from nowhere. This is one of the sheerest, narrowest gorges on the continent.

Here is one of Colorado's best-kept secrets—its cliffs looming big over the river below. For perspective, the Painted Wall outstrips both the Eiffel Tower, France, and the Empire State Building, New York City, in height.

Staring into the Black Canyon elicits a dizzying sense of the earth moving. You can't always see to the bottom—the name comes not from black walls, but because sunlight scarcely reaches the river below. That river, the Gunnison, is responsible for the canyon's existence, patiently carving it into surrounding volcanic rock over eons.

Play of light and shapes

Most people approach the park from the paved South Rim Road, but the North Rim is equally spectacular. Both sides have campgrounds, hiking trails, opportunities for kayaking and rock climbing, and jaw-dropping views. Trails on the canyon edges run through an arid landscape of fragrant juniper and pinyon pine to vertiginous viewing platforms—peer into the chasm onto a seemingly tiny river below.

Every inch of these sheer cliffs is fascinating, with ribbons of vivid pink and black, plus a spectrum of colors that changes as the light shifts. There are even different shapes discernible within the walls, from square blocks to triangular chips to paperlike layers that resemble neat stacks of books.

As you study the cliff walls, keep an eye out for peregrine falcons and their nests. These raptors are often seen from the Chasm View nature trail on the North Rim, as well as from Tomichi Point Overlook and Chasm View Overlook on the South Rim (both wheelchair-accessible). You might see them nesting on rocky ledges or hunting by swooping down on other flying birds. The imaginative visitor may also see a camel—that is, the Kneeling Camel, a rock formation visible from the North Rim.

FOCUS ON

Astronomy Festival

The park was certified an International Dark Sky Park in 2015. The lack of light pollution makes it ideal for stargazing any time, but enthusiasts aim for the Astronomical Society's annual dark-sky celebration, with educational talks and solar daytime viewing. After dark, there are guest speakers and kid-friendly programs. Volunteers supply the telescopes.

Above Visitors stand on a pinnacle that seems to hang precariously over the void

Left This out-of-the-way gem in western Colorado has some of the steepest cliffs, oldest rock, and craggiest spires in North America

2,722

The depth in ft (829 m) at Warner Point—the canyon at its finest.

Right Carving a route through beautiful sections of deciduous forest, the Ohio & Erie Canal Towpath Trail makes for a pleasant family bike ride

Below A steam locomotive on the Cuyahoga Valley Scenic Railroad creates a picture-perfect scene

FAMILY FUN

Cuyahoga Scenic Valley Railroad

Trains on one of the longest-running railways still in operation today offer activities for all ages, ranging from cookie-decorating rides to the chance to learn about the park's flora and fauna. You can even step back in time on the historic Nickel Plate Road 765 steam locomotive.

Did You Know?

The Ohio & Erie Canal that runs through the park was created by laborers working for a mere 30 cents a day.

Ohio

CUYAHOGA VALLEY

ESTABLISHED 2000

Rich in history and culture, this undeveloped landscape bursts to life out of a neighboring metropolis, serving up a world of adventure and seasonal beauty to relish at any time of the year.

With a unique location between the two large cities of Cleveland and Akron, this national park is somewhat of a hidden gem. At the center of it all is the Cuyahoga River valley, where small groups of quaint houses, scenic roadways, and enchanting northern forests sprawl across vistas of rolling hills.

Once in its grasp, it's hard not to fall in love with the diverse natural features that locals have long treasured. Not wanting to see development overtake the area's value, residents fought to have the park protected. A National Recreation Area was established in 1974, and houses that already stood in this designated spot still remain—an unusual thing to see in a national park.

A park for all

While the park's charming history draws people in, what keeps them coming back are the endless opportunities for fun. This is a park that truly celebrates all seasons. Waterfalls gush in the spring, inviting the choruses of wading birds and raptors, and all summer long, outdoor enthusiasts walk, run, cycle, and hike through lush woodlands. During the fall, the park transforms into a sea of red, orange, and yellow as trees erupt in vibrant colors—a favorite scene for photographers who flock here during peak leaf season. When snow blankets the land in the winter, sports lovers head to the hills for prime sledding and skiing conditions.

To enjoy the park's recreational and historic glory year-round, travel alongside the scenic Ohio & Erie Canal. Completed in 1832, this multistate crossing provides 101 miles (162 km) of recreation—some of which cut through the park on the Towpath Trail. And there's more: art exhibits, musical shows, and horseback riding make Cuyahoga Valley perfect for the entire family.

Right Leaves carpet the
pretty boardwalk trail,
which gets swamped after
the floods hit the park

NORTH CAROLINA

○ Greenville

Columbia ○ ⊙ CONGAREE

SOUTH
CAROLINA

○ Charleston

GEORGIA

Atlantic
Ocean

South Carolina

CONGAREE

ESTABLISHED 2003

At Congaree, when you stop and listen, it seems as
if you can hear every breath of wind, every branch
twist and fall, and every tiny bird whistle and chirp.
The park is a sensory delight, filled with glorious
trails through ancient floodplain and forest.

A singing natural world unfolds at Congaree,
nestled among a forest of bald cypress
trees where battles were lost and won.
Congaree American Indians, whom the park
was named for, lived on the Congaree River
until European settlers arrived in the 18th
century. In the next century, the lumber
industry would come calling but, thanks to
the park's remote location and lack of usable
waterways, most of the trees were spared

Today, under old-growth canopies, shy
wildlife hides in the trees while amphibians,
reptiles, and fish make their way through
the floodplain, formed when the Congaree
and Wateree rivers are swelled by heavy
rains. Insects fill the air during hot summer
months, Spanish moss drips from the
cypress trees, glistening in the humidity,
and scores of bird species' fly through this
International Biosphere Reserve. In the

morning, reflections of the trees are precise
in the stillness of the water. At night, head
out on "owl prowls" to listen for echoing
calls of barred owls.

A landscape to roam

Cast-fishers can drop a line anywhere
in the park (except for Westin Lake), and
serene spots include Cedar Creek and
oxbow lakes where bowfins, bluegill, and
yellow perch are pulled up regularly. For
a leisurely adventure, paddle out on a
ranger-guided outing to explore 15 miles
(24 km) of waterway on the Cedar Creek.

If you'd rather stay on dry land, the
wheelchair-accessible Boardwalk Loop Trail
passes myriad tree species, from loblolly
pines to tupelo trees, which shelter some
of the microorganisms that make up this
ecologically fascinating environment.

150

The surface temperature of the sand in summer can reach 150°F (66°C).

−20

On a winter night, the temperatures can drop to lows of −20°F (−29°C).

Colorado

GREAT SAND DUNES

ESTABLISHED 2004

Like a lost piece of the Sahara Desert that's been
dropped into a Colorado valley, the Great Sand Dunes,
with their steep mountain backdrop, are equal
parts baffling and beautiful.

When you first see the dunes, the obvious question is: how on earth did they get here? The tallest dunes in North America nestle between the San Juan and Sangre de Cristo mountains, the byproduct of a huge lake that once covered the San Luis Valley and later drained into the Rio Grande. A sand sheet was left behind when the lake disappeared, and prevailing winds blew the sand toward lower passes in the Sangre de Cristo Mountains. Frequent storms brought wind from the opposite direction, and the two opposing forces caused the sand to form vertical dunes. Vegetation across the valley floor has since slowed the process, but the landscape is far from static. Even today, parabolic dunes form in the sand sheet and migrate toward the dune field.

They might look barren, but the dunes support a surprising amount of life. Only the top few inches are dry; rainfall keeps the lower layers moist and allows hardy plants like Indian ricegrass, blowout grass, prairie sunflowers, and scurfpea to thrive, as well as animals such as salamanders, kangaroo rats, and tiger beetles. Beyond the dunes, there's even more diverse flora and fauna in the park's wetlands, lakes, rivers, and alpine tundra ecosystems.

Above A solitary camper leaves a footprint trail in the pristine sand

Left Wild deer survive on plant life and scrub in the arid climate

Far Left Not just a story of unusual geology, the dunes are also a fabulous recreational area

FLORA AND FAUNA
Tiger Beetles

Endemic to the park, the tiger beetle is a sand obligate that thrives in this protected habitat, hunting down ants, mites, and other beetles with amazing speed. Key markings are its iridescent green head and dark, violin-shaped pattern on the back.

Sandbox playground

Unlike many fragile natural environments, the dunes suffer no ill effects from being trampled, hiked across, and even sledded down. The Great Sand Dunes National Park and Preserve encourages visitors to rent special sleds or sandboards for surfing or sledding down the dunes. Of course, to come down, you first have to hike up, and this can feel like a Sisyphean task. There's something deceptive about distance here—even the shorter, nearer dunes that look easy to reach can take surprising effort to climb. The payoff is the downhill spree.

If you prefer to travel both directions on your own two feet, you can reach Star Dune, the tallest in the park (and in North America), in about five hours round trip; find the trailhead by hiking 2 miles (3 km) south along Medano Creek to the dune's base, then follow a ridge to the summit. With a permit, you can camp overnight— imagine the starry skies and nocturnal species you'll see from a campsite.

Trails outside the dunes, such as the Mosca Pass Trail, provide a taste of the nearby landscape. A hike to Upper and Lower Sand Creek lakes starts north of the park boundary and visits two alpine lakes framed by 13,000-ft (4,000-m) peaks. The 8-mile (13-km) hike is a good place to spot pikas.

Kids in particular will enjoy splashing in Medano Creek, which flows from early spring into summer. Wading, swimming, tubing, and sand sculpting are all popular.

Below Like its winter counterpart sledding, sandboarding is a downhill speed thrill

Three Hikes

Montville Nature Trail ▷
0.5 miles (1 km) round trip. An easy, shaded loop from the visitor center with views of the first row of dunes.

Wellington Ditch Trail
1.8 miles (2.9 km) round trip. Branching off from the Montville Nature Trail for another mile, this trail is good for spring wildflowers and dune views.

Mosca Pass Trail ▷ 7 miles (11 km) round trip. From a trailhead near the visitor center, this trail follows Mosca Creek through forest and meadows—an especially good place for spotting grouse, wild turkeys, and songbirds.

History of the San Luis Valley

History casts a long shadow here: prehistoric Clovis and Folsom Complexes, the Ute, Spanish, and other Europeans have all made their mark.

AD 900–1650

The indigenous peoples are mostly Ute, who live in hunter-gatherer societies. Comanche, Apache, Navajo, Arapaho, and Cheyenne come to trade, hunt, and raid.

1694

▽ Spaniard Don Diego de Vargas provides the earliest surviving written record of the area, detailing his encounters with the Ute and his wonder at bison herds.

10,000 BC

Paleo-Indians migrate to the valley, where they hunt the ancient bison and mammoths with spears launched with an atlatl (spear-throwing tool).

5500 BC

Climate fluctuation leads to population growth and technical innovations. Still nomadic, people experience greater stability in what is called the Archaic Stage.

1598

After reports of gold in the San Luis Valley, Spanish explorer Juan de Oñate claims all land surrounding the drainage from the Rio Grande for Spain.

1807

△ Army officer Zebulon Pike enters the San Luis Valley to explore the Southwest and the Spanish settlements in New Mexico. He spots the peak later named for him.

The Great Sand Dunes was named an International Dark Sky Park in 2019, and the nighttime stargazing is epic. Hike the dunes, too, under a full moon, when it's so bright no flashlight is needed.

Sandy seascape

People have been interacting with this park long before it was a park—at least 11,000 years. Stone Age nomadic hunter-gatherers roamed the San Luis Valley, as evidenced by spearpoints used to hunt mammoths. More recently, Ute, Apache, and Navajo inhabited the area. The "living artifacts" of peeled ponderosa pines tell how they used bark for food and medicine. Spanish explorers arrived in the 1600s and 1700s, followed by Zebulon Pike (of Pike's Peak) in 1807. Pike's journals describe the appearance of the dunes as "that of the sea in a storm."

Above The idllyic and aptly named Star Dune is a remarkable 750 ft (229 m) from base to summit

1845—48

The US annexes Texas, which achieves statehood. The San Luis Valley is part of the annexation. The Mexican-American war sees Mexico lose vast tracts of land.

1876

▽ Within a month of the nation's Centennial, Colorado becomes the 38th state in the Union. Known as the Centennial State, its territory includes the San Luis Valley.

1876—79

African American Buffalo Soldiers patrol the Great Sand Dunes area to keep peace between the settlers and Indian tribes, who coined the soldiers' catchy moniker.

1821

△ The Mexican War of Independence ends New Spain's dependence on Old Spain, severing ties. The San Luis Valley is now fully part of the new nation of Mexico.

1821—22

Fur trader Jacob Fowler travels the valley observing the animal and plant life, white settlers, and American Indians. The *New York Times* reviews his published journal.

1932

President Herbert Hoover signs a proclamation giving Great Sand Dunes monument status. The status protects the delicate ecosystem from gold and silver mining in the area.

2004

△ The monument becomes the national park and preserve you see today, acquiring surrounding land to reach its current size of 168 sq miles (434 sq km).

California

PINNACLES

ESTABLISHED 2013

Don't underestimate this smaller and younger park. This is where the California condor soars, swerving around volcanic outcroppings. Lace up your walking boots and embark on steep climbs around the park's trademark cliffs and explore its hidden talus caves.

Forged from the forces of volcanic eruptions and tectonic uplift, the unique landscape of Pinnacles National Park brings you closer to California's fascinating and tumultuous geological past. Topping it all are the volcanic spires that were formed 23 million years ago when a volcano the size of Mount St. Helens formed close by. The nearby San Andreas Fault split the volcanic mass of the Pinnacles-Neenach volcanic field in two, while wind and water transformed the rock into the spectacular formations you see today. It's little wonder, then, that President Theodore Roosevelt declared this park a National Monument over 100 years ago.

Small but mighty

Pinnacles may be one of the smallest parks in the United States, but there's more to explore than just the signature cliffs. There are forests of tangled chaparral, rolling hills, and valleys that drop to as low as 824 ft (251 m) along South Chalone Creek

before climbing back up to the park's high point on North Chalone Peak at 3,304 ft (1,007 m). Below the surface, there's a phenomenal network of eerie talus caves just waiting to be discovered.

All this topographic variety makes Pinnacles a magnet for abundant wildlife. Little compares to spotting a wild California condor in its native habitat, hearing a cacophony of acorn woodpeckers and over 20 species of raptor, or glimpsing bobcats, gray foxes, and black-tailed deer. The real thrill, though, is the remarkable sight of Townsend's big-eared bats roosting in the darkness of the talus caves.

Given the park's easy access to San Francisco, it's a great spot for a short family vacation. With immense rock features to scramble on, expansive hiking trails, and the chance to camp out under the stars (with specialized ranger-led nighttime activities on offer), Pinnacles is an adventure playground for everyone.

Right The superlative rock formations at Pinnacles are a massive draw for climbers

Far Right Bear Gulch is a talus cave, formed by the spaces between fallen boulders

Below Volcanic rocks at High Peaks make up the park's varied topography

Three Hikes

Easy ▷ Moses Spring to Rim Trail Loop, 2.2 miles (3.5 km) round trip. This short, family-friendly trail leads up through a superb selection of rock formations and talus caves, and past the reservoir. Climb through the Bear Gulch Cave to sight residing bats.

Moderate High Peaks Trail, 6.3 miles (10 km) loop trail. Follow a steep and narrow path through the heart of the park's pinnacle formations on this signature trail. Crossing streams and delving into talus caves, this hike is beautiful at every turn, but the panoramic views of the looming rock spires jutting out along the top of the ridgeline are unparalleled.

Challenging ▷ Chalone Peak Trail, 9 miles (14.5 km) round trip. Stretch yourself with this long day hike, passing stunning wildflowers to the top of the park's highest peak for seemingly boundless vistas. This peak is a popular haunt for the California condor, so have your binoculars at the ready.

IOWA

ILLINOIS

Kansas City

GATEWAY ARCH

KANSAS

MISSOURI

ARKANSAS

Right The massive Gateway Arch, until 2018 known as the Jefferson National Expansion Memorial, is mirrored in the reflection pool

Missouri

GATEWAY ARCH

ESTABLISHED 2018

Soaring high above a Civil Rights landmark on the banks of the Mississippi River, the elegant, silver-steel Gateway Arch is a gleaming memorial to the westward expansion of the United States in the 19th century.

The graceful silver arch is a symbol of St. Louis and the centerpiece of one of the few urban national parks. It was conceived in the 1930s as a tribute to President Thomas Jefferson, whose purchase of the Louisiana territory beyond the Mississippi River in 1803 opened up the westward movement of explorers and pioneers.

The magnificent arch, designed by renowned architect Eero Saarinen, was built in 1963–65. On a bright day, when its tapered form shimmers in the sunlight and reflects in the waters of this mighty river, it is a perfect tribute to a visionary president.

Like a silver rainbow, the arch towers above another venerable landmark, the Old Courthouse. Two benchmark Civil Rights cases were heard in this historic 1828 building: the infamous Dred Scott Case, and, in 1872, Virginia Minor's challenge of the state's male-only voting laws. Both cases went to the US Supreme Court, which ruled against the plaintiffs.

Look West

For a thrilling way to experience the arch, squeeze into a capsule-like tram car and ride up inside the dark, narrow legs to the top. Here, small windows on either side afford you incredible views over the Mississippi, the city, and beyond. From this lofty vantage point, you'll gaze out at the great westward expanse that was Jefferson's legacy to his country.

630
In ft (192 m), the height of the arch.

43,000
The weight in tons (39,000 metric tons).

630
Width at the base in ft (192 m).

60
Depth in ft (18 m) of the foundations.

FOCUS ON

The Dred Scott Case

Dred Scott and his family were born into slavery, but they were taken into free territories, where they lived for many years. Under the "once-free, always-free" doctrine, they sued for freedom in 1846. The landmark case dragged on 11 years, making it to the Supreme Court. Its ruling against the Scotts provoked widespread anger and helped fuel the start of the Civil War.

MICHIGAN

INDIANA
DUNES ⊙

ILLINOIS

○ Fort Wayne

Indianapolis ○

OHIO

INDIANA

KENTUCKY

Indiana

INDIANA DUNES

ESTABLISHED 2019

At this cherished pocket of Indiana you'll cross an amazingly rich natural world where grasses grow from ancient sand and into the sky. Prepare to fall in love with one of the most biodiverse parks in the system.

Hugging Lake Michigan in northern Indiana, layer upon layer of fascinating features cascade across the landscape with as much intensity as a falling Midwestern sunset. This park, formerly a National Lakeshore, was named for its dunes. They started forming over 13,000 years ago during the last Ice Age when glaciers retreated, creating the Great Lakes. Made of gravel, sand, and pulverized boulders, the vegetated slopes protect the shores from storms and shield beaches from invasive species that crawl in from the wetlands.

If the landscape alone wasn't exceptional enough, you may be astonished to sight five model homes nestled in the dunes. Created for the "Homes of Tomorrow" exhibit for the 1933 World's Fair in Chicago, they were moved by barge to the Indiana Dunes to promote new development at Beverly Shores.

Above The gorgeous Art Deco Florida Tropical House is one of the park's "Homes of Tomorrow"

Above Hikers are treated to spectacular panoramas of vegetation painted in vibrant shades of auburn and green in the fall

Most know the newly minted national park and neighboring state park as a retreat from nearby cities, where the beaches become shoreside playgrounds in the summer. The lake holds 1,200 cubic miles (5,000 cubic km)

Bring a macro lens to capture intricate details of an enormous population of plant species and wildflowers in the spring.

of water, causing it to act more like an ocean than a protected body of freshwater (to the delight of sailors and body surfers). Away from the water, nature lovers are entranced by world-class biodiversity— with marshes filled with birds, squishy bogs that birth carnivorous plants, and more than 1,100 flowering plants throughout.

Hikers are gifted with 50 miles (80 km) of trails, snaking through forests to lush beaches where the dunes wait to be climbed. The tricky "Three Dune Challenge" leads to the tops of the highest dunes here: Mount Jackson, Mount Holden, and Mount Tom, with some of the most breathtaking views in the whole park a welcome reward.

PARK PIONEERS

Henry Cowles

A botanist from the area, Cowles published an article in 1899 bringing attention to fragile ecosystems in the region, inspiring a legacy of preservation that led to federal protection in 1966. He is known as "the father of plant ecology."

New Mexico

WHITE SANDS

ESTABLISHED 2019

At America's youngest national park, a rolling sea of white spreads across the New Mexico desert, as if a snowy avalanche toppled from distant mountains yet refuses to melt beneath a relentless sun. This is more than just a park: this is an ethereal world.

The mountain-ringed Tularosa Basin hoards a rare white jewel: the largest gypsum dune field on earth, much of it contained within White Sands National Park. These magical dunes were formed after the evaporation of an ancient sea, leaving behind gypsum in the form of selenite crystals. Weathering and erosion break down the crystals into grains, which are carried by winds to form the dunes. Every day the dune field reinvents itself as the winds reshape the contours.

The most peaceful time to visit is October, when summer crowds have departed, days are sunny, and it's the last month of the year for full-moon hikes.

White Sands has witnessed a remarkable span of human history and technological advancement. More than 10,000 years ago, Paleo-Indians were hunting mammoths here with hand-thrown spears. Today the park borders White Sands Missile Range, site of the first atomic bomb detonation and birthplace of America's space program. The earliest tests on rockets that paved the way for a journey to the moon were conducted amid these pale and peaceful dunes.

Despite the harsh conditions, more than 800 animal species eke out a living here. Most, like the kit fox, are nocturnal, leaving patterns of tracks for you to decipher in the daytime. Small animals such as the Apache pocket mouse have evolved a white coloration, concealing them from predators, and plants also adopt strategies to survive in the ever-shifting sands. A visit to this incredible park offers a glimpse of a different world, where the scars of the land are healed with every single breeze.

Did You Know?

The White Sands pupfish survives in micro-habitats in and around the park, and nowhere else in the world.

Ways to Explore

Camp ▷ Nothing beats the otherworldly vision of the sun rising and setting over the alabaster dunes. Experience this glory by grabbing a permit, hiking to the heart of the dunes, and pitching your tent on the sparkling sand.

Picnic Head to one of the tables dotted around the park for a dining spot with heavenly vistas. Since gypsum doesn't absorb heat from the sun, the dunes remain cool, so kick off your shoes to feel the sand between your toes.

Sled ▷ Don't resist the urge to go sledding in this glistening wonderland. Waxed plastic snow saucers work best, so purchase one at the park's gift shop and enjoy the ride.

Walk Marvel at the park's expanse on one of its short walking trails. Loop through the bright sand interspersed with shrubs on the Dune Life Nature Trail, or follow the leisurely Interdune Boardwalk, a wheelchair-accessible connector between two large dunes.

Night watch ▷ Once a month rangers lead a short hike to witness the rising of the full moon. Seeing the dunes awash in milky moonlight is a sublime experience you will long remember.

Hike The strenuous Alkali Flat Trail, a 5-mile (8-km) loop, plunges into the dune field, skirting the edge of parched Lake Otero. Set off before sunset to see the dunes painted in delicate hues.

Left Waves of white gypsum dunes push toward a distant horizon at the park, extending for 276 sq miles (715 sq km)

INDEX

ACKNOWLEDGMENTS

Dorling Kindersley would like to thank the National Park Service, Steve Crozier, and Tom Morse whose help and assistance contributed to the preparation of this book, plus the following authors for their words:

Greg Benchwick is a travel and adventure writer based in Colorado. When he's not looking for the next great trail, rafting remote rivers in Utah, or climbing to the top of Lost Spires in California, Greg works for the UN Development Programme on climate change.

Terra Breeden is a journalist, travel writer, and avid outdoors-woman. Aside from writing about her beloved national parks, Terra is usually exploring the Sierra Nevada Mountains surrounding her home in Lake Tahoe, California.

Donna Dailey is an award-winning travel writer who has been exploring national parks since she was a child. She has backpacked through the Canyonlands, climbed the highest peak in Rocky Mountain, and lives near Saguaro. She has worked on many DK titles.

Mike Gerrard divides his time between England and Arizona, where he lives near Saguaro National Park— where he had his first close encounter with a rattlesnake. His favourite parks are Olympic and Shenandoah. Mike has worked on various US-based guides for DK.

Candy B. Harrington is based near Yosemite, and has covered accessible travel exclusively for the past 25 years. She's the founding editor of *Emerging Horizons*, and the author of a series of national park guides for slow walkers and wheel-chair-users (*www.emerging horizons.com/books*).

Stephen Keeling has been exploring America's national parks since 1991 (50 so far). He worked as a financial journalist for seven years before writing his first travel guide, and has since worked on numerous titles for DK, including award-winning *DK Eyewitness New York City*. He lives in the Big Apple.

James Edward Mills is a freelance journalist who specializes in environmental conservation and outdoor recreation. With a particular interest in diversity and inclusion, his work centers upon the narratives of those often forgotten throughout the enduring legacy of public land management and our natural heritage.

Roger Naylor is an award-winning Southwest author and travel writer. He specializes in state and national parks, lonely hiking trails, twisting back roads, diners with burgers sizzling on the grill, small towns, ghost towns, and pie.

Becky Ohlsen is a travel writer and has been visiting national parks since childhood. She's studied faces in the rock formations at Arches, tried sledding down the Great Sand Dunes, spotted a grizzly bear at Glacier, and gazed into the abyss at the Black Canyon of the Gunnison.

Stefanie Payne is a communications strategist at NASA. When not telling the story of exploration in space, she writes about exploration on Earth. In 2016, she road-tripped to every US national park to document America's treasured lands.

Access Tips and Resources

All national parks have an accessibility guide on their homepage. US residents with a permanent disability can get a free lifetime pass good for admission to all national parks. Proof of residence and disability is required (*www.nps.gov/ planyourvisit/passes.htm*).

Service animals, as defined in the Americans with Disabilities Act, are welcome at all national park facilities. Emotional Support Animals are considered pets and must abide by park pet regulations (*www.nps.gov/ planyourvisit/service-animals.htm*).

It's sensible to book directly with official park concessionaires for national park lodging reservations, rather than third-party sites.

For more information and additional resources, visit *www.nps.gov* or *www. barrierfreenationalparks.com*.

Leave No Trace Seven Principles

1. Plan Ahead and Prepare
2. Travel and Camp on Durable Surfaces
3. Dispose of Waste Properly
4. Leave What You Find
5. Minimize Campfire Impacts
6. Respect Wildlife
7. Be Considerate of Other Visitors

www.lnt.org

The publisher would like to thank the following for their kind permission to reproduce their photographs:

(Key: a-above; b-below/ bottom; c-centre; f-far; l-left; r-right; t-top)

123RF.com: arinahabich 236br; Alberto Loyo 201cra.

4Corners: Jordan Banks 2-3; Susanne Kremer 144b.

Alamy Stock Photo: Accent Alaska.com 201cr, 205tr; Agefotostock / George Ostertag 167tr,/ Juan Carlos Muñoz 172bl,/ Mireia Romaguera 30bl,/ Michele Wassell 187bl; Allegra 81cra; Alpha Stock 137crb; Arco Images GmbH / J. Pfeiffer 150bl; Art Collection 2 18–19b; Mary Liz Austin 130; B.A.E. Inc. 226crb; Russ Bishop 93cr, 238tr; Pat & Chuck Blackley 101tr, 119r, 232tc; Francisco Blanco 226br; Peter Blottman 54bl; Rick & Nora Bowers 141c; Simon Browitt 84bl; Anthony Brown 42–3b; Mike Byrne 150crb; Cavan Images 246–7c,/ Aurora Open / Rich Crowder 75bc,/ Aurora Photos / Carol Barrington 74bl,/ Menno Boermans 86–7t,/ Steve MacAulay 163cr,/ Alexandra Simone 76,/ Ethan Welty 210l; Mike Cavaroc 176bl; Chronicle 181br, 214bl; Serhii Chrucky 244bl; Cultura Creative (RF) / Seth K. Hughes 139bc,/ Mike Tittel 239t; Cultura Creative Ltd / Victoria Zeffert 247tr; Ian G Dagnall 14, 39tr, 75cb, 102br; Tim Dahl 219bc; DanitaDelimont.com / Chuck Haney 185br,/ Adam Jones 118b; Danita Delimont, Agent / Jamie And Judy Wild 22bl; dbimages / Roy Johnson 100–101t; deadlyphoto.com 110bc; Design Pics Inc / Alaska Stock / Scott Dickerson 205crb / Patrick Endres 199tr / Michael Jones 202–203b / Amber Johnson 210crb/ Kevin Smith 204–205c,/ Matt Hage 203tl,/ Nick Jans 204bl; Trent Dietsche 173cra; Cody Duncan 165tr; Everett Collection Historical / CSU Archives 43br; Everett Collection Inc 223br,/ Ron Harvey 16bl; EyeEm / Chavalit Likitratcharoen 8cr,/ Caleb Weston 49tr; Clint Farlinger 136; Hudson Fleece 133tr; Lee Foster 147tr; Ben Fox 53crb; Dennis Frates 150–51tl; Larry Geddis 97cr; georgesanker.com 36cb; GL Archive 238crb; Glasshouse Images / Circa Images 23tl; Granger Historical Picture Archive / NYC 17b, 19tr, 79ca, 223cra, 239clb,/ Kolb brothers 23tr,/ Fred Mang 63br; H. Mark Weidman Photography 89cr; Nick Hanna 95br; hemis.fr / Pascal Ducept 161b; Heritage Image Partnership Ltd / Werner Forman Archive / Mesa Verde National Park Museum 62cb; Janette Hill 36crb; History and Art Collection 60tl; Michael Hudson 101cra; George H.H. Huey 62crb; IanDagnall Computing 150br; imageBROKER / Stefan Auth 174l,/ Michael Runkel 214–15t,/ Ingo Schulz 173br,/ Michael Szönyi 85bl,/ Moritz Wolf 29tl, 40–41c; Images By T.O.K. 57cb; Kerrick James 148–9c; Inge Johnsson 69bl; Don Johnston_ WU 181tr; Jon Arnold Images Ltd / Michele Falzone 149cra; Steven J. Kazlowski 87cb; Raymond Klass 178–9cr; Ivan Kuzmin 111cb; Fred LaBounty 141cb; Lebrecht Music & Arts 121cb; Dianne Leeth 181crb; K.D. Leperi 26cra; mauritius images GmbH / Marco Isler 80bl; Matt May 148bl; Michael DeFreitas North America 201cb; Constance Mier 145bc; Mint Images Limited 206bl; Jeff Mondragon 191bc; Andrew Morse 65br; Marc Muench 149tr, 191crb; William Mullins 213c; National Geographic Image Collection / Barrett Hedges 87cr,/ Jonathan Irish 136tr,/ Patrick Kelley 82–3c, 84br,/ Tim Laman 131cb,/ Rich Reid 189tr, 189crb; Natural History Archive 91bl, 238cra; Natural History Collection 40bc; Natural History Library 24bl, 125cb, 125bc, 206bc, 247crb; Nature and Science 92tl; Nature Picture Library / Jack Dykinga 115cr,/ Kirkendall-Spring 109cra; Ron Niebrugge 92–3cr, 200–201c; Boyd Norton 201br; NPS Photo 25tr, 238cl; M. Timothy O'Keefe 134–5c, 135ca; George Ostertag 81crb; George Oze 149cr, 151cb; Efrain Padro 119br; Panther Media GmbH / Diana.K 94ca; Ronald S Phillips 196–7c; Photo Resource Hawaii / Debra Behr 217cr; PhotoAlto sas / Jerome Gorin 154bc; Pictorial Press Ltd 229br; The Picture Art Collection 151bl, 238bc; Pictures Now 103bl; PJF Military Collection 20bl; Norman Pogson 151bc; The Print Collector / Heritage Images 84cb; Purestock / Don Paulson Photography 165cra; © Radius Images 58–9t; The Reading Room 151crb; Lee Rentz 131cla, 160cl, 189cr, 218bl, 219cb; Bryan Reynolds 141br; Whit Richardson 211tr; Robertharding / Gary Cook 174cra,/ Neale Clark 48b,/ James Hager 36bc,/ Michael Runkel 85bc; Marc Romanelli 109tr; James Schwabel 146bl; Science History Images 28bl, 85br,/ Photo Researchers 15clb, 121cr; Andre Seale 217tl, 217cra; Robert Shantz 141crb; Spring Images 57br, 132–3t; Stephen Saks Photography 103bc, 241cr; Stocktrek Images, Inc./ John Parrot 63clb; Benjamin Sy 57cr; Tetra Images, LLC / Peathegee Inc 31br,/ Rob Tilley 50br; TMI 50bc, 52–3c, 171tr; Togwotee 111bl; Morgan Trimble 201c; D. Trozzo 107cb; Richard Uhlhorn 162br; Greg Vaughn 167br; Ventu Photo 212bl; Frank Vetere 69br; George Ward 213cra, 213br; WaterFrame_ mus 191cb; Jason O. Watson 59cr; James Weber 141cra; Leon Werdinger 150cb; Jim West 95crb; Westend61 GmbH / Fotofeeling 84tr; Regula Heeb-Zweifel 83tl.

Ardea: © Nature's Images / Science Source 120bc.

AWL Images: J.Banks 99crb; Danita Delimont Stock 81tl, 185crb; Christian Heeb 159tr.

Bridgeman Images: Granger / Fred Mang, Jr. 63bc; © Look and Learn 214cb,/ J A Hammerton 214bc.

Depositphotos Inc: zrfphoto 180–81t.

Dorling Kindersley: Colin Keates 177br; Peter Wilson 103cb.

Dreamstime.com: Cheri Alguire 59br; Arinahabich08 236bc; Patrick Barron 147cra; Benkrut 191tl; Jon Bilous 124–5t; Philip Bird 66–7; Francisco Blanco 145cb; Tom Branting 69cb; Tristan Brynildsen 64–5t; William C. Bunce 191tr; Cathywithers 169crb; Crackerclips 39l; David Crane 212–13t; Shelley Dennis 239crb; Christina Felschen 160tl; Anton Foltin 176–7t; Sandra Foyt 103t, 190bl; Giovanni Gagliardi 147cr; Esteban Martinena Guerrero 165crb; Yuval Helfman 221br, 240–41b; Melanie Hobson 154–5t; Laurens Hoddenbagh 65crb; Tom Jaksztat 12–13; Leonardospencer 25crb; Edmund Lowe 163l; Margaret619 63t; Mariakray 145tr; Nat693 43tr; Oksanaphoto 131crb; Sean Pavone 115b; Pix569 221cra;

Psnaturephotography 121bc; Rixie 41tr; Jason P Ross 71cra; Joe Sohm 133cr, 231tr; Kenneth Sponsler 232–3b; Michael Ver Sprill 101cr, 101br; Spvvkr 45tl; Andrei Gabriel Stanescu 241br; Vadim Startsev 147crb; James Vallee 159crb; Wilsilver77 121crb; Wollertz 49cb; Colin Young 38b; Zhukovsky 107bc.

Getty Images: 500px / Hervé DUCHENNE-CRETIER 8br,/ Stass Gricko 80–81t,/ Federico Robertazzi 146–7t,/ Robert Szumlakowski 57c; Archive Photos / Robert Alexander 227bl,/ Buyenlarge / Carol M. Highsmith 222–3t,/ Harvey Meston 93crb,/ Transcendental Graphics 63bl; Aurora Open 129cr; Blend Images - Michael DeYoung 99bl; Brand X Pictures / Gallo Images 87c; Cavan Images 107cra; Corbis Documentary / Robert Holmes 83cr,/ Merrill Images 95tl,/ Scott T. Smith 107crb,/ Stuart Westmorland 128–9t,/ VCG / Roger Ressmeyer 85clb; Corbis Historical 79cb,/ Library of Congress / VCG 223cb; De Agostini / DEA PICTURE LIBRARY 62bl; Design Pics / Scott Dickerson 198–9t, 199cr,/ Mark Emery 193br; DigitalVision / Matteo Colombo 158–9b,/ The Good Brigade 221crb,/ Jordan Siemens 6, 129b; Gustaf Emanuelsson / Folio 164–5c; EyeEm / Natalia Kochina 72–3,/ Michael Lewis 65cra,/ Silke Reitz 107bl,/ / William Slider 174cr,/ Steven Swinnen 36cl; Gallo

Images / Danita Delimont 56tr; The Image Bank / Juan Carlos Munoz 142–3,/ James O'Neil 5, 45br,/ Don Smith 152–3c; imageBROKER / Moritz Wolf 53cr; James + Courtney Forte 203crb; Patrick Lienin 236–7t; The LIFE Picture Collection / Alfred Eisenstaedt 151br; Lonely Planet RF / Matthew Micah Wright 27; David McNew 221cr; Moment / Bryant Aardema -bryants wildlife images 36br,/ photo by Chris Axe 54–5t,/ Antonio Busiello 187crb, 188–9b,/ Yiming Chen 83cra,/ Jeff R Clow 111bc,/ David Rius & Núria Tuca 174br,/ Diana Robinson Photography 126bc, 171br,/ Work by Zach Dischner 159br,/ Dean Fikar 90–91t,/ Photo by Mike Kline 243,/ Daniel Viñé Garcia 106,/ Donald E. Hall 129tr,/ Troy Harrison 111crb,/ Jeremy Cram Photography 170–71t,/ Daniel A. Leifheit 88,/ Sandra Leidholdt 76crb,/ Matt Anderson Photography 108–109,/ Nico De Pasquale Photography 172–3t,/ Laura Olivas 247cr,/ Daniel Osterkamp 8bl,/ Posnov 81cr, 213cr,/ Gary Samples 96bl,/ Putt Sakdhnagool 116br,/ Lea Scaddan 203cr,/ Deb Snelson 138–9t, 140–41b,/ Sam Spicer 122–3,/ Scott Suriano 124bl,/ Bill Swindaman 120–21,/ Tony Shi Photography 171cra; Moment Open / Lidija Kamansky 57cra,/ Daniel Osterkamp 171cr, / Posnov 135cb; National Geographic

Image Collection / Michael Melford 196clb; NurPhoto / Patrick Gorski 244–5t; Photodisc / Michele Falzone 153cr,/ Stephanie Hager - HagerPhoto 133cra,/ LWA 114cla,/ Linka A Odom 231l,/ Jordan Siemens 166–7b; Photographer's Choice RF / Alan Majchrowicz 208–09,/ Bryan Mullennix 223bl; Robertharding / Jordan Banks 110–11t,/ Michael Runkel 216,/ David Tomlinson 168–9t; Stockbyte / Michele Falzone 96–7; Stone / Peter Adams 34–5,/ Per Breiehagen 178cl,/ Ed Freeman 99br,/ David Madison 197tr,/ Alan Majchrowicz 228–9t,/ Tegra Stone Nuess 163tr,/ Andrew Peacock 46–7,/ Jordan Siemens 68–9t, 99cr, 126–7,/ Peter Unger 69crb,/ WIN-Initiative 182–3; Chris Swartwood 116-17; Mike Tauber 30-31bc; Tribune News Service / Anchorage Daily News / Marc Lester 206–207t; Universal Images Group / Prisma by Dukas 220–21c; Valentin Wolf 98–9t.

Grand Canyon Conservancy: Mindy Riesenberg 91br.

iStockphoto.com: AvatarKnowmad 131bl, 213cb; benedek 186–7t; CampPhoto 62tl; Dennis_Casey 69tr; DigitalVision Vectors / bauhaus1000 121ca; E+ / Adventure_Photo 175tr,/ aimintang 104–105,/ benedek 78–9t, 189cra, 224–5,/

Matt Dirksen 77tr,/ JeffGoulden 53cra,/ mantaphoto 89tr,/ pchoui 139br, 187bc, 226l,/ tobiasjo 156–7,/ Jorge Villalba 85cb,/ VisualCommunications 8tl; ericfoltz 234–5; FatCamera 55br; gkuchera 184–5b; JeffGoulden 56–7b; jenjen42 52bl; july7th 50–51t; Katie-Dobies 39cra; kellyvandellen 55crb; Chris LaBasco 70–71t; lightpix 185tr; Prolixus_Luminis 49bc; MicheleVacchiano 173c; mixmotive 203cra; MNStudio 84crb; mtnmichelle 71crb; NNehring 36–7t; RomanKhomlyak 32–3; sarkophoto 192–3t; SeanXu 74–5t; SumikoPhoto 227tr; Shelley Wales 210br; wanderluster 60–61c, 62br; Michael Zeigler 187cb.

Library of Congress, Washington, D.C.: LC-DIG-pga-13831 / P.S. Duval & Co. 239bc.

Nat Geo Image Collection: 189tl.

Courtesy of National Park Service, Lewis and Clark National Historic Trail: 20–21tc, 64bl, 205cra, 205cr, Eugene Barton 79br, Kurt Moses 241tr, Diane rennkin 39cr, Janice Wei 85t.

plainpicture: DEEPOL by plainpicture 76br, 109crb, / Ryan Tuttle 241tl; Design Pics / Doug Lindstrand 87cra; Minden Pictures / Yva Momatiuk

& John Eastcott 87br; Tandem Stills + Motion / Andrew Peacock 89crb.

Rex by Shutterstock: AP 135br,/ Ed Andrieski 63cb.

Robert Harding Picture Library: Adam Burton 44; Michael Nolan 194–5.

Shutterstock.com: Andriy Blokhin 103crb; Nat Chittamai 129cra; Jim David 70bl; Everett Historical 21tc, 91cb,/ Truman Ward Inger 181cr; Lloyd Wallin Photography 214crb; Doug Meek 112–13, 115cra; Mia2you 218–19t; Oscity 168bl; PhilGatesPhotography 169br; Richard Seeley 131bc; ShuPhoto 94b; Karel Stipek 65cr; STS Photography 223c.

SuperStock: Alaska Stock - Design Pics / Kevin Smith 199br; Minden Pictures 150cl.

Cover images:

Front: Alamy Stock Photo: john lambing

Back: Alamy Stock Photo: Cultura Creative Ltd / Victoria Zeffert cb; Kerrick James c; Fred LaBounty tl; Marc Muench bc. Getty Images: Gustaf Emanuelsson / Folio bl; Moment / Jeremy Cram Photography tc.

For further information see: www.dkimages.com

Senior Editors Lucy Richards, Michelle Crane
Senior Designer Ben Hinks
Editors Margaret Parrish, Zoë Rutland
Project Designers Abi Read, Van Le
Proofreader Stephanie Smith
Indexer Hilary Bird
Senior Picture Researcher Ellen Root
Picture Researchers Naomi Bristow, Sumita Khatwani, Vagisha Pushp
Senior Cartographic Editor Casper Morris
Jacket Designer Maxine Pedliham
Senior DTP Designer Jason Little
Senior Production Controller Stephanie McConnell
Managing Editor Rachel Fox
Managing Art Editor Bess Daly
Art Director Maxine Pedliham
Publishing Director Georgina Dee

First edition 2020
Published in the United States by DK Publishing,
1450 Broadway, Suite 801, New York, NY 10018
Copyright © 2020 Dorling Kindersley Limited
A Penguin Random House Company
20 21 22 23 10 9 8 7 6 5 4 3 2 1
All rights reserved.

No part of this publication may be reproduced, stored in or introduced into a retrieval system, or transmitted, in any form, or by any means (electronic, mechanical, photocopying, recording, or otherwise), without the prior written permission of the copyright owner.

A CIP catalog record for this book is available from the British Library.

A catalog record for this book is available from the Library of Congress.

ISSN: 1542 1554
ISBN: 978 0 7440 2449 4

Printed and bound in China.

www.dk.com

MIX
Paper from responsible sources
FSC™ C018179